THE HISTORY OF THE
TWENTIETH (LIGHT) DIVISION

MAJOR-GENERAL W. DOUGLAS SMITH, C.B.

THE HISTORY OF
THE TWENTIETH
(LIGHT) DIVISION

BY

CAPTAIN V. E. INGLEFIELD

WITH AN INTRODUCTION BY

LIEUT.-GENERAL

THE EARL OF CAVAN

K.P., G.C.M., K.C.B., M.V.O.

London

NISBET & CO. LTD.

22 BERNERS STREET W.1

First Published in 1921

PREFACE

THIS history has been compiled from the official records and from the notes of many of those who took part in the operations described. The fighting troops of the Division necessarily occupy the chief place in the narrative, but it must be remembered throughout that the achievements of these troops would have been impossible without the co-operation of the Royal Army Service Corps, Army Ordnance Corps and Army Veterinary Corps units, and the good work of the Field Ambulances and stretcher-bearers.

Of the great number of honours won, and of the still greater number of gallant actions performed, only a few have been mentioned. These must be taken merely as typical of the many brave deeds which there is no space to record.

The rank of officers and non-commissioned officers given is that which they held at the time of the events described. Every effort has been made to ensure accuracy in this and in all other respects. For any inaccuracies or omissions I offer my apologies.

I wish to thank the many officers of the Division who have helped me by reading the narrative and by giving me most useful information, in particular

Lieut.-Colonel A. E. Erskine, whose assistance throughout has been invaluable. I wish to thank also the publishers, Messrs Nisbet & Co., for the interest they have shown and the trouble they have taken in the production of this book.

V. E. I.

INTRODUCTION

WHEN one feels a personal affection for a Division such as I do for the 20th, it is the pleasantest of tasks to record it publicly.

The 20th Division never failed me, and never failed its neighbours, during the time that I had the honour of commanding the XIVth Corps.

How can one say more?

I owe the Division my undying thanks, and I trust this book may perpetuate its great deeds, as an incentive to all to show an equally bold front in the day of trouble.

GUARDS CLUB,
S.W.1.

CONTENTS

LIST OF ILLUSTRATIONS

MAPS

AT END OF BOOK

HISTORY OF THE 20TH (LIGHT) DIVISION

CHAPTER I

THE FORMATION OF THE DIVISION AND TRAINING IN ENGLAND

4th August 1914 to 19th July 1915

ON the 4th of August 1914 war was declared between England and Germany. Two days later Parliament sanctioned an increase of 500,000 men to the army, and in a letter to the nation on the 7th of August Lord Kitchener appealed for the immediate enrolment of 100,000 men.

The ready response to this appeal soon supplied more than sufficient men for the first six divisions of the New Army, eventually numbered 9 to 14. New battalions continued to be raised to absorb as far as possible the stream of recruits and on the 11th of September the formation of six additional divisions —the 15th to the 20th—was authorised. Thus the 20th (Light) Division came into existence. It was to be composed entirely of Rifle and Light Infantry battalions—formed into the 59th, 60th, and 61st Infantry Brigades—and Divisional troops. A few changes were made later, and the order of battle of the Division as finally constituted was as follows :—

59th Infantry Brigade

10th (Service) Battalion the King's Royal Rifle Corps.

11th (Service) Battalion the King's Royal Rifle Corps.

10th (Service) Battalion the Rifle Brigade.

11th (Service) Battalion the Rifle Brigade.

60th Infantry Brigade

6th (Service) Battalion the Oxfordshire and Buckinghamshire Light Infantry.

6th (Service) Battalion the King's (Shropshire Light Infantry).

12th (Service) Battalion the King's Royal Rifle Corps.

12th (Service) Battalion the Rifle Brigade.

61st Infantry Brigade

12th (Service) Battalion the King's (Liverpool Regiment).

7th (Service) Battalion Prince Albert's (Somerset Light Infantry).

7th (Service) Battalion the Duke of Cornwall's Light Infantry.

7th (Service) Battalion the King's Own (Yorkshire Light Infantry).

Pioneer Battalion

11th (Service) Battalion the Durham Light Infantry.

Divisional Artillery

90th Field Artillery Brigade.

91st Field Artillery Brigade.

92nd Field Artillery (Howitzer) Brigade.

93rd Field Artillery Brigade.

Divisional Engineers

83rd Field Company Royal Engineers.
84th Field Company Royal Engineers.
96th Field Company Royal Engineers.

Signal Service

20th Divisional Signal Company Royal Engineers.

Divisional Transport and Supply

20th Divisional Train.

Medical Units

60th Field Ambulance.
61st Field Ambulance.
62nd Field Ambulance.

Originally the 12th King's did not belong to the Division, but were an attached battalion of army troops; the 11th D.L.I. then formed part of the 61st Brigade. Towards the end of 1914 a pioneer battalion was added to each division. Being composed largely of miners, the 11th D.L.I. became the pioneer battalion of the 20th Division, and the 12th King's then took their place in the 61st Brigade.

The Division was formed at Blackdown in September 1914. The first officer of the Divisional Staff to join was Major J. E. B. Martin, M.V.O., who at first had charge of the musketry, and who served with the Division in France as A.P.M. until September 1918. Within a few weeks Major-General R. H. Davies, C.B., a New Zealander, who had commanded the 6th Brigade in France through the critical fighting of August and September, was given command of the Division. Major-General Davies applied himself whole-heartedly

to the work of training ι. new command, and by his
personality won the complete confidence of his officers
and men. It is largely due to him that the 20th on
arrival in France was a thoroughly efficient division.
He was ably assisted by his two senior staff officers,
Lieut.-Colonel W. R. N. Madocks, G.S.O. 1, and Lieut.-
Colonel F. C. Dundas, A..Λ. and Q.M.G., both of whom
served with the Division for over two years. At this
time the 59th Brigade was commanded by Colonel G.
Leslie, the 60th by Colonel A. E. W. Colville, C.B., and
the 61st by Colonel O'D. C. Grattan, D.S.O. Brig.-
General John Hotham became the C.R.A. and Colonel
E. R. Kenyon the C.R.E. Early in 1915 the 20th
Divisional Ammunition Column was formed under
Lieut.-Colonel J. R. Foster, who although over sixty
years of age commanded the column until the end
of the war.

The whole of the Division was not concentrated in
one area. The 59th and 60th Brigades were at Blackdown, and the artillery near by at Deepcut. The
battalions of the 61st Brigade were at Aldershot and
later at Woking; the R.E. units were trained at
Chatham. The field ambulances remained at Aldershot, where they carried out nearly all their training,
joining the Division only ι. the following June, a little
over a month before embarkation for France.

Throughout the period of training, but particularly
in the early days at Blackdown, there was the greatest
difficulty in getting clothing and equipment. No
uniform was available until November, when a suit
of emergency blue was issued to each man. A certain
number of old rifles for drill purposes became available
about the same time. There were so few S.M.L.E.
rifles in some battalions that only one or two companies
could fire at a time, and even then each detail after

MAJOR-GENERAL R. H. DAVIES, C.B.

[To face p. 4.

firing had to hand over the rifles to another detail waiting to fire. The artillery at first had only enough harness for one six-horse team in each brigade. The shortage of saddles was made good to a certain extent by private gifts. Each brigade had two 90-mm. and two 15-pr. guns, but these had no sights. Wooden sights and wooden guns were improvised to carry out battery gun drill. It was not until February that one 18-pr. gun was issued to each battery.

There was no lack of men in the Division, many units being well over establishment; the main difficulty to be contended with was the shortage of regular officers and N.C.O.'s to carry out the training. For a few weeks one or two experienced officers and a few re-enlisted N.C.O.'s in each battalion and artillery brigade were confronted with the task of turning a thousand totally untrained men into an efficient and well-disciplined fighting force. The task was made possible by the unbounded enthusiasm of the men, all of whom had volunteered immediately after the outbreak of the war and whose one desire was to learn their job and to get out to France.

In February 1915 the Division moved to Witley. Some of the units were encamped or billeted near Guildford and Godalming; others, after marching to Witley in the pouring rain, went into a camp there described as a sea of mud with damp and leaky huts. The training now became more interesting, and included tactical schemes. Officers and N.C.O.'s had joined or had been promoted, and the issue of service dress begun at Blackdown was completed. A large number of horses, guns and equipment for the artillery became available, the stamp of draught horse obtained at this time being particularly good. The Divisional Ammunition Column had to be completed with mules.

At the beginning of April the Division moved by road to Salisbury Plain, covering the sixty-three miles in four days—a creditable performance, as the weather was warm and the roads were dusty, and the men marched for the first time in full marching order. Three months of hard work followed; field firing and night operations were carried out in addition to tactical exercises which often involved a long march to the training area and back.

At this time the number of field companies per division was increased to three, and the 96th Field Company, which had originally formed part of the 26th Division, joined the 20th on the 15th of May.

The three field ambulances, having completed nine months of hard training at Aldershot, often under most unpleasant conditions, joined the Division on Salisbury Plain in June.

Meanwhile the transport and equipment of units were being completed, and everything pointed to an early departure. The Division was finally inspected by the King towards the end of June, and a month later embarked for France.

CHAPTER II

THE LAVENTIE SECTOR

20th July 1915 *to 21st January* 1916

Arrival of the Division in France—Further training in trench
warfare—The Division in the Laventie Sector—Operations
in conjunction with the Battle of Loos—Raid—Gas attack
—Move out of IIIrd Corps Area.
(*Vide* Sketch A.)

THE leading units of the Division left Amesbury
on the 20th July. The route followed was
either by Folkestone and Boulogne or by
Southampton and Havre, and then by train from the
ports of disembarkation to the area west of St Omer.
The various stages of the journey—embarking men and
horses, entraining and detraining in France, marches to ·
rest camps and billets—were all accomplished satisfactorily if not without some discomfort, chiefly due to
the rough and rainy weather. On the 22nd Divisional
Headquarters was established at Lumbres, and the
Division was concentrated in this area by the 26th.

The next day orders came for a further move eastwards, and on the 28th the Division started on a hot
and trying march into the area of the IIIrd Corps
(Lieut.-General Sir W. P. Pulteney), which formed
part of the First Army and which was holding a line
between Neuve Chapelle and Armentières.

By the 30th the various units had moved into
billets in the area bounded roughly by the line
Hazebrouck - Bailleul - Steenwerck - Neuf Berquin, with
Divisional Headquarters at Merris.

The situation on the British front at this time was briefly as follows :—

The Third Army under Sir Charles Munro held the right of the line from the Somme, where it was in touch with the French, to a point south of Arras. Between this point and Grenay (four miles north-west of Lens) the French Tenth Army intervened, cutting off the Third Army from the First, which, under Sir Douglas Haig, continued the line to near Armentières; north again, Sir Herbert Plumer's Second Army held the left of the British line as far as the right of the French troops at Boesinghe.

The IIIrd Corps, consisting now of the 8th, 27th and 20th Divisions, was in touc' on the right with the Indian Corps near Fauquissart; thence the line ran in a general north-easterly direction parallel to the Rue Tilleloy and some 200 to 500 yards on the south-east side of it, until, opposite Picantin, it turned east for about a mile. North of Rouge Bancs it began to turn north-east again, and kept this general direction, passing close in front of La Cordonnerie Farm, La Boutillerie and Rue du Bois to a point on the Armentières-Lille road about half a mile north-west of Wez Macquart.

The 20th Division, like other troops in England, had been trained largely with a view to open warfare, so that on its arrival in France schools and courses of instruction had to be organised to carry on the training in trench warfare and in those forms of fighting that had lately come into use. Thus bombing was started almost at once, and the instruction given was thorough. Officers and N.C.O.'s went to the 8th and 27th Divisions for a course of training; bombing schools were opened in the Division, and brigade and battalion bombing officers appointed. Brigade bomb-

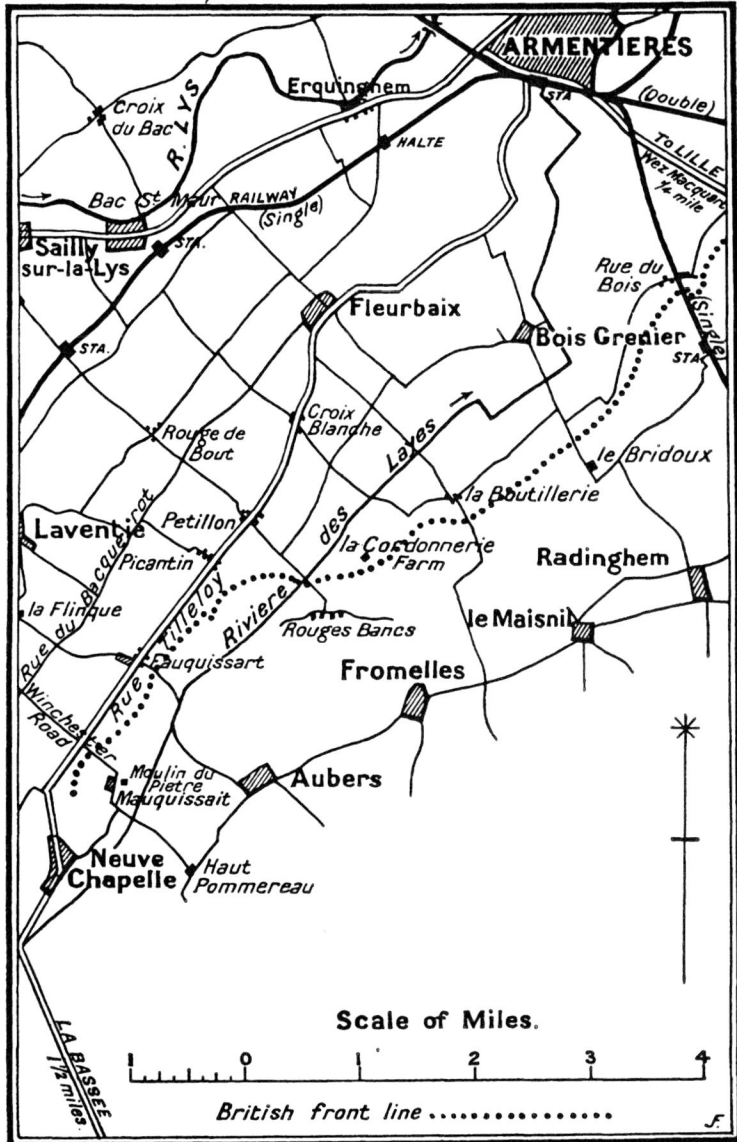

LAVENTIE, 1915. Sketch A.

ARMENTIÈRES

Croix du Bac

Erquinghem

R. LYS

(Double)

HALTE

TO LILLE

Wez Macquart ¼ mile

Bac St. Maur RAILWAY (Single)

Sailly sur-la-Lys

STA.

Rue du Bois

Fleurbaix

Bois Grenier

STA.

STA.

Rouge de Bout

Croix Blanche

le Bridoux

Layes

la Boutillerie

Laventie

Petillon

la Cordonnerie Farm

Radinghem

Picantin

des

la Flingue

Rouges Bancs

le Maisnil

Fauquissart

Fromelles

Rue du Jacquinot

Rivière

Rue Tilleloy

Winchester Road

Moulin du Pietre Mauquissait

Aubers

Neuve Chapelle

Haut Pommereau

LA BASSÉE 1½ miles

Scale of Miles.

1   0   1   2   3   4

British front line ....

F.

ing officers at the end of each course picked out any men who were likely to become really expert and kept them for a further course. The rest went back to their battalions as battalion or company bombers. The training was carried on under some difficulty at first, as nothing was provided. No bombs were available for instructional purposes, and therefore they had to be improvised. Machine-gun classes were also formed, and from time to time officers and N.C.O.'s went to Wisques for a course in the use of machine guns in the field. Gas-mask drill was very strict, and was practised every day. Demonstrations and lectures were given, and as many men as possible were made to pass through gas. In addition to these special courses of instruction, ordinary training was carried out.

Between the 2nd and the 17th of August all units, from brigade headquarters downwards, were attached to the 8th and 27th Divisions in the line, thus introducing officers and men to the realities of trench warfare.

By the 18th all units had returned to the Divisional area with the exception of the 83rd and 96th Field Companies R.E. and the 11th D.L.I. (Pioneers), who were working on the defences. The 90th Field Artillery Brigade (Colonel E. Pollock), however, instead of undergoing a tour of instruction, went straight into the line on the 2nd of August, and that night came into action near Laventie in rear of the 19th Infantry Brigade, which held the right of the 8th Division line.

On the 9th of August the Division lost the services of A/92 (Howitzer Battery), which was transferred to the 27th Division.

Between the 15th and 17th the 59th Infantry Brigade moved into the line, taking over the right of the 8th Division front from the 19th Brigade, which

went to join the Ist Corps. The 59th Brigade came
under the orders of the 8th Division, and Brigade
Headquarters was opened at Laventie. The line,
after some readjustment on the 18th, ran from near
Fauquissart to a point east of Petillon, and was held
by two battalions in the front trenches, a third in a
line of defended posts about the Rue Bacquerot, and
the fourth in reserve at Laventie. Reliefs between
battalions took place every four to seven days.

It was not until the end of the month that the
Division took over a sector of the line, and while
waiting in the reserve area three battalions of the
61st Brigade, as well as the R.E. and 11th D.L.I.,
were employed as working parties at various points
in the IIIrd Corps area.

On the 22nd of August orders came for the Division
to move forward. The IIIrd Corps was extending its
right by taking over a part of the Indian Corps front
as far as a point just north of Mauquissait. This line
was to be held by three divisions—the 20th on the
right, the 8th in the centre and the 27th on the left,
each division keeping one brigade in reserve. The
20th Divisional Artillery (Brig.-General Hotham) began
moving to the new area on the night of the 23rd/24th.
By the 28th the move of all units was completed,
and Divisional Headquarters was opened at Nouveau
Monde, near Estaires.

The Divisional front ran from the corps right flank
near Mauquissait to Petillon. The 59th Brigade (Brig.-
General C. D. Shute), with its left at Petillon, then
became the left brigade of the Division. On the right
was the 60th Brigade (Brig.-General J. W. G. Roy)
in touch with the 59th just east-north-east of Fauquissart. The 61st (Brig.-General C. Ross) was in
reserve at Estaires, where the battalions which had

been detached rejoined it—the 7th K.O.Y.L.I. and the 7th D.C.L.I. on the 28th, the 12th King's on the 6th of September. The artillery was organised in two groups, the La Flinque group supporting the right of the line and the Laventie group the left, with head-quarters at Estaires. Of the field companies R.E., the 84th and 96th were in the 60th Brigade area, and the 83rd with the 59th Brigade.

Both the 60th and 59th Brigades had two battalions holding the front trenches, with the others either in reserve or holding a line of defended posts which ran about a mile behind the line. These posts were either entrenched positions or farm-houses, more or less battered about but still habitable. They were put into a state of defence, and occupied by a platoon or half a company, and in a few cases the civilian inhabitants of the house went on living there at the same time as the military garrison.

The country in this sector was flat and low—an expanse of grass or mud intersected by small ditches. Though at this time of the year the surface was still very hard and dry, the water level was only some three or four feet below the ground, and this made the normal form of trench, in the southern part of the area, out of the question. Instead, breast-works of sand-bags were built up and strengthened with loose earth. Dug-outs, as known in later times or even then in some parts of the line, did not exist. Small recesses in the breast-work and some splinter proofs behind were all that could be made. Many breastworks had no parados to give cover from the backward effect of shells bursting behind, and this had to be made. Fortunately the shelling of the front trenches in this area was not severe except on the 25th of September and during a feint attack in October.

In consequence very few casualties were due to this lack of cover from the rear.

The German front line was much on the same level as our own, and anything from 80 to 250 yards away. Behind that, the ground rose gently to the long low ridge running by Aubers, Fromelles and Radinghem— not more than 50 feet above the rest of the country, but for all that a commanding height completely overlooking our positions.

The artillery was to the east and south-east of Laventie, where clumps of trees, orchards and hedges gave good cover for the guns. Excellent observation was obtained from the ruined houses along the Rue Tilleloy.

On the whole of the British front the year 1915 was really a time of preparation. The hard fighting of 1914 and the first four months of 1915 had caused a considerable drain on the personnel of the army, and though many reinforcements had come out both as drafts and as units—the latter for the most part Territorial troops—yet the great bulk of the New Army was still in England, and could not be expected to turn the balance decisively in our favour until well on in 1916. Nevertheless there was much fighting, especially in certain parts of the front such as the Ypres salient and about La Bassée and in the battles of Neuve Chapelle and Loos.

The sector about Laventie during the autumn and winter of 1915 was one of the quietest on the British front. The first month that the Division spent in the line was uneventful, though there was continued activity in some form or other; mining was always being carried out by both sides, and enemy sniping never ceased. The latter caused a certain number of casualties, so that steps had to be taken to deal with it by training sniper of our own. These worked in pairs, the same pair always working on the same ground, so that they got to know every yard of it.

The Germans undoubtedly had an excellent system of intelligence. They seemed to know exactly what reliefs were being carried out, for they often shouted the names of regiments that had just come in, and on one occasion correctly whistled the regimental march. This is explained by the fact that they had listening sets of which at that time we knew nothing. Later many orders were issued to prevent leakage, and open earth circuits were strictly forbidden.

Just at the time when the Division took over this sector, a deserter came in and reported that the Germans were mining against us near Mauquissait, and also had gas cylinders there, and were preparing to attack us on the 30th. To meet this it was decided to fire a camouflet on the 29th and to follow up with a bombardment of the enemy trenches in order to damage them sufficiently to show whether or not he had a gas attack in preparation. The bombardment was carried out by the La Flinque group, in conjunction with the Meerut Divisional Artillery and a brigade of 9·2 howitzers.

It was a hazy day with fine rain falling, and observation was difficult, so the bombardment was curtailed and was resumed on the 30th under better conditions on a section of trench somewhat further south. Considerable damage was done. A part of the parapet was demolished and a magazine exploded, but no evidence of gas was found.

The 93rd Field Artillery Brigade (Lieut.-Colonel A. T. Anderson) and one section of each battery of the 92nd Brigade (Lieut.-Colonel H. G. Ricardo) moved on the 30th to positions south and south-east of

Fleurbaix in the 8th Division area. Here they came into action during the first two nights of September, and later, on the 25th of the month, supported an attack by the 8th Division.

On the 5th of September the 61st Brigade relieved the 23rd Brigade of the 8th Division, and took over the line running east and then north-east from the left of the 59th Brigade to a point about 600 yards south-west of La Boutillerie. The line was held by three battalions, with the fourth battalion in support. At first Brigade Headquarters was at Rouge de Bout, near Laventie, but a heavy shelling on the 9th compelled a move to an estaminet some little distance away.

On the night of the 12th/13th the 7th Somerset L.I. relieved the 12th King's in the front line. At 5.30 A.M. the enemy blew up a mine under a small salient of the front trench held by a platoon of " B " Company. About twenty men were buried by the explosion. In spite of heavy artillery, machine gun and trench mortar fire which the enemy poured into the area of the explosion, the crater was occupied at once, and the rest of the company began to rescue their buried comrades, five of whom were killed and twelve injured. The casualties among the rescuers were two killed and five wounded. Lieut. B. E. F. Mitchell, the platoon commander, was awarded the M.C., and Lance-Corporal C. Ward, who was in charge of the company stretcher-bearers, the D.C.M. for conspicuous gallantry under heavy fire. Major R. P. Preston Whyte, commanding "B" company, received the written congratulations of the Divisional Commander.

The 84th Field Company R.E. (Major H. S. Christie) moved to Rue Biache in the 61st Brigade area. Each field company was now with an infantry brigade, the 96th (Major A. C. Scott) with the 60th Brigade, the 83rd (Major L. E. Hopkins) with the 59th, and the 84th with the 61st, and henceforward this arrangement was kept, each brigade and its field company working together. Similarly the 60th Field Ambulance (Lieut.-Colonel A. C. Osburn), the 61st Field Ambulance (Lieut.-Colonel W. J. S. Harvey), and the 62nd Field Ambulance (Lieut.-Colonel J. G. Gill) worked respectively with the 59th, 60th and 61st Brigades.

The two companies of the 11th D.L.I. (Pioneers), which had remained to work under the R.E. when the Division came into the line, returned in the beginning of September.

Meanwhile, plans had been made for operations on a considerable scale further south, to begin on the 25th of September. The general plan was that the French were to advance in Champagne, and in conjunction with this the British troops were to attack near Loos on a front from about Grenay to the La Bassée canal.

Along the rest of the front subsidiary operations were to be carried out :—

(1) By the 2nd Division of the First Army near Givenchy.

(2) By the Meerut Division (Indian Corps) near Neuve Chapelle.

(3) By the 8th Division (IIIrd Corps) near Le Bridoux.

(4) By the Vth Corps near Bellewarde Farm, east of Ypres.

It is with the operations of the Meerut and 8th Divisions, on the immediate right and left of the 20th, that we are now concerned.

The Meerut Division was to assault the enemy's

trenches about Mauquissait with the ultimate objective, should the enemy show signs of demoralisation, of the high ground between Haut Pommereau and La Cliqueterie Farm. This would pave the way for a further advance of the Indian Corps in a south-easterly direction, breaking the enemy's line and assisting the advance further south by turning the La Bassée defences. The Gharwal Brigade was detailed to attack on the right and the Bareilly Brigade on the left.

The 8th Division, on the left of the 20th, was to attack the German line from about La Boutillerie to Le Bridoux. Its further objective was the capture of Bas Maisnil, Le Bridoux and Ferme Houssain, to prepare the way for a possible advance of the whole corps to the Aubers-Radinghem ridge. This operation was to be carried out in the first instance by the 25th Brigade.

Between these two operations the 20th Division was to co-operate :—

(1) By making a smoke screen along the whole front, so as to conceal the true points of attack.

(2) By covering its own front and the advance of the assaulting columns on its flanks by fire.

(3) By cutting wire at certain points, both to deceive the enemy and to facilitate a possible advance.

(4) By being prepared to assault the enemy's line on the right or left and to press forward in the centre, according to the progress made by the divisions on the flanks.

The attack was preceded by a four days' bombardment of the enemy's lines. His front and support trenches were badly damaged ; strong-points and houses in and behind his line were breached and lanes cut in his wire. Although considerable damage was observed to have been done, the enemy made very little retaliation.

During the bombardment, various means were adopted with the idea of deceiving the enemy as to the actual time of attack. Rapid fire was opened by the artillery as if for the final bombardment, and searchlights were turned on to the enemy's parapet which was then brought under fire. One night, having fired a rocket, the troops in the front trenches immediately began cheering, showing bayonets over the parapet and throwing empty jam tins into the wire in order to induce the enemy to man his parapet. One round was then fired by each gun on the enemy's front line.

On the night of the 24th/25th, headquarters of brigades proceeded to their advanced report centres, and units in reserve were moved up to support and assembly trenches which had been dug close behind the front line so as to be ready, if necessary, to assume the offensive.

One battalion of the 59th Brigade was kept at Laventie to form, with the 11th D.L.I. and the Divisional Mounted Troops, the Divisional reserve.

Of the two attacks on the flanks of the 20th Division the first to be launched was that on the left. At 4.30 A.M., the 8th Division advanced and soon gained a footing in the enemy trenches, with the exception of a detached force (on the immediate left of the 61st Brigade) which was unable to get forward.

The 59th and 61st Brigades found the line opposite to them strongly held by the enemy, whom they engaged with rifle and machine-gun fire. No advance was possible on this part of the front.

B

About 10.30 A.M., the 8th Division asked for machine-gun fire to be opened on its flank. During the afternoon it seemed to have difficulty in holding the line it had gained, and the 61st Brigade and the guns in support of it assisted by bringing artillery and machine-gun fire to bear on parts of the enemy line near Bas Maisnil. About half-past four a counter attack drove back the 8th Division troops, who were reported at 6.40 P.M. to be again holding their original line.

On the right of the 20th Division two battalions of the 60th Brigade were able to advance. Astride the Winchester road the German line ran out into a sharp salient, protruding into a wider re-entrant in our own line. Opposite the north face of this salient, a sap had been dug for a short distance out from the 60th Brigade trenches. It was intended in the case of an advance of our troops, to continue this sap through to the German line and make a fire trench of it, so connecting up the line already held with the ground newly won.

Zero was fixed at 5.50 A.M. on the 25th. Two minutes before this a mine was exploded in the enemy salient, and at zero the final bombardment of the enemy line began. Six minutes later the smoke barrage was started all along the front of the Division. This was effected by means of smoke candles lighted on the parapet, or by phosphorus bombs and grenades of all descriptions thrown by catapults and trench mortars. At 6 A.M. the Bareilly and Gharwal Brigades attacked.

The smoke barrages possibly helped the brigades on the right to advance, but made it very difficult to observe from our line what was going on. About 7 A.M., however, the troops of the Meerut Division were known to be making good progress, and at their

request orders were issued at 7.30 A.M. for the 12th
R.B. to advance and connect up with the left of the
Bareilly Brigade.

" D " Company of the 12th R.B. was ordered into
the fire trench to prepare for assault, with " B " and
" C " in support, while " A " Company was detailed
to work on the sap.   The actual order to assault was
sent to " D " Company at 8.10 A.M. but telephone
communication with the front line had broken down,
and the message had to go by orderly and so did not
arrive till 8.25 A.M. when the assault began.

By this time the smoke barrages had cleared and
all companies, especially those in support, as they
appeared in the open, suffered heavy casualties both
from shelling and from rifle and machine-gun fire
which enfiladed them from the left.

All three companies were across by 9.30 A.M., and
once they had gained the enemy's trenches they met
with little immediate opposition, and began to consolidate a line running north and east of Mauquissait.
They gained touch with the left of the Bareilly Brigade
and bombers were pushed forward along the enemy
trenches.

At the request of the Bareilly Brigade, the bombing
officer and some bombers of the 12th R.B. were sent
forward towards the Moulin du Piètre and joined the
bombers of the Black Watch.

Meanwhile " A " Company had been working on the
sap, but little progress had been made owing to the
heavy enfilade fire from the German trenches.   The
first two sections who worked on this sap lost all their
men except two.

As soon as it was seen that the Bareilly Brigade
had gained a footing in the enemy trenches, a platoon
of " A " Company got across to the salient and began

to sap back towards our line so as to meet the trench which the rest of the company was making. This work also was found to be impossible. The parapet was broken through and the sap pushed some six or eight yards out, when work was practically brought to a standstill by heavy fire further along the German line.

At 9.45 A.M. " A " Company of the 12th R.B. was relieved by " B " Company of the 6th K.S.L.I., who continued to work under heavy fire. The difficulties under which these parties worked were very great, and the sap was never completed.

" A " Company of the 12th R.B. on being relieved from work on the sap re-formed behind the parapet, and two platoons went forward. They were, however, held up about half way across and had to take cover in a ditch.

On the advance of the 12th R.B. the 6th K.S.L.I. occupied the trenches just vacated along the Rue Tilleloy and later were ordered to advance. At 11.30 A.M., just as the leading company reached the trenches forming the north face of the salient, the Germans launched a strong bombing attack against the Bareilly Brigade, which was forced to retire to its original line. The second company advancing in support came under very heavy fire, and was forced to take cover in a ditch where it was pinned to the ground.

It was then about midday, and the survivors of the Bareilly Brigade had got back to their own trenches. The right flank of the 12th R.B. was thus uncovered, and the battalion was heavily attacked by bombers on the front and on both flanks. The supply of bombs in the battalion ran short, and casualties were heavy.

At 12.30 P.M., the 12th R.B. and the two companies of the 6th K.S.L.I. were forced to retire. While doing so all companies again lost heavily, though the retirement was gallantly covered by detachments of both battalions from the reverse slope of the enemy's parapet. These men held their ground until the enemy came within a few yards of them, and eventually got back by working their way along the ditches that ran by the side of Winchester Road.

The bombers and machine gunners of the brigade worked under the brigade bombing and machine-gun officers, and did very good work. The brigade bombing officer—Lieut. Shaw—blocked one of the enemy's trenches on the left of our position in the salient. He held this block for nearly two hours, and did not withdraw until he and his sergeant were the only two left and all his bombs, including such German ones as he could find, had been used. Lieut. Hankey of the 12th K.R.R.C. also distinguished himself. For his excellent work in covering the withdrawal, he was awarded the Legion of Honour.

Every effort had been made to cut the sap through between our line and the enemy's salient, but the work went very slowly. All digging in the open was immediately stopped by enfilade machine-gun fire, and even the continuation of the work by sap incurred casualties from shelling. The wounded had to be carried back along the narrow trench and this caused constant interruptions, so that when the retirement began little progress had been made.

After all the other troops had got back, a few men were left in occupation of the saphead until between 3 and 4 P.M., when they also were withdrawn.

The Divisional Artillery did most valuable work during the day, by keeping under fire the enemy's trenches on the left of the attack, and so reducing the very heavy casualties that must otherwise have been inflicted by the machine guns on that flank.

In the light of later experiences some details of the signal communications are interesting. Advanced Brigade Headquarters was within 300 yards of the original front line, and single trench cables were used up to that line. The shell fire was so local, that on the whole these cables were maintained during the battle without great difficulty. Behind Brigade Headquarters the line was never cut.

The retirement of the 12th R.B. and the 6th K.S.L.I. to the original line was over by 2 P.M., and ended the day's fighting. The operations had been successful in holding the enemy to his ground, and in preventing him from sending reinforcements to the scene of the main attack. The brunt of the fighting fell on the 12th R.B., who held on with great determination when their flanks had become exposed, and who throughout the day fought splendidly, thoroughly earning the congratulations sent them by the Divisional Commander.

The casualties were heavy considering the number of men actually engaged—19 officers, and 542 other ranks in all; the 12th R.B. alone lost 7 officers and 332 men; the 6th K.S.L.I. lost 4 officers and 59 men. During the day the enemy shelled the front trenches heavily, and caused a considerable number of casualties among some of the battalions that were not actively engaged. Of these the 12th K.R.R.C. suffered the most; they lost altogether 3 officers and 75 other ranks.

The 61st Field Ambulance (Lieut.-Colonel W. J. S. Harvey) which was attached to the 60th Brigade worked extremely well, and all the wounded were cleared during the day. Lieut. G. A. Maling, R.A.M.C., won the V.C. for his continuous bravery during these operations. He " worked incessantly from 6.15 A.M.

on the 25th till 8 A.M. on the 26th, collecting and treating in the open under heavy shell fire more than 300 men. At about 11 A.M. on the 25th he was flung down and temporarily stunned by the bursting of a large high explosive shell which wounded his only assistant and killed several of his patients. A second shell soon after covered him and his instruments with débris, but his high courage and zeal never failed him, and he continued his gallant work singlehanded." [1]

It was expected that there would be a renewal of the fighting the next day, but no further operations took place. On the contrary, a demonstration that had been ordered for the 27th was cancelled the afternoon before, and orders were issued that no gun ammunition of any kind was to be expended for the time being except to repel attack or for retaliation.

The casualties of the day's fighting had materially reduced the strength of the 60th Brigade, and on the 26th the 11th D.L.I. (Pioneers) were attached as an extra battalion, and for the next six weeks took their turn with the other battalions of the brigade in the front line trenches. The excellent pioneer work that this battalion had done was marked by letters of appreciation received on the 28th from the C.E. IIIrd Corps and from the Corps Commander.

As Divisional reserve a brigade of the 23rd Division was attached to the 20th. This was later reduced to two battalions, but was not completely dispensed with until the 10th of November.

On the 28th the whole Division side-stepped about a mile to the right. This brought the right flank to a sunken road about half a mile north-east of Neuve Chapelle and the left to a point some quarter of a mile north of Rouge Bancs. The line was held by the three

[1] *London Gazette*, dated 18th November 1915.

brigades in the same order as before, each brigade
having two battalions in the front trenches.

The Divisional Artillery was now complete again,
the 93rd Brigade and the sections of the 92nd having
returned from Fleurbaix, and was divided into four
groups. On the right was " Tyler's Group," which
became " Ricardo's Group " on the 11th of October,
then the La Flinque and Laventie Groups with the
Croix Blanche Group on the left.

The movements necessitated by this rearrangement
of the Divisional front were much hindered by the state
of the ground. There had been a good deal of rain in
the last few days, and the communication trenches
were thick in mud and in places nearly knee-deep in
water. The night was very dark and the trenches—
especially in the area taken over from the Meerut
Division—were complicated by the labyrinth of assembly
and forming-up places which had been made for the
attack on the 25th. The relief was completed by
3.30 A.M. on the 29th, though minor adjustments were
made the next day.

At one point in the 59th Brigade front the line took
a sudden turn back for a short distance and then ran
on in its original direction. A corner was thus left
which at night might very easily come under fire from
further down the line. To prevent this a red lamp was
hung out every night at the corner of the trench, which
so came to be known as the Red Lamp Salient.

A very gallant act was performed here on the 1st
October when a mine shaft got full of foul air and
the R.E. listening post was overcome. Captain G. H.
Gilbey, Sgt. Toole and Pte. Holmes of " C " Company,
11th R.B., descended the mine shaft at great risk
and succeeded in rescuing three out of the five men
of the listening post. They persevered in this work

until they were exhausted. Captain Gilbey was given the M.C. and Sgt. Toole and Pte. Holmes the D.C.M.

After the 25th of September there was no further offensive action on the Laventie front to assist the operations that were still going on south of the La Bassée Canal. Various measures, however, were adopted from time to time with the purpose of leading the enemy to expect an attack and of holding his troops to this part of the line.

Thus on the night of the 8th/9th of October an attempt to cut the enemy's wire at two points with gun-cotton torpedoes was made by the 59th Brigade.

Lieut. Hugh Jones and Lieut. Grant, both of the 96th Field Company, R.E., directed the operations, and escorts were found by the 10th R.B. and the 11th K.R.R.C. The enemy was very alert, and the right party under Lieut. Grant was unable to reach the German lines owing to the activity of hostile patrols. Eventually at 2.10 A.M. the charge was fired in an enemy sap, where it did considerable damage; the party then got away under heavy fire without casualties. Lieut. Hugh Jones with the left party reached the wire at 1.30 A.M. and placed the torpedoes in position. He attempted to fire them, but was delayed by a faulty fuze. Suddenly the enemy opened a heavy fire at point-blank range. Lieut. Hugh Jones was badly wounded, but he made another attempt to fire the charge and only when this also failed and two of his four men had been wounded did he withdraw. For his action on this occasion he was awarded the M.C.

Still with the idea of holding the enemy to his ground a demonstration was made on the 13th of October by the IIIrd and Indian Corps. On the 20th Division front the line of the 60th Brigade near Mauquissait was

chosen as the scene of a feint attack in which the
assaulting troops were to be represented by dummies.
During the preceding night a false parapet was built
across a re-entrant in the line. At 7 A.M. on the 13th
the Divisional Artillery opened fire, cutting the wire
very effectively and shelling various points in rear
of the German position. The intense bombardment
which began at 12.30 P.M. badly damaged the enemy's
front line, and one gun firing on certain of his trenches
in enfilade is believed to have caused much loss to his
troops as they manned the parapet. At the same time
a smoke barrage was started along the whole of the
60th Brigade front. Boxes of free phosphorus had been
put out during the night between the lines and these
were fired electrically from the trenches, while catapults
and trench mortars helped by throwing smoke bombs.
The screen was very effective, and covered the front with
a thick cloud for nearly two hours.

The 60th Brigade front line was at this time held
by the 6th K.S.L.I. on the right, the 11th D.L.I.
in the centre, and the 12th R.B. on the left. Two
battalions—the D.L.I. and the R.B.—used dummies
which were made of sacks stuffed with straw and
clothed with old salvaged greatcoats and with caps
either salvaged or else lent by the men.

On the front of the D.L.I. the smoke was too thick
for the dummies to be seen except for the first few
minutes, when they were effectively used.

Opposite the 12th R.B. on the left the smoke was not
continually dense, and in the clearer intervals the
dummies were a great success. They were stuck on
bayonets, put over the parapet and then withdrawn ;
they were rolled over the parapet as if shot, and then
pulled back by strings when the smoke became thick
again ; they were poked out of the sally ports, moved

up and down a sap in front of the trenches and laid out in ditches in front so as to be just visible.

When the smoke barrage began the enemy opened heavy rifle and machine-gun fire which he kept up for half an hour. Judging from the intensity of this fire he must have been manning his parapet in strength. At the same time the enemy field guns and howitzers severely shelled our trenches, creating a barrage along the 60th Brigade front. Most of the shells seem to have fallen on the support trenches and on the old assembly places, for the 12th R.B. had only two casualties, and this they attribute to the fact that all men of this battalion were kept in the front trenches during the bombardment and none behind in support. The trench mortars also came in for fairly heavy shelling. One of the detachments had bad luck, for when the gun was being packed up the officer and two men were killed and the third man wounded by the last shell that the Germans fired in the course of these operations. Our bombardment ceased at 2.10 P.M. and by 2.45 all was quiet.

There is no doubt that the demonstration was a success. The enemy must have suffered a good deal from our shell fire, while the casualties in the 20th Division were only about 50. The dummies were most realistically worked so that the enemy was thoroughly deceived and certainly concentrated his artillery on the area of the 60th Brigade. A German communiqué dealing with this demonstration came later into our hands. It ran: " A strong attack by the enemy was stopped at his trenches."

All this time mining, sniping, and other activities inseparable from trench warfare continued on both sides. Patrols were constantly at work at night examining the German line, noting the state of the wire

and the position of new works and showing much coolness
and daring in collecting all the information they could.
2nd Lieut. M. L. Cope of the 11th R.B. won the M.C.
while out with a patrol on the night of the 16th of
October. He raided and bombed a German listening
post, killing two of the enemy and routing the rest,
and obtaining two greatcoats and a rifle. When his
bombs were exhausted he followed up with his revolver
and emptied the chambers into the Germans at six
yards' range. Having no more ammunition he immediately went to the assistance of a severely wounded
man, whom he helped into cover. The action for which
Lieutenants G. Meredith and H. H. de D. Monk, both
of the 11th K.R.R.C., were awarded the M.C. may also
be given here, though it occurred on the night of
the 24th–25th of November. These two officers were
reconnoitring with their company officer when the
latter was killed. For over an hour, under continuous
and heavy fire and over flooded and difficult ground,
they dragged the body back until they reached our
trenches.

On the 31st a new breastwork was made in order to
straighten off a re-entrant near the Duck's Bill—a
projecting trench on the extreme right of the Divisional
line. The Meerut Division on the right carried on the
work towards the south. One thousand men of the
20th Division were employed in three reliefs, and
between 8 P.M. and 3 A.M. they built the breastwork
throughout the whole length to a height of four feet.
The work was continued the following night until
stopped by heavy and continuous rain.

Brig.-General Ross, who had commanded the 61st
Brigade since June 1915, left the Division on the 13th
of November to take command of the 6th Division.
He was succeeded by Brig.-General W. F. Sweny.

During November two more changes were made in the extent of the Divisional front. On the 10th the Indian Corps was relieved by the XIth Corps, a division of which—the Guards—took over the right of the 20th Division line on the 14th. The 60th Brigade thus relieved moved to Laventie in Divisional reserve. The two battalions of the 23rd Division being then no longer required returned to their own area. At the same time the 11th D.L.I. took up their regular duties again as a pioneer battalion.

A further move between the 21st and the 24th left the Division holding the sector from east of Picantin to west of Le Bridoux with the Guards Division on the right and the 23rd on the left. Divisional headquarters was now at Sailly-sur-la-Lys. Two brigades were in the line and one in reserve, and they relieved each other in regular sequence every ten days. The headquarters of the Divisional Artillery moved to Sailly on the 27th, by which date the artillery units were settled in the new area and organised in two groups, the right and the left, with C/92 Battery acting as a counter-battery.

During the remaining two months which the 20th Division spent in this area operations were chiefly confined to artillery bombardments. There was a raid by the 59th Brigade in December, and a modified gas attack was carried out the night before the Division moved out of the line, but otherwise the task of keeping the enemy occupied and damaging his defences fell principally to the artillery, whose accurate fire also played an important part in supporting the infantry raid. On the 20th of November the enemy's line had been shelled with the object of destroying his mine shafts and as much as possible of his trenches. Other bombardments in which the Divisional Artillery took part were carried out on the 28th and 30th. Although considerable damage was done there was very little retaliation. Between the 6th and the 10th of December the German position at Turk's Point Salient, just south of La Boutillerie, was shelled with good results, the heavy artillery co-operating both in this bombardment and in another which took place on the 3rd of January.

On the night of the 15th/16th of December a raid was carried out by the 59th Brigade. For seven days beforehand the artillery fired on the German wire, cutting eight lanes in it though only four of them were intended to be used. These lanes were kept under machine-gun fire at night, but in spite of this the Germans put up a certain amount of new wire which had to be cut by infantry parties on the night of the raid. A detailed reconnaissance was carried out and all arrangements were made with the greatest care.

The attack was originally timed to be launched at 1 A.M. but was put off till 2 to allow the moon to set. The night was then dark with a little rain falling, and a slight wind blowing from the German trenches.

Two attacks were made, one by the 10th R.B. on the right, the other by the 11th K.R.R.C. on the left.

The right attack under Major Lascelles had much further to go than the other—about 500 yards—and on this side it was found that the wire had not been so effectively cut. Lieut. C. E. S. Rucker volunteered to take out two wire-cutting parties and proceeded to open the lanes through which the raiding parties were to pass. The wire-cutting parties did most excellent and arduous work, but the task took longer than was expected and before it could be completed the 11th K.R.R.C. on the left had entered the enemy's trenches.

The Germans, now thoroughly alert, manned a listening post just inside their wire. As surprise was impossible it was decided to abandon the raid of the 10th R.B. Lieut. Rucker then took out a bombing party, again volunteering for this task, and under heavy fire threw six bombs into the listening post from a distance of a few yards, almost certainly killing all the men inside it. He was awarded the M.C. for his gallantry in carrying out these duties.

The left attack was under Major J. F. R. Hope. Patrols sent out before the assault found only the centre gap open; the other gaps had to be cut by wire-cutters —a difficult task—to clear a passage through. The attack was divided into three parties. The one on the right was cutting the last strand at the time of the assault, and being discovered in the enemy's wire did not get in, though severe losses were inflicted on the enemy by bombing from the parapet. About 24 men of the other two parties got in and finding the trenches strongly held had sharp fighting, while the artillery put down a most accurate curtain of fire which effectually prevented the enemy from being reinforced. Once in the trench, these two parties turned inwards, fighting their way along until they met. They then retraced their steps, and the thoroughness with which the trench was cleared and the effectiveness of the barrage are shown by the fact that they came out unmolested.

Very soon, however, the Germans opened fire, making the work of bringing in the wounded difficult and dangerous. Lieut. F. W. Warre of the 11th K.R.R.C. received the M.C. for his gallant conduct in getting all casualties back to our line. Not only was he the last man to return, but on finding that some wounded had been left behind he went back under heavy fire and

collected them.   He was wounded when returning the
second time.

The Germans were completely surprised, but fought
with determination.   Their trenches were found to be
very neat and well made, but with a foot of water in the
bottom.

The raid was made under most difficult conditions.
Rain had flooded the ditches, forming pools in places
thirty yards or more across.   Not only had the men to
crawl over the mud for 180 yards, but also they had to
lie down and wait for the time to attack.   Their hands
became so numbed with cold that when they reached
the objective they had great difficulty in withdrawing
the pins from the Mills bombs, and some were seen
sitting on the fire step under heavy fire pulling out the
pins with their teeth, while an officer was unable to let
off his revolver.   In spite of all this at least 39 Germans
were killed by the raiding parties, and the artillery,
trench mortars, and machine guns must have accounted
for a good many more.   Our casualties were 5 men
killed and 1 officer and 10 men wounded.

The artillery was excellent.   The infantry report
stated :   " It would be impossible to have got more
accurate and ready support."

The moral effect of the raid was very good.   It was
the first fighting that this brigade had seen, and keen as
the men were it was a source of great encouragement
to them to prove by experience that man for man
they were better than the Germans.

For their conspicuous gallantry and ability throughout the operation, Sgt. E. G. Wimpey, Sgt. O. Green
and Pte. H. Skeele, all of the 11th K.R.R.C., were
awarded the D.C.M.

One of the reasons which made the Divisional Artillery
so thoroughly dependable and effective, not only at

this time but throughout the war, was the close touch which was always maintained with the infantry. A spirit of real camaraderie existed between the two arms ; artillery officers would frequently come to the dugouts of infantry commanders and discuss with them the best means of giving them all possible assistance. The excellent results of this system were proved over and over again.

In the middle of December preparations were made for a gas attack which was to be delivered on the first suitable night after the 20th of the month, in conjunction with raids by four small columns of the 59th Brigade. By the 20th 800 cylinders had been brought up to the front line near Cordonnerie Farm and 50 to the parapet astride the La Boutillerie road, and all preparations were complete.

The operation, however, was delayed for nearly three weeks by a constantly unfavourable wind. Meanwhile orders arrived for the relief of the 20th Division by the 8th. The move was to begin on the 9th of January. Accordingly on the 6th and 7th 450 gas cylinders were withdrawn from the front trenches. Then, on the 8th, the wind changed, and as by 2 P.M. it was blowing from the north-west, orders were immediately issued that the attack should take place that night with the 400 cylinders which still remained in position.

At this time the Divisional front was held by the 60th Brigade on the right and the 61st on the left. The 59th Brigade, which was to provide the raiding parties, was in reserve. As the number of cylinders had been so much reduced, it was decided to send forward only one raiding party instead of four.

The gas was turned on at 2 A.M. on the 9th, but

c

went slowly, and was blown by gusts of westerly wind across the front of the trenches to be attacked. As the right flank of the raiding party would then have been exposed, and as the enemy throughout showed himself to be particularly alert, the raid was finally abandoned.

Smoke barrages were made at 2.10 A.M. on the flanks of the gas, and the artillery and trench mortars carried out a most excellent and accurate bombardment. Machine guns assisted with indirect fire which was good and never dropped. At 2.40 A.M. the gas was turned off and the smoke barrages and machine gun and trench mortar fire ceased.

During the time spent in the Laventie sector good work was done by the Divisional Mounted Troops— Headquarters, " D " Squadron and the Machine Gun Section, 1/1st Westmoreland and Cumberland Yeomanry —under Lieut.-Colonel C. Beddington. Parties of " D " Squadron (Major E. B. Lees) frequently did a tour of duty in the trenches, and the Machine Gun Section was regularly employed in the line. On the 25th of September Lieut. Leighton acted as Divisional Observation Officer and Captain Curtis as Liaison Officer between Divisional Headquarters and the Meerut Division. On the 8th of December Major Lees was invalided home and Captain C. A. C. Hazelhurst took command of " D " Squadron. By the 16th of January the squadron had 54 trained bombers—72 per cent. of the men available for bombing instruction.

The 20th Divisional Cyclist Company, under Captain C. H. M. Johns, in addition to providing orderlies, police and men for salvage and other duties, provided working parties almost every day and night from the middle of October, and put up a large amount of wire.

The gallant conduct of Lieut. Hankey, 12th K.R.R.C., while instructor at the 60th Brigade bombing school, should be mentioned here.   On three separate occasions Lieut. Hankey saved lives by picking up and throwing away lighted bombs which had been dropped or had fallen short.   He was later awarded the Albert Medal for these acts.

On the 9th the relief of the 20th by the 8th Division began, and by the 13th all units were in the reserve area, with Divisional Headquarters at Blarnighem Château.   Here they stayed for a week carrying out training.   Suddenly, on the 20th of January, the Division was ordered to move north to the Second Army, having been specially selected by Lord Cavan to form part of the new XIVth Corps.

CHAPTER III

THE YPRES SALIENT

22nd January to 26th July 1916

The left sector of the XIVth Corps front—German attacks on
the left of the line—Arrival of the Machine Gun Companies and Medium Trench Mortar Batteries—Major-
General Davies succeeded by Major-General Douglas
Smith—Attack on the 7th D.C.L.I.—The Division in
reserve—Reorganisation of the artillery—The sector north
of Hooge—Attack on the 7th Somerset L.I.—Attack on
the Canadians at Hooge—Gas attacks and raids by the
Division—Move south.
(Vide Map I.)

ALTHOUGH the Division began its march north
into the Ypres Salient on the 22nd of January
1916, it was more than a fortnight before any
of the troops took over a part of the front line. Twelve
days were spent in the area round Cassel. During this
time, in order to learn the ground and the local conditions, parties of officers and N.C.O.'s were attached for
two or three days at a time to the 14th Division, which
was holding the left sector of the VIth Corps front, and
which the 20th was under orders to relieve. On the 3rd
of February the Division moved to the Reserve Area
vacated by the 49th Division, with Headquarters at
Château Esquelbecque—an interesting old house built
in 1606 and occupied by General Grant with the 15th
Hussars for two years after the battle of Waterloo.
Next day the VIth Corps handed over to the newly-

formed XIVth, which consisted at this time of the
Guards, 6th and 20th Divisions.

The new line, held by two brigades with one in reserve,
was the left sector of the British front and ran on the
north side of Ypres from a point 1500 yards due north
of St Jean to the canal bank about 1000 yards south-
east of Boesinghe. On the right was the 6th Division
and on the left the French Thirty-sixth Corps. The
difference between this sector and the area about
Laventie immediately became apparent from the daily
casualty lists. During the first month alone at Ypres
the Division suffered 1000 casualties, equal to the whole
number sustained during the five months at Laventie.

In order to make clear the operations that followed,
it is necessary to describe in some detail the trenches on
this front. They were numbered from the right, B 15
to 17, D 19 to 22, and E 23 (just south-east of Krupp
Farm) being in the area of the right brigade. The
left brigade trenches—those with which we are at first
chiefly concerned—were E 24 to 29 and F 30 to 35.
The ground between the canal and the German lines
was nothing but a quagmire. It was therefore impossible
to construct continuous front line trenches, and those
that did exist had in many places been blown in. These
isolated sections of trench, separated from each other by
gaps which in places were 80 yards or more across,
were held by parties varying in strength from 8 or 10
men to a platoon. They were narrow and shallow, the
parapets low and rarely bullet-proof, with very little
wire in front of them. There was only a very small
parados in some places and hardly anywhere any
revetment. There were practically no dugouts. Communication trenches were few and bad; they were
extremely difficult to drain and were constantly being
demolished by shell fire, so that rations, R.E. material,

etc., had to be brought up a long way from the dumps under very difficult conditions. The Germans had constructed concrete block-houses all along the front at short intervals, and their position on the Pilckem ridge entirely dominated the whole ground as far as Ypres, rendering any movement in the front areas very difficult.

The 60th Brigade, under Brig.-General Roy, moved into these trenches on the night of the 11th/12th of February, coming under the orders of the G.O.C. 14th Division for the following day until the rest of the 20th had come up into the line and Major-General Davies had taken over command. The 6th K.S.L.I. were on the right of the front line and the 12th R.B. on the left. The relief began about 9 P.M. and was still in progress when the Germans opened a very heavy bombardment on the left of the line where the 12th R.B. were taking over from the 9th K.R.R.C. A bombing attack then developed against the two trenches F 34 and F 35 on the extreme left, accompanied by artillery and trench mortar fire on the communication trenches leading to the canal bank. The attack on F 34 came from the right, from the front and from the left front, but failed. In F 35 the number of available bombs soon ran out, owing to two bomb stores having been blown up by shells, and great difficulty was experienced in getting up a further supply through communication trenches knee-deep in mud. The Germans bombed their way up the whole of the trench, at the end of which they were stopped by rifle fire. Major H. L. Riley, commanding the 12th R.B., then asked the 12th K.R.R.C. for two bombing sections ; with these in support Lieut. Gribble, the bombing officer of the 12th R.B., counter-attacked, and after half an hour recaptured the whole of F 35 as well as a German bombing post. Lieut. Gribble, who received the M.C. for his action on this day, was severely wounded while making a block in the trench. During this attack valuable help was given by the 20th Divisional Artillery, which had begun moving into the line as early as the 9th of the month.

Having been driven out of F 35, the Germans withdrew and began bombarding the trench with guns and trench mortars. Gradually they blew it in, necessitating successive withdrawals and causing many casualties. Several blocks were built during the 12th, and these were used as one section of the trench after another became untenable. Eventually, when the whole of F 35 had been practically obliterated, a position was taken up a little further back. During the morning of the 12th three bombing sections of the 12th K.R.R.C. and three of the Oxford and Bucks L.I., with two platoons of the 12th K.R.R.C., were sent up to reinforce the 12th R.B., and the garrisons of the trenches in rear were strengthened. The difficulties of communication were increased by the telephone wires having been broken during the bombardment. The 12th R.B. lost three officers and about 100 other ranks, but they made a fine stand—recognised by the Commander-in-Chief and the Army, Corps, Divisional and Brigade Commanders in the messages which they sent next day. One of these messages ran : " The Commander-in-Chief and the Corps Commander both wish to express their gratification at the most successful action of both the artillery and infantry of the 20th Division yesterday under novel conditions which might have placed them at a disadvantage."

Another, addressed to the 12th R.B., was as follows : " Corps and Divisional Commanders convey thanks and congratulations to all ranks for good work done yesterday under trying conditions. Brigadier also thanks all ranks for excellent work."

About 3.30 P.M. on the 12th an intense bombardment was put down on the trench F 30, held by 2nd Lieut. Fish and 30 men of the 12th R.B. After ten minutes the barrage lifted, on which about 200 Germans, under cover of heavy machine-gun fire, crossed to an unoccupied trench on the right. A small party reached the right sentry group but was driven back. Later, between 4 and 5 P.M., two bombing attacks were repulsed by 2nd Lieut. Fish and his garrison—reduced during the day to one sergeant and seven men. During the whole time the machine gun of this party was out of action. On request for reinforcements 30 men of the battalion were sent up at 9 P.M., and the garrison worked all night strengthening the parapet and barricades. 2nd Lieut. Fish was awarded the M.C. on the 2nd of March.

The 59th Brigade took over the right of the Divisional front on the night of the 12th/13th, after some delay caused by the heavy shelling of Poperinghe and Vlamertinghe. Next day the 61st Brigade went into the reserve area in and about Poperinghe; Divisional Headquarters moved on the 12th into hutments about two miles north-east of the town, and at 8 A.M. on the 13th Major-General Davies took over command of the sector from the G.O.C. 14th Division.

Infantry action was over for a few days, during which the necessary reliefs were carried out and work on the trenches begun. There was, of course, a tremendous amount to be done to make a good line. Sixteen hundred men of the 59th Brigade worked almost every night at this time, and good progress was made during the month. The line of the 60th Brigade was worse than ever after the recent bombardments, which had destroyed the parapets in many places, and in all parts of the Divisional front shelling continued daily, hampering the working parties and necessitating still more work. The canal bank was under enfilade fire from some German guns, which did a good deal of damage there and caused many casualties on the night of the 12th/13th. The only bridge in the left sub-sector which could be used by day was broken on the 13th, so that communication across the canal on this flank was cut off until the R.E. had repaired the damage at 10 P.M. that night.

All companies of the R.E. and of the 11th D.L.I. were kept working hard during the time spent in this sector, reclaiming the front line system and improving communications. The field companies, working in the areas of their brigades, constructed among other things extensive breastwork trenches in No Man's Land and a large number of framed machine-gun emplacements with concrete head cover. The amount of work that was done by the R.E. and infantry is indicated by the fact that at one time an average of four tons of material was taken up to the line each night from the workshops and dumps of the 96th Field Company alone. The artillery did a great deal of work constructing new observation posts and improving communications and battery positions. The 11th D.L.I. were employed in digging and revetting trenches, putting out wire, making dugouts and machine-gun emplacements, sinking wells, and repairing and relaying tramways. Later, in April, one company of the battalion was sent to each of the brigades in the front line, and a letter received from the C.R.E. on the 9th of the month especially praised the work of these companies.

The system of communications taken over by the Signal Company was in keeping with the general condition of the trenches. Shallow buried cables were found in the back areas and open cables forward of brigades. As these were continually being cut, the work of the company became increasingly difficult. The forward communication trenches were so overlooked from Pilckem Ridge that lines could not be mended in daytime. As subsidiary methods which were adopted in later times were not then used, the standard of communication was necessarily less high than it had been in the Laventie area.

The Germans renewed their activities on the extreme left of the line on the 19th, when they made another attack on F 34. This was now no more than a post, quite isolated and in a very exposed position, not more than 20 yards from a strongly held German trench, with which it was connected by a sap. It was held by one officer and 30 men of the 12th K.R.R.C., who had relieved the 12th R.B. four days before. About 4.30 P.M., after sweeping the parapet of F 34 with machine-gun fire, the Germans seem to have come up the sap from their own line and rushed the post. The S.O.S. call was sent, whereupon the artillery, assisted by the French, put down a barrage from the canal bank round trenches F 34 and 33, five batteries of the Divisional Artillery alone firing over 1200 rounds. Another party of the enemy—they were estimated at 200 in all—got in on the right of F 34 and also on the right of F 33, between which post and the next, F 30, there was a gap of 300 yards in dead ground where the intervening trenches had been destroyed. The N.C.O. and 12 men in F 33 were thus cut off, and all except one man were captured. The first intimation received that these men had been taken prisoner came from the German wireless communiqué. F 30 was then isolated. As the Divisional Commander decided that owing to the exposed position of the captured trenches no counter-attack should be made, the garrison of F 30 was ordered to withdraw.

On the 20th of February began a series of most successful artillery bombardments, which were carried out daily up to the 25th, and continued after that date at frequent intervals as long as the Division remained in this sector.

These bombardments produced retaliation from the German guns and trench mortars, which did a good deal of damage to our positions. Infantry action was confined to patrols which were frequently out and did good work.

Meanwhile, on the 18th of February, the Division had received orders to extend the line to the right, taking over as far as Pratt Street, just north-west of Wieltje Farm, from the 6th Division. This added some 1500 yards to the front and included a pronounced salient, the right of which rested on the road 500 yards north of the Farm. The rearrangement was made by each brigade extending its right, the 60th putting three battalions into the front line and the 59th keeping two in front and two behind. The necessary alterations were carried out on the 21st and 22nd, and on the 23rd the 60th Brigade on the left was relieved by the 61st and went into Divisional reserve.

On the 3rd of March an addition was made to the fighting troops of the Division by the arrival from England of the three Brigade Machine Gun Companies. They went to join their respective brigades, with which they served until, under a new organisation in 1918, they became the 20th Battalion of the Machine Gun Corps.

At this time also three Medium Trench Mortar Batteries (X/20, Y/20 and Z/20) were formed, under

Captain Buckley, the D.T.M.O. On the 8th Major-General Davies handed over command of the Division. His successor was Major-General W. Douglas Smith, C.B. During this month also Lieut.-Colonel A. Rolland succeeded Colonel Kenyon as C.R.E.

While the trenches were being made more secure and more habitable by hard and continual work, another unpleasantness was added to life in the Salient by a change in the weather. On the 21st of February it became cold and frosty. Two days later snow fell and a hard frost followed, covering the canal with ice. After another fall of snow on the 26th a thaw set in, leaving the ground sodden and the trenches in a very bad state. Cold weather came again at the beginning of March, and snow fell at intervals throughout the month. In these conditions the problem of keeping the troops warm and giving them hot food had to be solved. All rations were carried from dumps near the canal bank in sandbags. Fires in the front line were impossible, as any smoke at once drew hostile artillery fire. The difficulty was met by buying oil and spirit stoves, and by supplying " Thermos " cases and food containers. In this way it was found possible to provide hot tea and food daily.

At 4 P.M. on the 11th of April the enemy began a bombardment of the front trenches of the left sub-sector, held by the 61st Brigade. The fire increased in intensity about 6 P.M., trench mortars being used as much as artillery. Trench E 28, held by the 7th D.C.L.I. in four posts, was destroyed. Most of the men in this trench managed to work their way either to a bombing post on the left or into E 27 on the right, but those in the centre who could not get out were either killed or wounded. The enemy then attacked E 28. The first line, about 70 strong, was caught in enfilade by a party of 12 men of the D.C.L.I., who had taken up a position at the end of the trench, and was practically wiped out before the second line was over the parapet. On receiving the S.O.S. signal the French as well as the Divisional Artillery immediately opened a very accurate fire. The second German line, about 30 men carrying entrenching tools, was caught by the artillery fire and turned back.

At the same time two parties attacked trenches E 25 and 26. These trenches were separated by a gap, in front of which was a large crater caused by a trench mortar. Some Germans got into this crater, but were bombed out again. About 30 more were seen in front of E 27 and 28, and a small party of 15 crawled up and attempted to enter one of the other trenches, but all were driven off. In the course of the evening two platoons of the 7th Somerset L.I. went up to bring ammunition and to reinforce the garrison. During the whole time the enemy kept up a barrage in rear of the trenches attacked, and much courage and coolness were shown by officers and men in passing through this very heavy shell fire and in bringing wounded out of it.

Second Lieut. R. Tawney received the M.C. and Sgt. J. Bristow the M.M. for their gallant action at this time.

The casualties in the D.C.L.I. were about 60. The enemy must have suffered much more heavily, as in front of trenches E 27 and 28 alone 30 dead were found.

The next day a message was received from the Army Commander conveying his appreciation of the gallant defence made by the 7th D.C.L.I., and the quickness of the artillery in supporting them. Recognition of individual acts of courage in this battalion came later, on the 15th May, when Captain W. W. Forestier and 2nd Lieut. L. E. Oudin, who

was afterwards killed on the Somme, were awarded
the M.C., and Sgt. C. W. Hood, Company-Sgt.-Major
W. Burman and Pte. H. Morris the M.M., for their
action on this day.

The Division then went back for a month's rest.
The relief by the 6th Division began on the 15th, and
units moved into the reserve area some miles west of
Poperinghe, with Divisional Headquarters at Esquelbecque. During this time brigade groups went in turn
to Calais, first the 61st, then the 60th, and then the
59th, for periods of a week or ten days each. The
Division was in turn in G.H.Q. and in Corps reserve.
and spent the time training and refitting. The
Divisional Band was formed at this time, and Sgt.
Eldridge, 11th D.L.I., was appointed Bandmaster. On
the 3rd of May it played for the first time in the square
at Esquelbecque.

On the 5th Brig.-General the Hon. L. Butler took
over command of the 60th Brigade from Brig.-General
Roy.

On the 12th the Divisional Artillery held a horse
show, which proved a great success. The condition
of the artillery horses and the excellence of their
turnout evoked the admiration of the whole Corps.
Organised sports, horse shows, bombing and bayonet
fighting competitions were also held at this period
by the brigades at Calais. The march of the 59th
Brigade from Calais, on the 13th of May, was rather
a severe test, and showed the state of fitness to which
the men had been brought. Orders reached battalions
only two to two and a half hours before the move,
which began at 7 P.M. The brigade marched 16
miles that night in the rain, arriving in billets at 4 A.M.
on the 14th. Starting again at 11 A.M., the troops
covered another 17 miles, and got into billets between

six and seven in the evening. Thus 33 miles had been done in twenty-four hours. Hardly any men fell out and the march was continued in the morning.

Next day the following letter arrived from Corps Headquarters: " The Corps Commander has heard with great pleasure of the soldier-like way in which the 59th Infantry Brigade tackled the difficulties of a sudden move and a wet night march. It was only to be expected of a brigade like the 59th, but it reflects great credit, all the same, on all concerned."

During May an alteration was made in the organisation of the artillery. The Brigade Ammunition Columns disappeared, and the Divisional Ammunition Column, under Lieut.-Colonel Foster, was divided into a first échelon (Nos. 1, 2 and 3 Section), and a second échelon (No. 4 Section), the latter supplying the wants of the infantry alone.

This was followed by a reorganisation of the batteries. The 92nd Brigade was to be a howitzer brigade no longer. The 91st, 92nd and 93rd Brigades were each to consist of three 18 pdr. batteries and one howitzer battery, and the 90th Brigade to consist of three 18 pdr. batteries. Each battery, as before, consisted of four guns.

On the 20th of May it was arranged to work the ammunition supply from a central dump at Divisional Ammunition Column Headquarters, whence issues would be made to sections, the sections delivering to battery gun positions and to infantry brigade transport lines.

In May the Divisional Mounted Troops left the Division. Headquarters and " D " Squadron of the Westmoreland and Cumberland Yeomanry, after a fortnight's training with the 2nd Cavalry Division, moved on the 15th to join the remaining squadrons

as a regiment under XIth Corps. The Divisional
Cyclist Company from the 26th of May became
absorbed in the XIVth Corps Cyclist Battalion.

On the 18th of May the Division began to relieve
the Guards in the right sector of the Corps line. The
G.O.C., 20th Division, took over command of this
sector on the 21st. The 60th Brigade was on the right,
the 61st on the left, and the 59th in reserve, with
Divisional Headquarters at the Mairie in Poperinghe.
On the right of the 20th was the Canadian Corps ;
on the left the 6th Division.

The line ran from some 400 yards north-west of
Hooge in a general north-westerly direction, passing
in front of Y Wood, through the east of Railway Wood,
and just in front of Crump and Warwick Farms
and the village of Wieltje. A few hundreds of yards
north-west of Wieltje the sector ended at the point
where the Divisional right had formerly rested.

The German front line ran at a general distance of
250 to 400 yards from our own, with, however, certain
important variations. A sharp German salient at the
north-east corner of Railway Wood ran to within 70
yards of the British trenches ; opposite Verlorenhoek
the lines were a little over 200 yards apart. About 300
yards north of Warwick Farm a sharp triangular salient
projected from the German line, and there was a rather
blunt German salient on the south-east side of the
Wieltje road.

On the night of the 20th/21st of May three bombing
attacks covered by the fire of six machine guns were
made against the 7th Somerset L.I. in the left sub-
sector. This battalion had moved into the trenches
the night before, and was still under the G.O.C. Guards
Division. The attacks were made simultaneously at
11.45 P.M. against the right, centre and left of the

battalion line, and were driven off chiefly by the
bombing sections, which had been placed at the weak
points in the trench. On the right, a party estimated
at 20 tried to force the barricade on the Ypres-
Zonnebeke road, but was driven off by two bombing
sections and the fire of Lewis guns. The attack in
the centre failed to reach the trenches. On the left
one of the sentries, Pte. Harris, heard the enemy
coming up an old communication trench which ran
towards the German lines. As soon as a wiring party
which was out in front had been recalled, Pte. Harris
began throwing bombs, whereupon the enemy came
out of the communication trench and tried to get
through the wire. The bombing section stationed in
this part of the trench was now reinforced by another,
and between them they drove back the attack. Sgt.
Tanner then led the two sections up the communication
trench in pursuit of the Germans, who, however, had
retired to their own line. In the course of the night
the Somersets had 1 man killed and 3 officers and 16
other ranks wounded. The G.O.C. Guards' Division,
in his report on these attacks, wrote : " The Somerset
L.I. deserve great credit for the manner in which their
bombing sections were organised, and for the immediate action taken. . . . Sgt. Tanner and his bombing sections showed initiative in at once pursuing the
enemy."

June was a month of much greater activity, which
began with the German attack on the Canadians at
Hooge. On the 2nd of the month, when this action
began, the 60th Brigade was still holding the
right of the Divisional front, in touch with the 3rd
Canadian Division ; the 59th Brigade had relieved
the 61st about a week before, and was holding the left
subsector.

D

On this day Brig.-General Sweny, Major R. Dashwood, his Brigade-Major, and Captain Beddington, his Staff-Captain, were all unfortunately wounded by a shell in Ypres. Brig.-General Hobkirk temporarily took over command of the 61st Brigade.

At 8.50 A.M. on the 2nd the Germans opened an intense bombardment on the Canadians and the 6th K.S.L.I., the right battalion of the 60th Brigade. Our artillery responded so effectively that the enemy, who tried to advance on the right of the 6th K.S.L.I. front, was unable to get forward, and lost heavily. At 12.30 P.M. the Germans attacked the Canadians, and during the day succeeded in taking two lines of trenches, including Hill 62 and Sanctuary Wood.

This advance compelled the temporary abandonment of two forward guns of C/92 Battery which had been placed in Maple copse, close to the Canadian front line, in order to enfilade " No man's land " opposite the front of the 20th Division.

Nearly all the gunners were killed or wounded, the sergeant in charge eventually receiving the M.M. for his gallant defence. The guns, when eventually recovered some days later, were riddled with bullets and badly smashed by shell-fire.

At 9 A.M. on the 2nd the 61st Machine Gun Company at Brandhoek was ordered to stand to. Although the transport was three-quarters of a mile away, the company was ready to move fifty minutes after the order had been received. Later, at 1.30 P.M., one section of this company was sent up through Ypres, which was being severely shelled, to the 60th Brigade, to strengthen the right flank.

" A " and " B " Companies of the 12th K.R.R.C., under Captain D. Gardiner, were sent forward through a heavy barrage at 2 P.M. to reinforce the Canadian

Division, and suffered rather severely going up. They
rejoined their battalion on the 5th.

The enemy artillery and trench mortars were unusually active all along the line during the day, but
no further attack developed on the Divisional front.
During the night the Canadians made several counter-
attacks, and on the 3rd were reported to have got back
some of the lost trenches. Fighting continued about
Hooge and Sanctuary Wood on the 4th and 5th, which
were, however, comparatively quiet days on the front
of the 20th Division. The 6th K.S.L.I. were relieved
by the 6th Oxford and Bucks L.I. on the night of the
3rd/4th of June.

At 12.30 P.M. on the 6th the enemy opened an
intense fire on the 60th Brigade line ; it lasted till
3.45 P.M. On the right, on the front of the 6th Oxford
and Bucks L.I., the shelling was chiefly on the support
trenches, leaving the front line little damaged, but
the front trenches of the 12th R.B. on the left were
breached in several places. Telephone communication
from this battalion headquarters to all companies was
broken.

At the same time the enemy attacked the Canadians,
and the 6th Oxford and Bucks L.I. several times got
rifle and machine-gun fire well in to parties of Germans
moving towards Hooge.

About 2.30 the enemy came over his parapet towards
the lines of the 12th R.B. and of the 11th K.R.R.C.,
who were holding the right of the 59th Brigade front.
Rifle fire was opened on them, and the artillery immediately barraged the trenches in answer to the
S.O.S. A party of about thirty, advancing towards
the 11th K.R.R.C., was seen to turn back hurriedly
into cover, under the fire of our Lewis guns. Most
of those who attacked the 12th R.B. dropped into

long grass when fire was opened, and tried to crawl back ; none reached our line.

About 3.15 P.M. the enemy exploded two mines. One was well in front of the 6th Oxford and Bucks L.I. line, and did no damage ; but the other, under the trenches of the 12th R.B., about Gully Farm, destroyed fifty yards of trench, and buried Second-Lieut. Messenger and 22 men. Only Second-Lieut. Messenger and 10 men survived.

Meanwhile the main attack, which was being delivered with great determination against the Canadians, was meeting with some success. At 3.26 P.M. the 3rd Canadian Division reported that the enemy was advancing north of the Menin road and through Sanctuary Wood ; and at 7.55 P.M. that the Germans had captured Hooge.

The 7th K.O.Y.L.I. left Poperinghe at 4.10 P.M. for Vlamertinghe, and came under the orders of the 60th Brigade. At 10 P.M. the 12th R.B. were reinforced by two platoons of the 12th K.R.R.C. and two Lewis guns ; and a working party of 100 men of the 12th K.R.R.C. was sent up to them.

Throughout the operations of this day the trench mortar batteries did most valuable work, Captain Buckley, the D.T.M.O., and Captain Traill, commanding Y/20 Battery, both receiving the M.C.

In the course of the fighting some of the Canadian communications broke down. Fortunately, with the help of recently completed buried cables, some laid in the sewers of Ypres, the 20th Divisional Signal Company was able to maintain communication for the Canadians for a considerable time during the most critical period of the fighting.

During the night the damage done to the trenches was repaired and a new line dug. Patrols searched the front, bringing in prisoners, and discovering parties of the enemy consolidating their line. These parties were brought under fire from our machine guns and snipers, and suffered much loss. Touch with the Canadians, which had been lost during the day's fighting, was re-established, and was maintained throughout the night.

The casualties of the 60th Brigade were about 100, of which 77, including 25 killed, were in the 12th R.B.

On the 10th of June the following message was received from G.O.C. 3rd Canadian Division : " I am writing on behalf of the whole of the 3rd Canadian Division to thank you most heartily for the immediate and substantial assistance which the 20th Division gave us on June 2nd and on the subsequent days, and to ask you also to repeat our thanks to General Butler and to the 12th K.R.R.C., who sent two companies to strengthen our line. We shall always remember with gratitude the help given so promptly and freely by your Division."

The next few days were spent in harassing the enemy parties working on their new positions, and in work on our own trenches. On the 8th and 9th the 60th Brigade was relieved by the 61st in the right sub-sector. Though the 60th went into reserve, the troops had not much rest, for by the 10th, 600 men of the Brigade were working nightly on the new line from Cork Cottages to Dragoon Farm, and 200 men were employed in burying cables. On the 11th an additional 600 men (300 from the artillery and 300 from the reserve brigade) were required to bury cables for the XIVth Corps.

The last phase of these operations was carried out on the 13th, when the Canadians attacked in order to regain the lost ground. To assist them, the 20th

Division was ordered to discharge gas and smoke along its front and then push out patrols, following these up by larger raiding parties if possible, at four selected points in the German line. Zero was 1.30 A.M. on the 13th. Owing to the short notice that had been given, it was found impossible to get all the gas cylinders into the trenches in time. By some mistake in one part of the line, the smoke bombs were thrown three minutes before zero. This unfortunately gave alarm to the enemy, who thus had time to put on gas masks.

The gas, discharged at zero from 130 cylinders, went well and quickly. In three minutes practically all the rifle and machine-gun fire from the German trenches had ceased. The artillery barrage also began at zero, and was most effective. After twenty-five minutes it lifted to allow our infantry raiding parties to go forward.

On the right one party of the Somerset L.I., under Captain J. N. C. Peard, was held up by the wire near Railway Wood. Owing to the gas this party had to put on gas masks, and while attempting to cut a passage through the wire 3 men were killed and Captain Peard and 10 men wounded. All the wounded, however, were brought back safely. A party of the 11th K.R.R.C. under Lieut. H. A. Denison got in at the Mound (southwest of Verlorenhoek), which was found to be practically obliterated by our trench mortar bombardment. This party beat off a counter attack, and returned with only five slight casualties. The left party got as far as the German wire and reconnoitered the position, but, being only a small patrol, did not attempt to enter the trenches.

The 1st Canadian Division in a most successful attack regained Mount Sorrel and Observatory Ridge. On the 24th of June the Division began a series

of operations—bombardments and raids—against the
enemy. The first day was devoted to wire cutting—
very successfully done by the artillery and trench
mortar batteries. On the 25th the enemy lines were
shelled during the day, and at 10 o'clock that night
a raid on the enemy salient east-south-east of Wieltje
was carried out by three columns of the 10th K.R.R.C.,
with the assistance of 1 officer and 4 men of the 84th
Field Company R.E. The assaulting troops—3 officers
and 80 men—were under the command of Captain
R. S. Cockburn; the three raiding parties were led
by Lieut. F. V. Le Pavoux, Lieut. R. L. Jones (both
of whom were wounded during the raid), and Lieut.
G. A. Langley. The R.E. party was under Lieut.
Manisty.

This raid had been previously practised against
facsimile trenches in the back area, and Lieut.-Colonel
Blacklock, D.S.O. (later promoted Major-General), who
commanded this battalion, had carefully supervised
the training for this operation. It was in a great
measure due to him that the raid proved so successful.

All three parties entered the enemy's lines and went
thoroughly through the salient, suffering very few
casualties. The German trenches had been badly
knocked about by our artillery fire, but a great deal
of work had evidently been expended on them. They
were found to be deep and strong, well revetted, and
absolutely dry. Seven prisoners—including an officer
—were taken, but the officer was killed and five of the
men were wounded by a German shell after they had
reached our lines. A considerable amount of loot—
equipment, papers, etc.—was also brought in. Captain
R. S. Cockburn, Lieut. F. V. Le Pavoux, Second-Lieut.
R. L. Jones, Second-Lieut. G. A. Langley and Lieut.
Manisty, were all awarded the M.C. The M.M. was

given to Lance-Cpl. J. Frost, Lance-Sgt. F. W. Webb, and Rfm. E. Coates, of the 10th K.R.R.C., Sgt. A. McKay, 84th Field Company, Sapper H. Holland, 20th Divisional Signal Company, and Rfm. J. P. Mansfield, 59th Trench Mortar Battery. Our casualties during the raid were 1 officer and 3 other ranks. Unfortunately the parties on their return came into the enemy's barrage on our front and support lines, and lost a good many men. This brought the total casualties to 3 officers and 38 other ranks. The raid was a great success in every way, the information alone which it secured being of the greatest value.

Another raid was carried out on the night of the 29th/30th of June by the 6th K.S.L.I., commanded by Lieut.-Colonel E. A. Wood, D.S.O. A bombardment by the Divisional Artillery and the heavy guns of the XIVth Corps during the day and night did great damage to the trenches and provoked considerable retaliation, especially on Railway Wood. Under cover of these bombardments the trench mortars effectively cut the German wire.

Two raiding parties went forward, each composed of 2 officers and 40 men of the 6th K.S.L.I. They were all volunteers, and had been specially trained for this raid at Vlamertinghe on a model of the German trenches to be attacked. Special equipment was carried, such as revolvers, knobkerries, explosives, rockets and torches, and one party had bells and the other rattles, to be used as the signal to withdraw. The two parties were commanded by Lieut. D. S. A. McKimm on the right and Captain H. M. O'Connor on the left, and were accompanied by a party of the 83rd Field Company R.E., under Second-Lieut. H. Y. V. Jackson, and some of the 177th Tunnelling Company R.E. They moved out at midnight, and on the barrage lifting, made for the enemy trenches.

The right party got in first, and found the line badly knocked about. Lieut. McKimm and his men thoroughly searched the trenches, blocked the enemy's communications, and did as much damage as possible. Eleven Germans were bayonetted emerging from a shelter into the trench, six dug-outs with parties of four to six inside were bombed, and other casualties caused and prisoners taken. By 12.30 A.M. the party had returned without casualties.

Captain O'Connor's party also successfully entered German lines. One section, under Corporal Richards, who gallantly continued to lead his men although wounded early in the raid, bombed seven dug-outs and took six prisoners, pushed forward against strong opposition, and then held on until the order to retire was given. Other sections dealt similarly with all the enemy they met. Lance-Cpl. Walker was killed while making a splendid fight with his section, which was able to account for 35 of the enemy.

The casualties of this party were 2 killed, 1 missing and 9 wounded. In the course of the raid 60 or 70 prisoners were taken.

The artillery support was all that could be desired. During the barrage, half the guns fired on the front line and half on the support lines, so as to prevent the enemy from recognising when the lift took place, and the raiding parties, entering as soon as the barrage lifted, took the enemy completely by surprise.

The whole operation was very well carried out, and all ranks showed extraordinary keenness and determination to make the raid a success.

Among the many honours awarded to officers and men of the 6th K.S.L.I. for their services on this

occasion were the following: M.C., Captain H. M.
O'Connor, Lieut. D. S. A. McKimm; D.C.M., Cpl. R.
Richards.

All these raids and bombardments entailed harder
work on the troops behind the front line. R.E. material
was constantly required for the trenches, but owing
to the operations transport for it was difficult to obtain.
The ammunition requirements, too, during June were
heavy. Great credit must be given to the officers and
men of the Divisional Ammunition Column, who were
kept working at very high pressure during the whole
month.

On the 5th and 6th of July the 59th Brigade relieved
the 61st in the left sub-sector.

On the night of the 10th a minor operation was
carried out by the 59th Brigade. Gas was turned on
at 10.30, accompanied by a smoke screen and an
artillery and trench mortar barrage, while four raiding
parties formed up ready to go forward. This time
the enemy seemed to be well prepared. As soon as
the gas was discharged he lighted fires along his parapet
to make the cloud rise. Severe artillery, rifle and
machine-gun fire prevented the raiding parties from
reaching his lines except at one point. This was at
the Mound, where Second-Lieut. Rudd and a party
of the 11th K.R.R.C. successfully bombed their way
up one of the communication trenches.

On the 12th the Germans severely shelled the
Wieltje salient. Great damage was done, and one
company alone—" A " Company of the 10th R.B.—lost
25 casualties, one-third of its whole strength. On the
12th and 14th the town of Poperinghe was heavily
bombarded; over 200 shells fell near the square and
railway station on the 12th, so that on the 14th,
under the orders of the Corps Commander, all troops

moved out of the town. Divisional Headquarters moved to a camp about 1000 yards to the north.

On the night of the 13th/14th, orders were received directing the 60th Brigade to move to Steenwerck, to be placed under the orders of the IInd Anzac Corps. The brigade, with its machine gun company and light trench mortar battery, entrained next morning at Poperinghe, which was being shelled at the time, but fortunately got away without casualties. The troops detrained at Steenwerck, and marched from there to Erquinghem. The 12th R.B. went straight into the trenches, the 6th K.S.L.I. and 6th Oxford and Bucks L.I. extending the line to the left on the 15th, when Brigade Headquarters and the 12th K.R.R.C. went into billets at Fleurbaix. The Brigade held a line running north-east and east from La Cordonnerie Farm on the right to just north of Le Bridoux ; covering this line were three attached batteries of the 24th Field Artillery Brigade, of the 6th Division.

The next two days were spent in registering the guns and in cutting the wire, in preparation for an attack which was to be made by the 61st Division and the 5th Australian Division on the right of the 60th Brigade. On the 19th, after a bombardment during the day, a mine was sprung opposite La Cordonnerie Farm at 7 P.M., and the assaulting troops went forward. Delangre Farm was the left of the attack, so that the 60th Brigade was not involved in these operations beyond firing on the Germans, who stood to in their trenches north of the farm and offered a good target for the machine guns. The ground gained could not be held by the attacking troops, who were back in their own trenches by 6.15 A.M. on the 20th.

On the night of the 22nd/23rd the 60th Brigade was relieved and marched back to billets about Bailleul.

Meanwhile, the rest of the 20th Division, with the exception of the artillery, had been relieved between the 14th and the 18th by the 6th Division, and had moved to an area west of Poperinghe, with headquarters at Esquelbecque. Here a warning order was received on the 17th that the Division, less artillery, would be required in the next few days to move to the area of the Vth Corps, to which the 84th Field Company R.E. had been attached since the 15th. On the 19th the move began, and on the 20th Major-General Douglas Smith took over from the G.O.C. 24th Division a line facing Messines and Wytschaete, and extending from the river Douve a little west of the Ploegsteert-Messines road to a point just south-west of the cross-roads at Kruisstraat.

The G.O.C. had not assumed command of this sector more than an hour, and the relief was not yet completed, when he received verbal instructions that the 20th Division would be required to move south as soon as it had been relieved by the 36th and 50th Divisions. Definite orders arrived next day, and the relief began at once. On the 23rd and 24th, units concentrated in the back area about Steenwerck and Hondeghem, where the 60th Brigade rejoined, and on the 25th and 26th the Division, leaving the artillery still at Ypres, went south to Doullens.

CHAPTER IV

THE SOMME

24th of July to 7th of September 1916

The line between Beaumont Hamel and Hebuterne—Move to
the Somme area—Battle of Guillemont.
(*Vide* Map II. and Sketch B.)

AS soon as all units were concentrated in the
district round Doullens, the 20th Division was
ordered to relieve the 38th in the hilly country
between Beaumont Hamel and Hebuterne. Accordingly
the 29th of July found the Division once more in the
line, though not yet in the area of the great offensive
which had been progressing since the first of the month
between the Ancre and the Somme.

Brig.-General W. E. Banbury, C.M.G., took over
command of the 61st Brigade on the 28th of July
from Brig.-General Sweny, who had returned to the
Brigade a few days earlier, but was still suffering from
the effect of his wounds.

The right of the new line rested about half a mile
north-west of Beaumont Hamel on the south side of a
spur known as Redan Ridge, overlooking the village,
which lay in a narrow valley some hundred feet below.
From the crest of Redan ridge the line ran rather east
of north into somewhat lower ground, facing Serre
and extending to a point 1200 yards north-west of it.
Here it formed a salient and turned back, rising to the
Divisional left flank at a place known as Sixteen Poplars
on the Hebuterne-Puisieux road about 1000 yards

from Hebuterne. The 61st Brigade held the right of this line, the 60th the centre opposite Serrre and the 59th the left, with Divisional Headquarters at Couin. The 38th Divisional Artillery remained in the line to support the 20th Division, whose own artillery was still at Ypres. The Division was now once more in the XIVth Corps, which had taken over that day from the VIIIth, and which consisted of the Guards, 6th, 20th and 25th Divisions; on the right of the 20th was the 25th Division and on the left the 56th.

Although this country was now outside the main battle area, attacks had þeen made on the 1st of July between the Ancre and Serre and north of Hebuterne, with a view to holding the enemy reserves and occupying his artillery. To meet these attacks the enemy had concentrated a large force of artillery, with the result that when the 20th Division took over the line the trenches were in an appalling state and the ground still covered with dead. The front line could be held only by advanced parties, and it had to be reclaimed; in places where it was too much damaged and full of dead bodies it had to be filled in and a new line dug in front of it. Communication trenches had to be put in good order for 500 yards behind the front line, deep dug-outs made, the battlefield cleared and a new line built within 200 yards of the enemy, wherever there was a greater distance than this between the opposing trenches. To assist in this task the 3rd Battalion Grenadier Guards was attached to the 20th Division from the 1st to the 7th of August; on the departure of this battalion, a field company of the Guards Division came to help. The field companies of the Division were employed in the areas of their respective brigades, and the 11th D.L.I. and large parties from the battalions in reserve were constantly at work.

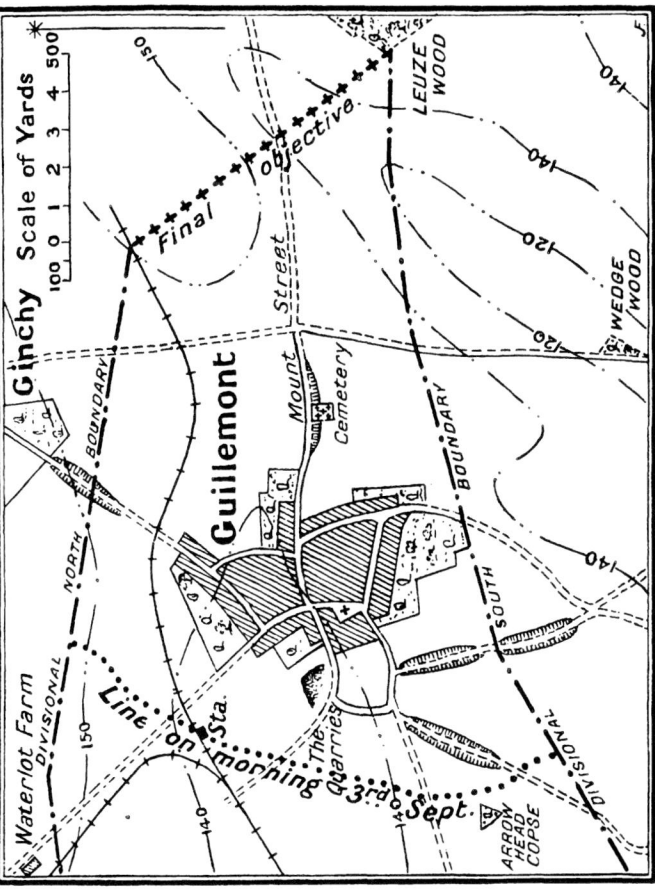

CUILLEMONT, 3RD-4TH Sept. 1916.   Sketch B.

Ginchy   Scale of Yards
100   0 1 2 3 4 500

Final objective

LEUZE WOOD

WEDGE WOOD

150

140

120

120

140

140

Street

Mount

Cemetery

Guillemont

BOUNDARY

NORTH DIVISIONAL

SOUTH BOUNDARY

DIVISIONAL

Waterlot Farm

150

140

140

Line on morning 3rd Sept.

The Quarries

Sta.

ARROW HEAD COPSE

[To face p. 62.

During the fortnight which the Division spent in
this sector the time was chiefly spent in improving
the line and in making preparations for a coming
attack. Accordingly the artillery and the troops in
the front trenches were kept fairly busy, while the
enemy trench mortars caused a good deal of fresh
damage and hindered the parties working at night.
The Divisional Signal Company was largely occupied
in an attempt to sort out a complex system of buried
cables left by the VIIIth Corps after the unsuccessful
attack at the beginning of the month. Wire cutting
by shell-fire was carried out daily for the first four
days of August. On the 4th our trench mortars and
Stokes guns and the 59th Brigade machine guns co-
operated with the artillery in a bombardment to
silence the enemy's trench mortars. That evening,
between 7 and 9.15 P.M., another bombardment was
carried out in order to assist the operations of the Ist
Anzac Corps at Pozières. It had been intended to
make a smoke and gas attack on the front of the 61st
Brigade, but the wind was unfavourable, so all that
could be done was to bring the enemy's trenches
under rifle and machine-gun fire. The 61st Machine
Gun Company fired 14,000 rounds, forming a barrage
behind the enemy's line between Beaumont Hamel and
Serre. The enemy's retaliation was slight at the time,
but at 11 P.M. he opened a heavy trench mortar fire.

On the 7th the 61st Brigade was relieved by the
74th Brigade of the 25th Division, and went into
Divisional reserve about Coigneux. On the same day
the 38th Divisional Artillery was relieved by that of
the Guards, whose left group fired 1000 rounds on the
German front line on the 8th to assist the operations of
the Fourth Army.

A good deal of preparation was made on the 13th to

meet an expected attack. The army operators at the listening sets overheard a conversation between two German officers, which seemed to indicate that a bombardment of our lines, to be followed by a raid, had been arranged to take place that night. The Germans actually shot tracing tapes by rocket across "No man's land," exactly bounding the front of the expected attack. Neither the bombardment nor the raid, however, came off, the night as a matter of fact being particularly quiet.

On the 14th the 61st Brigade relieved the 60th, and that night made a smoke barrage in conjunction with operations further south, while artillery, machine-gun and rifle fire was opened along the whole Divisional front, a barrage behind the enemy's support line being made by the 61st Machine Gun Company.

Two days later, on relief by the Guards, the Division went out of the line, and after a few days in the district known as " A " area, with headquarters at Beauval, moved towards the scene of the battle in which it was to make its name. On the 22nd of August the 20th relieved the 24th Division in the sector north of the Guillemont-Montauban road. The 6th Divisional Artillery, which had been attached to the 20th Division since the 17th, when it had replaced that of the Guards, moved also to the new area. Divisional Headquarters was opened on the 23rd at Minden Post, near Carnoy.

The 59th Brigade held with one battalion in the front line the right sector from the Guillemont-Montauban road just west of Guillemont village to the station, with Brigade Headquarters at the Briqueterie, about half a mile south-east of Montauban. The 61st Brigade had a battalion and a half in the front trenches, continuing the line to a point just south of the south-east corner of Delville Wood. Brigade Headquarters was north-east of Bernafay Wood. The 60th Brigade was in reserve at the Craters, close to the Carnoy-Montauban road, about 1000 yards from Carnoy.

In order to appreciate the important part which the capture of Guillemont played in the general scheme, we will review briefly the course of the fighting up to this date. The original British line enclosed Maricourt on the east and north, running thence westward as far as Fricourt, which was in the hands of the enemy. It then turned rather west of north, past La Boisselle, Thiepval and Beaumont Hamel, all of which formed part of the German front line defences. Between the British right flank and the Somme the fighting was carried on by the French. The attack of the 1st of July gave us Montauban, Mametz, and a sharp salient each side of La Boisselle. These gains were increased in the fighting of the next fortnight to include Fricourt, Mametz Wood, Contalmaison, Ovillers-la-Boisselle and all ground between these places. On the left flank the German defences on the high ground south of Thiepval held out for many weeks. A second attack just before dawn on the 14th of July yielded very important results ; a footing was gained on the great ridge which extends between Combles and Thiepval, and part of the enemy's second defensive system was broken.

Sir Douglas Haig in his despatch [1] divides the battle of the Somme into three phases. In the first, which ended with this advance on the 14th–18th of July, the success of the attacks evidently came as a surprise to the enemy, who must have considered his defences practically impregnable. The second phase was a severe struggle for the possession of the main ridge, ending with the capture of Guillemont and Ginchy on the 3rd and 9th of September respectively. By this time the enemy

[1] Sir Douglas Haig's Despatches, p. 23.

E

had begun to bring strong reinforcements on to the
scene, so that on the 18th of July, at the close of the
first phase, his 62 battalions had been increased to 138,
and by the end of August, when the 20th Division came
into the fighting, his original 6 divisions on the front
of attack had been reinforced by 30 divisions more.[1]
The third phase was the exploitation of the success.

The line gained by the 18th of July, at the close of
the first phase, included Trônes Wood, Delville Wood,
and Longueval; it then turned to the west, passing on
the north side of Bazentin-le-Grand and Bazentin-
le-Petit to join our original trenches near Ovillers-la-
Boisselle. This left a dangerously sharp salient about
Longueval and Delville Wood, overlooked by the enemy
all round from the south-east to the north-west.
Behind this salient ran the French communications
as well as our own, and many guns and much ammunition had here to be crowded into a confined space.
It was evident that the enemy might well cause us heavy
loss by bringing concentrated artillery fire to bear on
this area, while if he could drive in the salient he would
get direct observation over the ground behind. Indeed,
in a heavy counter attack on the 18th he succeeded
in regaining part of Delville Wood and penetrated into
the northern half of Longueval, maintaining these
gains until on the 27th and 29th he was once more driven
back. It became particularly important, therefore, in
this struggle for the ridge, to straighten out the line
by the capture of Guillemont and Leuze Wood, so
bringing the right flank of the attack into line with
the centre.

With this end in view, while a further advance was
being made in the north towards High Wood and
Pozières, several attacks were made on Guillemont.

[1] Sir Douglas Haig's Despatches, p. 33 (Note).

The first, on the 23rd of July, failed. On the 30th of July, and again on the 8th of August, our troops entered the village but were unable to hold it. Lastly, on the 16th and 18th of August, attacks planned on a more comprehensive scale advanced the line to Guillemont station and to within a few hundred yards of the outskirts of the village, which, however, still remained in German hands.[1]

From this it will be seen that the capture of Guillemont—the task which the Division had been ordered to carry out—was no easy matter. The attack was to form part of a larger operation carried out by the whole Fourth Army, in conjunction with the French on the right. It was originally intended that the attack should be made on the 24th of August. Before it could be launched a good deal of work had to be done. The trenches, which had been much damaged in the recent fighting, had to be repaired, and a new line had to be dug to serve as departure trenches for the assaulting troops. The night of the 23rd/24th was spent in digging this new line; the work, however, was so much interrupted by the enemy that not much progress could be made. About 9.15 P.M. a heavy bombardment was opened all along the front and support lines, followed at 10.30 by an advance against the 11th K.R.R.C., who were holding the front line of the 59th Brigade. The enemy was easily driven back by rifle and machine-gun fire, but the trenches were rather badly damaged by the bombardment, which caused about 150 casualties in the battalion attacked. By 11.30 all was quiet, and work was continued. At 12.30 A.M., however, the shelling broke out again, effectually stopping all further work for the night. XIVth Corps therefore ordered the attack to be postponed, confining the

---

[1] Sir Douglas Haig's Despatches, pp. 32, 34 to 36.

activities on the Divisional front to a modified artillery
programme in support of operations which were
carried out by the divisions on the right and left.
On the evening of the 24th, after another heavy
bombardment, the enemy attacked between the
Quarries, on the west edge of the village, and the
railway, but was again driven off. chiefly by machine-
gun fire.

On the 25th and 26th the Division side-slipped to the
right, the new front extending from 500 yards south
of the Montauban-Guillemont road to 450 yards north-
west of the village. On the 27th the 60th Brigade
relieved the 61st in the left sub-sector. On the eve of
this relief a direct hit on the headquarters of the
12th R.B., when a conference was taking place, unfortunately wounded five officers.

Meanwhile preparations for the attack were being
pushed forward. Unfortunately, just at this time
bad weather set in, and this, with the continued and
heavy hostile shelling, in which gas shells were largely
used, made the work extremely difficult. The trenches
were deep in mud and water, and were constantly being
blown in ; some of the communication trenches were
impassable, and all were in a very bad condition, so
that it became a most difficult matter to bring up rations
and ammunition and to effect reliefs in the front line.
The state of the Carnoy-Montauban road was such
that at one time, on the 29th, thirty-seven vehicles broke
down and stuck in the mud. In addition to this, on
the 25th the 11th R.B. lost about fifty men including
their commanding officer, Lieut.-Colonel Harington,
when the enemy attempted, without success, to enter
their trenches, and the 12th K.R.R.C. had to repulse
an attack which was made during a thunderstorm on
the evening of the 29th against the right of the 60th

Brigade line. After the thunderstorm, during which two of our observation balloons were struck by lightning and brought down, the trenches were in a worse state than ever. Moreover both No Man's Land and the ground behind the trenches were covered with dead bodies which had been lying out for weeks, and the state of the whole line was foul. The men, too, were given little rest; on the night of the 28th/29th all available men of all three brigades were working in the forward area.

These very severe conditions told on the health of the troops, who were becoming so exhausted that it seemed doubtful whether they would be fit for the severe fighting which the capture of Guillemont would probably involve. Brig.-General Shute was asked whether, in view of the weakness of his units and the great strain to which the men had been put, he thought his brigade could take part in the attack. All ranks were keen to go through with the job which they had been sent to do, and it was decided that the operations could be carried out if the whole brigade might first go for a day or two right out of the line to rest. This was granted. The attack, after being postponed to the 29th, and again to the 30th, owing to the weather and the state of the ground, had been finally put off to the 3rd of September. The 10th R.B. and the 10th K.R.R.C. had been relieved on the 29th by the 7th K.O.Y.L.I. and the 7th D.C.L.I., and on the 31st the rest of the 59th Brigade was relieved by the rest of the 61st in daylight and under a heavy gas bombardment. The 59th marched back tired out, having lost just 600 casualties, not counting sick, in the nine days it had held this line.

The 60th Brigade had suffered so severely, and the strength of the units had been so seriously reduced, that on the 1st of September the Corps Commander decided that the 47th Brigade of the 16th Division should be used in the attack on Guillemont and that the 60th Brigade should be withdrawn into reserve. The relief was accordingly carried out that night. Passing through Montauban battalions again came under heavy shelling. Brig.-General Butler handed over his complete plans for the battle to the Brigadier-General commanding the 47th Brigade, and sent up his staff captain and signal officer to assist him. It was a great disappointment to Brig.-General Butler and the 60th Brigade to be taken out of the attack after all the work done and the hardships suffered in preparation for it, but the strongest battalion, the 6th Oxford and Bucks L.I., did not number more than 550 rifles, and the remaining three battalions together totalled only 1000. The 6th Oxford and Bucks L.I. were then attached as a fifth battalion to the 59th Brigade. All this involved a modification of the original operation orders, though the main features of the scheme remained the same, and new orders were issued on the 2nd of September. In spite of these changes such a short time before the attack, all the necessary arrangements were made and worked well during the battle.

Before describing the course of the battle it may be well to notice the lie of the ground and certain points that had an important effect on the operations. The enemy's line ran a little to the west and north-west of Guillemont, which being part of his original second line of defence, though by this time reduced to a mass of ruins, was very strongly fortified. The village lay on high ground, but in a slight depression which is really the head of a long valley running up from the west. To the north, high ground extends for 3000 yards, with the village of Ginchy at the highest point ;

GUILLEMONT STATION

[*To face p.* 70.

to the south, after forming a ridge from 400 to 1000 yards across, the ground falls sharply in a series of irregular spurs and re-entrants towards the Somme. The most important of these re-entrants is a narrow valley which runs from Wedge Wood towards the north-east, merging just west of Leuze Wood into the high ground which extends east of Ginchy, and, except for the depression made by the upper end of this valley, east of Guillemont. Further east again the ground falls to the valley north of Combles. About 600 yards south-east of Wedge Wood is Falfemont Farm ; 400 yards south-west of Guillemont are the remains of a small triangular plantation known as Arrow Head Copse, situated on the top of the ridge and overlooking the village. Running more or less south from the south-west corner of Guillemont are two sunken roads, which gave more trouble and cost more casualties than any other obstacle encountered both in this battle and in the previous attempts to take the village. The Quarries, on the west edge of the village, had been well fortified and formed a very strong point. It only remains to take note of two roads, one leading from Wedge Wood to Ginchy, and the other, known as Mount Street, running east and west through Guillemont to the north corner of Leuze Wood.

The Divisional boundaries and the front line are shown in Sketch " B." The boundary between the brigades was Mount Street.

The essence of Major-General Douglas Smith's plan was to attack Guillemont from the north side as well as from the west and on the south.

To carry out this plan it was essential to dig assembly trenches north of Guillemont station. These were completed in time, thanks mainly to the untiring efforts of the 11th D.L.I. and the R.E.

Acting on the plan designed by Major-General Douglas Smith, Brig.-General Shute decided to put only a weak force on his left, and to dispose his greatest strength on the right flank, so as to encircle the village. His operation orders were a model of lucidity.

The first objective may be taken as the west and north sides of Guillemont; it included the eastern sunken road, the Quarries, and a road bounding the north of the village. The advance to this objective was to be made at noon.

The second objective, to be attacked at 12.50, was formed by a road passing through the eastern outskirts of the village and branching off from the north-east corner of it towards Ginchy.

The third objective was the Ginchy—Wedge Wood road, the attack on which was to be made at 2 P.M.

The fourth and final objective was a line running from the western corner of Leuze Wood, north-west towards Ginchy, as far as the railway.

On the right of the 20th the 5th Division was to advance against Falfemont Farm and Leuze Wood; on the left the 7th Division was to capture Ginchy.

During the night of the 2nd/3rd of September the 59th Brigade, with the 6th Oxford and Bucks L.I., returned to its position in the line, and the troops of both the attacking brigades took up their battle positions. There was luckily very little shelling during this night—none with gas shells—and units were able to complete their assembly before dawn. The enemy seemed unaware of the concentration that was being carried out against him. This was largely due to the splendid work of our aeroplanes. The last two days had been warm and sunny, and a complete rest and plenty of good food had restored the men wonderfully. They showed remarkable keenness as they went back to the line.

The following was the disposition of the troops on the morning of the 3rd of September :

Right Attack.

59th Brigade (Brig.-General C. D. Shute), with head-quarters at the Briqueterie, south of Bernafay Wood.

Front line, from right to left, 11th R.B. (Lieut.-Colonel A. E. Cotton), 10th R.B. (Lieut.-Colonel W. V. L. Prescott-Westcar), 10th K.R.R.C. (Lieut.-Colonel C. A. Blacklock), plus one company of the 11th K.R.R.C.

In support, 6th Oxford and Bucks L.I. (Lieut.-Colonel E. D. White).

In reserve, 11th K.R.R.C. (Major F. L. V. Swaine) (less one company), in trenches just south-east of Trônes Wood.

The 96th Field Company R.E. (Major P. F. Storey) was divided, one section being placed at each end of the front line, and the remaining half company, with a company of the 11th D.L.I., being south of Trônes Wood.

Left Attack.

47th Brigade (Brig.-General C. E. Pereira), with head-quarters near the north-east corner of Bernafay Wood.

Front line, from right to left, 6th Connaught Rangers, facing east opposite the Quarries ; 7th Leinsters, facing south-east.

In support, 8th Munster Fusiliers.

In reserve, 6th Royal Irish, just east of the northern half of Trônes Wood.

The 83rd Field Company R.E. (Captain J. A. C. Pennycuick) and one company of the 11th D.L.I., attached to the 47th Brigade, were west of Trônes Wood.

Supports to Right and Left Attacks.

Two battalions of the 61st Brigade were placed at the disposal of the attacking brigades, the 7th Somerset L.I. (Lieut.-Colonel C. J. Troyte-Bullock) supporting the 59th, and the 12th King's (Lieut.-Colonel A. N. Vince) supporting the 47th.

Divisional Reserve.

The 61st Brigade (Brig.-General W. E. Banbury), less the two battalions supporting the attack, was in Divisional reserve, with headquarters in Bernafay Wood close to the west edge. The two remaining battalions of the brigade—the 7th D.C.L.I. (Major R. Mander) and the 7th K.O.Y.L.I. (Lieut.-Colonel B. B. Robinson)—were moving forward from the craters near Carnoy with a view to occupying the trenches vacated by the 7th Somersets and 12th King's as soon as these units should advance.

Near the 61st Brigade headquarters, but outside the wood, were the 84th Field Company R.E. (Major M. A. H. Scott) and the 11th D.L.I. (Major G. Hayes), less the two companies attached to the 59th and 47th Brigades.

The 60th Brigade (Brig.-General the Hon. L. Butler), less the 6th Oxford and Bucks L.I., was at the craters.

Artillery.

The attack was covered by the fire of the artillery of the 6th and 24th Divisions, under Brig.-General L. M. Philpotts, C.R.A., 24th Division, and of the Corps heavy artillery allotted for the purpose. Brig.-General Philpotts and his brigade-major were both unfortunately killed on the following day whilst visiting Guillemont.

The strength of the brigades in actual number of rifles at the beginning of the day was as follows :

47th Infantry Brigade	.	.	.	.	.	2400
59th ,, ,,	plus	6th	Oxford	and
		Bucks L.I.	.	.	2300
60th ,, ,,	less	6th	Oxford	and
		Bucks L.I.	.	.	1000
61st ,, ,,	.	.	.	.	.	2253
			Total	.	.	7953

The operations began at 6 A.M. on the 3rd with a deliberate bombardment of certain selected areas. A " Chinese attack " was made at 8.15 A.M., when all batteries delivered a burst of rapid fire on the enemy's lines. At 8.30 the whole of the 6th and 24th Divisional Artilleries concentrated an intense fire on an area on the north-east of Guillemont known as the "trap" area, which had purposely not been shelled before, while the howitzers opened with gas shell.

At 9 A.M. the 5th Division began to advance towards Falfemont Farm. This attack was at first only partially successful, but indirectly it was very useful in diverting the enemy's attention from Guillemont.

Zero hour for the 20th Division was noon. Just before this, liquid fire was projected and a " push pipe " mine was exploded with the object of destroying a German machine-gun emplacement in the line of the first sunken road opposite Arrow Head Copse — a formidable obstacle which had held up former attacks on this flank. The mine had evidently struck a stone in being run out and had turned back. The explosion made a shallow trench about 120 feet long, leaving intact the machine-gun emplacement, which was, however, destroyed by the guns and which gave no trouble in the advance.

At zero the artillery fire became intense. Half the field artillery guns were used for stationary barrages and half for creeping barrages. At the beginning of the advance towards each objective the procedure was the same; a stationary barrage was put down and a creeping barrage moved forward in front of the assaulting infantry at the rate of fifty yards per minute. The stationary barrage lifted at certain stated times, or whenever the creeping barrage came up to it.

At zero, too, the infantry advanced close under the creeping barrage. The first objective was quickly reached. On the right strong opposition was met at the first sunken road by the 11th and 10th R.B., who lost a good many men at this point. The 6th Oxford and Bucks L.I. now came up, and passing through the two Rifle Brigade battalions carried on the assault to the second sunken road, which was the first objective on this flank. They, too, suffered a good many casualties, the three leading companies losing all their officers and their company sergeant-majors before the second road was reached. On the left the 47th Brigade moved forward rapidly, reaching the German lines at one point just as the enemy was manning his parapet and mounting a machine gun. Here the enemy was completely surprised and surrendered freely. In their impetuous advance the Connaught Rangers on the right passed the Quarries without completely clearing them, and the left flank of the 10th K.R.R.C., attacking on the left of the 59th Brigade, was placed for a time in a difficult position. Lieut.-Colonel Blacklock, commanding this battalion, at once grasped the situation, and by detaching his reserve company and a platoon from one of the companies in the line to clean up the Quarries averted what might have been a very awkward state of affairs. Later he was awarded a bar to his D.S.O. for this action.

Both brigades had occupied the first objective by 12.30 P.M., at which time the situation was as follows. On the right the 6th Oxford and Bucks L.I. and the 10th K.R.R.C. held the second sunken road and the west side of the village as far as Mount Street, with the 10th and 11th R.B. in rear. On the left the 6th Connaughts and 7th Leinsters held the rest of the western and the northern sides of the village, supported by the 8th Munsters, while the 6th Royal Irish were moving up from Trônes Wood. The 7th Somerset L.I. had reached the first sunken road after losing a good many men in passing through the enemy barrage at Arrow Head Copse; the 12th King's, moving forward under severe shell fire, had entered the northern part of Trônes Wood; the 7th K.O.Y.L.I. and the 7th D.C.L.I. were marching up from their billets, the leading companies of the former being east of Bernafay Wood. An officer who saw the battalions of the 61st Brigade stated that they advanced through a very heavy barrage in perfect order as if on parade.

The attack on the second objective in the 59th Brigade sector was carried out by the 11th R.B., the 10th R.B., and one company of the 10th K.R.R.C., supported by the Oxfords and the 10th K.R.R.C., with the 11th K.R.R.C. in reserve. On the left the Munster Fusiliers moved to the assault, leaving the Leinsters and Connaughts to consolidate the positions won. The advance was timed to begin at 12.50 P.M., and very soon afterwards reports that the troops had reached their allotted positions began to come in. It seems clear that the whole of the second objective had been captured by 1.30 P.M. There was a good deal of hand-to-hand fighting in Guillemont itself and in the orchards on the south side of it, where the supporting battalions were engaged in clearing up and consolidating the village.

At 2 P.M. the whole line went forward up to the Ginchy—Wedge Wood road, which the 59th Brigade reached without heavy casualties in spite of many small parties of the enemy who were found in dug-outs along the road and at the cemetery east of the village and were made prisoners. On the left the Royal Irish passed to the attack through the other battalions of the brigade. They were joined by the Munsters, and these two battalions having got forward under a hot fire to within 70 yards of the road, rushed the position, where they captured a machine gun and more than 100 prisoners.

As soon as this line had been reached it became clear to the commanders in the front line of the 59th Brigade that for the time being no further advance could be made. The 5th Division should by this time have got forward to the line of Leuze Wood, and was reported to have done so. Many of the enemy could, however, be seen both in the wood itself and on the spur south-west of it on the right of the 20th Divisional line. Lieut. H. R. Hill, 7th Somerset L.I., received the M.C. for a valuable reconnaisance he made at this time into Leuze Wood, which he found strongly held. Lieut.-Colonel White, Oxford and Bucks L.I., who had been placed in command of the front line troops of the 59th Brigade, decided not to attack the fourth objective, but only to send forward patrols towards it until the right flank was more secure. About 2.20 P.M. XIVth Corps reported that Ginchy had been occupied by the 7th Division, and at the same time ordered Major-General

Douglas Smith to co-operate with the 5th Division in
clearing the trench running from the south-east corner
of Guillemont to Falfemont Farm by bombing down it
from the north. For this purpose an additional battalion
of the 61st Brigade—the 7th D.C.L.I.—was put at
Brig.-General Shute's disposal, to be used in case of
necessity. At 3 P.M. the left brigade of the 5th Division
was reported in the trench running north-west from
Wedge Wood, while the right brigade was about
to attack the line Wedge Wood—Falfemont Farm.
Brig.-General Shute had not by 3.45 P.M. gained touch
with the 5th Division, so he prolonged his line to the
right for some 300 yards with the Oxford and Bucks
L.I., and brought up the 7th D.C.L.I. to form a
defensive flank to the south-east. To the left of the
Oxfords the line was held by the 11th R.B., one company
of the 10th K.R.R.C., the 10th R.B., and a portion of
the 96th Field Company R.E., while the 10th and
11th K.R.R.C. were consolidating the position in
Guillemont.

On the front of the 47th Brigade the Royal Irish
held the Ginchy—Wedge Wood road to the north of
Mount Street, with the Munsters on their left, forming
a defensive flank towards Ginchy. The sharp fighting
among the ruins of Guillemont had caused a certain
amount of confusion. "B" Company of the 7th
Somerset L.I., under Capt. Mitchell, M.C., was therefore
detached to reinforce the right of the 47th Brigade,
and arrived just in time to beat off a counter attack
with rifle and bayonet. Two companies of the King's
who had reached Guillemont station were ordered up
to support the Connaught Rangers on the north of the
village, but by 3.45 P.M., although they had arrived
at this position, they had not got into touch with the
Connaughts.

The rest of the 96th Field Company and the company of the 11th D.L.I. with the right attack had reached Arrow Head Copse. Of the 83rd Field Company and the company of 11th D.L.I. with the left attack, half were assisting the Connaughts to consolidate the position in Guillemont, while half were still west of Trônes Wood.

By 3.50 P.M. the 47th Brigade reported that the Munsters had been ordered to advance and take the fourth objective. Guillemont was being heavily shelled at this time, but the Connaughts and Leinsters were in the village, and the 12th King's, who had reached our original front line, had sent two companies forward to support the Connaughts. The left flank, therefore, seemed fairly secure. Casualties in the 59th Brigade had latterly been heavy, but touch had been gained with the 5th Division, and orders had been sent out for the final advance. Meanwhile the Ginchy–Wedge Wood road was being consolidated. Major-General Douglas Smith had therefore every hope that the fourth objective would be taken.

Then the outlook was completely changed by two events, reports of which reached Divisional Headquarters within a quarter of an hour of each other. At 5.15 P.M. the 47th Brigade stated that the 7th Division had been driven out of Ginchy. This was confirmed at 5.30 P.M., when the further news arrived that the 5th Division had not succeeded in advancing to its objective—the edge of Leuze Wood; in fact, parties of the enemy could be seen on the spur south-west of the wood and on the right of the 59th Brigade, where, moving on the exposed slope, they formed excellent targets to our troops across the valley. The enemy also had machine guns on this spur, but their

fire was kept down most successfully by a section of the
61st M.G. Company, under Lieut. Pavier. Immediately
on hearing of the repulse of the 7th Division, Major-
General Douglas Smith asked for a barrage on the left
flank ; the prompt response of the artillery prevented
any counter attack developing before a proper defence
could be organised. He also ordered the 60th Brigade
to move up to the west of Trônes Wood. When he
learned of the situation on the right, he saw that with
both flanks in the air the position was too precarious to
admit of a further advance. He ordered the B.G.C. 59th
Brigade, who had already cancelled the orders for the
attack, to consolidate the Ginchy—Wedge Wood road,
pushing out patrols towards the fourth objective, and
requested the Corps heavy artillery to fire on the
Ginchy—Leuze Wood road. The 7th D.C.L.I. having
been drawn into the battle with the 59th Brigade, he
placed at Brig.-General Pereira's disposal the last
battalion of the 61st Brigade, the 7th K.O.Y.L.I.

The situation on the left flank was, as a matter of
fact, critical, and was saved by the prompt action
of an officer of the 12th King's, Captain C. D. R.
Cleminson, who had been sent up with the two companies of his battalion to reinforce the Connaught
Rangers. When he had reached the north of Guillemont
he was joined by about sixty men of the 7th Division,
who stated that they had been driven out of Ginchy.
Realising the danger to the left flank, Captain Cleminson
on his own initiative advanced towards Ginchy and
dug in on a defensive line facing the village. In
response to a message purporting to come from the
Royal Irish he sent forward a platoon to Ginchy
Wood, on the south-west side of Ginchy. During the
advance to this point the platoon commander and many

F

men were killed. Sgt. Jones, the platoon sergeant, took command, got his platoon and the Lewis gun into position, and reported to Captain Cleminson that no trace of the Royal Irish could be found. He then returned to the platoon, and held out in this isolated position, without food or water, for two days and two nights. On the second day, owing to his coolness and resource, his platoon drove back three counter attacks with heavy loss. On the morning of the 5th he was relieved. For this magnificent deed he was awarded the Victoria Cross.

Captain Cleminson was reinforced by another company of his battalion, and collected parties of stragglers from the 7th Division. With these troops he organised a strong defensive flank. He gained touch at 9 P.M. with a party of the Royal Irish on his right, and maintained this position until, on the 5th, he too was relieved. For his gallant action he was awarded the D.S.O.

From 5.30 P.M. onwards the Germans made repeated counter attacks against the left of the line ; all failed. Their efforts gradually became less vigorous, until they were finally driven off about 8.30 P.M. During these attacks two companies of the Somerset L.I. were sent to the assistance of the 47th Brigade, making the left flank practically secure.

When, at 8.10 P.M., the Divisional Commander learned that the 7th Division troops were back in their trenches, he decided to use the 60th Brigade to relieve the 47th, which had suffered very heavy casualties. During the night the 12th R.B. (Lieut.-Colonel H. L. Riley) and the 12th K.R.R.C. (Lieut.-Colonel A. I. Paine) took over the right of the 47th Brigade line, relieving the Royal Irish and the Munsters, who went

back to their original positions in Bernafay Wood
and at Carnoy. He also ordered the 48th Brigade,
which had been put at his disposal some two hours
earlier, to move to the Craters; later, in view of
possible counter attacks, he ordered this brigade
further forward, the two leading battalions to be
about Bernafay Wood by 6 A.M. on the 4th.

During the night the 96th and 83rd Field Companies R.E., the two companies of the 11th D.L.I.
with them, and the 7th D.C.L.I., were employed in
Guillemont consolidating the village. The 84th Field
Company and the 11th D.L.I. (less two companies)
were wiring the front line and improving the communications back to Guillemont.

The 6th K.S.L.I. (Lieut.-Colonel E. A. Wood)—the
last battalion of the 60th Brigade—were approaching
the village at 2 A.M.

Orders for the operations to be carried out on the
4th arrived early that morning. The 20th was to
co-operate with the 5th and 7th Divisions in the afternoon, by sending out strong patrols to establish themselves on the line of the fourth objective. The troops
of the 59th Brigade were by this time becoming very
exhausted. As it was evident that the brigade could
not be relieved by fresh troops for some time, Major-
General Douglas Smith sent up the remainder of the
11th D.L.I. at 10.50 A.M. to take the place of the units
which were most tired out. By 11 A.M. the K.O.Y.L.I.
had reached the front line of the 47th Brigade. At
this time troops of the 7th Division were reported to
have entered Ginchy, but an hour and a half later
they were driven out once more. An attempt by the
enemy to work round the left flank was defeated by
the 12th King's.

Owing to the state of the trenches and to casualties among the runners, the orders for the operation did not reach battalions until after 6.30 P.M.—the hour at which it was due to begin. At 7.30, however, the patrols went forward under an intense creeping barrage and established themselves along the whole of the fourth objective. At the same time the 5th Division captured Falfemont Farm and pushed out strong patrols to Leuze Wood. The task assigned to the 20th Division was now accomplished, and with the 5th Division in line along the edge of Leuze Wood its right flank was safe. To complete the operations, it remained to capture Ginchy. This was carried out by the 16th Division on the 9th, when the crest of the whole ridge, from a thousand yards west of Combles to a thousand yards south of Thiepval, passed into British hands.

During the 4th of September the Divisional Commander had ordered the 47th and 60th Brigades to be relieved by the 48th, and the 59th by the last brigade of the 16th Division, the 49th, which had been placed at his disposal that afternoon. These changes were to be effected during the night of the 4th/5th, but owing to messengers being killed and guides losing their way, they could not be completed that night. The remaining units of the 47th Brigade were out of the line by 2 A.M. on the 5th. At 9.30 A.M., as soon as the 59th Brigade had been relieved, Major-General Douglas Smith handed over the sector to the G.O.C. 16th Division, and moved his headquarters to Forked Tree Camp. He left in the line, under the 16th Division, the 60th Brigade, the 7th Somerset L.I. and the 11th D.L.I. These troops rejoined their division on the 7th.

The casualties in the 20th Division during the battle were as follows :—

	Officers.	Other Ranks.	
59th Infantry Brigade	30	935 =	965
60th ,, ,,	20	402 =	422
61st ,, ,,	16	418 =	434
R.E.	2	50 =	52
D.L.I.	4	87 =	91
R.A.M.C.	1	8 =	9
	73	1900=	1973

These casualties, of course, threw a great deal of work on to the R.A.M.C., who carried out their duties very gallantly in spite of great difficulties. The conditions of this battle necessitated certain changes in the normal arrangements. The casualties in the Somme area were far greater than any with which the field ambulances had hitherto had to deal. The roads were so bad that cars could not get anywhere near the line, and wounded had to be carried a long distance over most difficult country, while the concentration of troops left few dug-outs for wounded or for R.A.M.C. personnel. The arrangements made were these. The personnel of all three field ambulances was pooled. Thus all the bearers were concentrated under one command at the bearer camp at Bronfay Farm, about a mile south-west of Carnoy. Advanced bearer posts were established at the Briqueterie near Montauban and at Bernafay Wood ; further forward still were posts at Waterlot Farm and in a trench east of Trônes Wood, and between these were relay posts. The medical officers of units had squads for the carrying of wounded at their regimental aid posts. There was a loading post at Montauban, which was as far forward

as the wagons could go, so that all stretcher cases had
to be carried back to there—sometimes as much as
5000 yards. The task of the stretcher-bearers was
indeed an appalling one. The magnificent way in
which they carried out their duties will always be remembered. From horsed ambulance wagons all cases
had to be changed into light motor ambulances before
they could reach a road on which the large motor
ambulances could travel.

Signal communication throughout the battle was
good, due to the excellent system devised by Major
F. J. M. Stratton, commanding the 20th Divisional
Signal Company R.E.

Division was in touch with brigades by telephone
practically without a break. Forward of brigades,
lines were laid as far as the original front line, with
runner posts and linesmen stationed at intervals along
them. The line to the left was broken only once;
that to the right was broken several times, but was
never out of action for more than ten minutes. Forward
of the old front line most messages came back by
runners; some were brought by pigeons, and a few
were signalled to aeroplanes. Arrangements were
made for visual signalling, and both brigades had wireless stations in touch with the Corps wireless at
Divisional headquarters.

The capture of Guillemont was a fine achievement,
for which the Commander-in-Chief, the Commanders
of the Fourth Army and of the XIVth Corps sent
messages of congratulation to the Division.

The importance of this battle is well shown by the
following extract from a leading article in one of the
London daily papers: " Guillemont is a strongly
fortified village near the end of the British line. It was
the most powerful of the German positions in the

neighbourhood of the Somme. . . . Two or three weeks ago the pessimists were wondering whether Guillemont would be taken this year. It has passed into the possession of Sir Douglas Haig so unobtrusively that few appear to understand that the fall of Guillemont is the most important event which has happened on the Somme for the last six weeks. Certainly the Germans are under no delusions about this conspicuous success."

CHAPTER V

THE SOMME (Continued)

29th July to 13th October 1916

Divisional Artillery in the Salient—Reorganisation into six-gun
Batteries—Move of Artillery to the Somme—Attack of
Division on " Blue Line " facing Morval and Lesbœufs,
16th to 18th of September—Line near Gueudecourt—
Attack on " Brown Line " overlooking Le Transloy, 7th
October.

(*Vide* Map II.)

WHEN the 20th Division moved out of the
Ypres Salient in July 1916, the artillery
remained in the line covering the infantry
of the 6th Division. Soon afterwards the XIVth Corps
went south, exchanging with the VIIIth, and the
remaining divisions which had composed the XIVth
Corps in the salient went with it, to reappear in the
Hebuterne area on their way to the Somme. Thus
on the 24th the Guards handed over to the 4th Division,
and on the 31st the infantry of the 6th was relieved
by the infantry of the 29th, on the front covered by
the 20th Divisional Artillery.

All through August the guns on both sides were very
active. Almost daily some part of our position in this
sector was heavily shelled, and our batteries were
occupied in retaliation, and in bringing under fire
various points in and behind the German lines. On
the 8th the enemy was particularly aggressive, and
shelled nearly all the battery positions. That night,

between 11 P.M. and midnight, he discharged gas on
the front of the 29th Division, which was unfortunate
in having a large number of casualties, though the 20th
Divisional Artillery had none.

On the 1st of September the Divisional Artillery,
while still in the line, was reorganised on the basis of
six guns to each 18-pr. battery. The three howitzer
batteries (the fourth, it will be remembered, had left
the Division in August 1915) remained unaltered, with
four guns each. This involved many changes; one
battery in each brigade was broken up to provide the
extra guns for those that remained; several others were
re-numbered, and the 90th Brigade, which had no
howitzer battery, disappeared. When the reorganisation was complete the Divisional Artillery, under Brig.-
General Hotham, was composed as follows :—

91st Brigade (Lt.-Col. F. A. Wilson). D.S.O.)	92nd Brigade (Lt.-Col. H. G. Ricardo).	93rd Brigade (Lt.-Col. A. H. D. West).
A/91.	A/92.	A/93.
B/91.	B/92.	B/93.
C/91.	C/92.	..
D/91.	D/92.	D/93.

On the 8th of September the 20th Divisional Artillery
was relieved by that of the 4th Division, and started
on a six days' march southwards to the Somme. On
the 13th it came again under the XIVth Corps, but
it was not to cover the front of its own infantry until
the end of the month.

After the operations at Guillemont the 20th Division
went back for a short period of rest, during which
time our hold on the main ridge was completed by
the capture of Ginchy. We now enter upon the third
phase of the battle, in which the British troops pushed

down the far side of the ridge and also gained ground
on the flanks of the attack. On the 15th of September
and the following days an advance on the whole front
of the Fourth Army brought the line on the right to
within assaulting distance of Morval, Lesbœufs and
Gueudecourt—the last of the enemy's original defensive systems—and on the left as far as High Wood,
Martinpuich and Courcelette. The attack was made
by the XIVth Corps on the right, the XVth in the
centre and the IIIrd on the left, and was the first
occasion on which tanks came into action. In the
XIVth Corps the 56th Division was on the right,
the 6th in the centre, the Guards on the left, and
the 20th in reserve.

The only unit of the 20th Division which fought on
the first day of the battle was the 91st Field Artillery
Brigade. On the 13th, as soon as the Divisional
Artillery had come into the XIVth Corps area, Brig.-
General Hotham was ordered to send one brigade to
reinforce the 56th Divisional Artillery on the extreme
right of the British line. Next day, accordingly,
while the 92nd and 93rd Brigades went into camp in
the Bois des Tailles, two miles south of Meaulte, the
91st Brigade, having marched already 35 miles, moved
up ten miles further to positions between Bois Favière
and Trônes Wood, where by 3 A.M. on the 15th all
batteries were dug in and ready to open fire. By the
time the teams had withdrawn to their wagon lines
they had covered well over 50 miles. This was a
very fine performance, reflecting the highest credit
on the spirit of the men and the fitness of the horses.
During the battle that day the brigade put down a
defensive flank barrage on Combles to assist the attack
of the 56th Division west of the village.

The headquarters of the 20th Division was at Forked

Tree Camp, two miles south of Fricourt, and the 92nd and 93rd Field Artillery Brigades remained in the Bois des Tailles.

The infantry of the 20th Division came into the fighting in the early hours of the 16th, when the 60th and 61st Brigades, having been placed under the orders of the G.O.C. Guards Division, moved forward, the 61st to the right of the Guards' line opposite Lesbœufs, the 60th into reserve at Waterlot Farm.

The three infantry brigades of the 20th Division had not yet received reinforcements to replace the great losses of the Guillemont fight and were in consequence very weak ; the 59th Brigade could put only 900 rifles in the line, and the other two brigades only 1100 and 1200, but they were still full of fight and confidence.

The first objective on this day was a " Blue Line " facing Morval and Lesbœufs and about 1200 yards west of these places. The second objective skirted Morval on the west and Lesbœufs on the east, ending at the cross-roads half way between Lesbœufs and Gueudecourt.

The 61st Brigade, under Brig.-General Banbury, was to attack on the right, the 3rd Guards Brigade on the left. On the left of the Guards was the XVth Corps.

The 61st Brigade was not in touch with any attacking troops on its right, as the 6th Division was still held up by the Quadrilateral—a well-sited and stubbornly defended fortification three-quarters of a mile east of Ginchy.

The 7th D.C.L.I. (Lieut.-Colonel J. G. T. Simcox, D.S.O.) were detailed to attack on the right of the line and the 7th Somerset L.I. (Major E. L. Lyon) on the left.

In support were the 7th K.O.Y.L.I. (Lieut.-Colonel
B. B. Robinson), who had orders to watch particularly
the exposed right flank. The 12th King's (Lieut.-
Colonel Vince) formed the reserve.

Owing to the late hour at which orders were received
on the 15th the battalions of the 61st Brigade had
not time to complete their assembly before dawn on
the 16th. As a result they had to face heavy and very
accurate machine-gun and minenwerfer fire, which
caused many casualties before the advance began.

The 7th Somerset L.I. lost Major Lyon and all senior
officers at this time. Second-Lieut. T. G. Jenne commanded the battalion throughout the operation and
was awarded the M.C.

Zero was at 9.25 A.M., when the assaulting troops
advanced to within 70 yards of the barrage. As soon
as the barrage lifted, they attacked the position. The
D.C.L.I., under Captain Macmillan, the second in
command, established themselves in the first objective,
where they captured 100 prisoners and 2 minenwerfer.
They found, however, that they were not in touch
with the Somersets, though they met an isolated company of this battalion. Due largely to the splendid
efforts of Lance-Cpl. R. V. E. Hill and Pte. C.
Barrow, who both received the M.M. for their gallant
action on this day, the Somersets gained the German
line on a front of 150 yards, taking 50 prisoners and
2 machine guns. They held their position while they
dug another trench just to the west of it ; then having
used all their own bombs and all that they had captured
from the enemy, they had to fall back to the new trench.

The time laid down for the advance to the second
objective was 10 A.M., but Captain Macmillan, 7th
D.C.L.I., seeing that the attack on the left was not
progressing, decided not to attempt any further advance.

It appears that, owing to the late hour at which the
orders were received and to the difficulty of effecting
the necessary reliefs, the Guards were late in launching
their attack, and then meeting with strong opposition
were unable to make much progress.

The Somersets came under very heavy machine-gun
fire, from which they suffered severely. As early as
half-past ten they were reported to have only two
junior officers left. In spite of running short of
bombs and ammunition, they held on in the trench they
had dug until they were relieved at night. The D.C.L.I.,
meanwhile, with a gap between them and the Somersets,
were left with both flanks in the air. They too had
lost heavily, and all battalion bombers had been wiped
out by minenwerfer. The K.O.Y.L.I. came up and
made their right flank secure, and when a counter
attack developed on their left they borrowed two
bombing sections from this battalion, and with their
help drove the enemy back. At 10.45 A.M. the 12th
King's went up to reinforce the line under very heavy
machine-gun fire from the front, right, and right rear.
About 6 P.M. the 84th Field Company R.E. came up
and constructed strong points on the flanks, and at
dusk a platoon of the K.O.Y.L.I. with a Lewis gun and
a bombing section dug in, with the assistance of a party
of R.E. on the left of the D.C.L.I. During the operations Lieut.-Colonel B. B. Robinson, commanding the
7th K.O.Y.L.I., was wounded by a shell which hit
the battalion headquarters, killing or wounding all
officers there. At night all units of the brigade were
relieved.

The casualties were heavy, but the brigade gained
and held its objective. It was a particularly fine
performance, and Brig.-General Banbury received high
praise from the G.O.C. Guards Division for the success

of the attack. With both flanks exposed the 61st
Brigade had successfully stormed, under heavy artillery,
rifle and machine-gun fire, a strong German position,
and in spite of numerous counter attacks had succeeded
in holding it until relieved.

Captain Macmillan, D.C.L.I., was awarded the D.S.O.
for his gallant leadership on this occasion.

On the night of the 16th/17th the 20th Division,
less the 61st Brigade, relieved the Guards in the left
sector of the XIVth Corps front, with the headquarters at Bernafay Wood. The 60th Brigade, under
Brig.-General Butler, took over the right of the line
from the 61st, which moved back into Corps reserve
at Carnoy, leaving the 84th Field Company at the
disposal of the C.R.E. ; the 59th, under Brig.-General
Shute, took over the left of the line from the 3rd Guards
Brigade. The Divisional reserve was formed by a
brigade of the 5th Division at Waterlot Farm. On
the right of the 20th was the 6th Division, and on the
left the 21st Division of the XVth Corps. The front
was covered by the Guards and two brigades of the
6th Divisional Artillery.

The relief of the Guards by the 59th Brigade was
most arduous. The situation here was very obscure ;
the guides had great difficulty in finding their way, and
the enemy was shelling the area with gas. The 11th
R.B., for example, had to march for a considerable
distance in gas masks, and took about five hours to
get from Trônes Wood to the line.

The headquarters of these four battalions were in
a ditch which the enemy shelled continuously on the
17th, and on which he obtained many direct hits.

During the day the enemy made several attempts
to enter the trenches of the 60th Brigade. A determined bombing attack launched at 1.30 P.M. against

the 12th K.R.R.C. was driven back with great loss after fighting lasting for an hour and a half. At the same time an attack was made against the 6th K.S.L.I. A party rushed the bombing post on the left of this battalion, while large numbers of men in small groups tried to come across the open from Lesbœufs. The latter were repulsed, and the N.C.O. in charge of the bombing post collected his men, who by out-throwing the Germans drove them back. Several other attempts were similarly defeated by the superior throwing of our bombers. The artillery opened fire, and accounted for many of the enemy. The casualties—due partly to these attacks and partly to hostile shelling—amounted to 3 officers and 35 other ranks in the 12th K.R.R.C., and 62 other ranks in the K.S.L.I.

On the same day three battalions of the 59th Brigade —the 11th R.B., the 10th R.B. and the 11th K.R.R.C. —were called upon to carry out a most difficult operation. The objective was some 800 yards of the Blue Line which still remained in the enemy's hands. The battalions from the first were placed at a serious disadvantage, as the trenches they had taken over the night before ran almost at right angles to the enemy's line ; they were, in fact, old communication trenches. British troops were reported to be holding the Blue Line on each flank of the objective, but it was not discovered until too late that this information was incorrect. The brigade on the left of the 59th was therefore unable to give the expected assistance by bombing down the flank of the enemy's line. Owing to the uncertainty of the situation and the difficulty of communicating with the front line, the companies did not receive their orders until a short time before the attack ; one company of the 11th R.B. did not take part in the operation, as all runners sent to this company were hit before they could reach it.   Moreover, owing to the little time available for the preparation of barrage tables and to the uncertainty of the ammunition supply, the artillery could not give the necessary support.

These three battalions, then, on leaving their trenches had to swing round on a forward slope.   As soon as they showed themselves, the enemy, obviously ready for the attack, put down an extremely quick and accurate barrage, and met the assaulting line with a hail of bullets.   Although nearly all the most advanced troops became casualties, some of the 11th K.R.R.C. fought their way forward to the objective, and Captain O. R. Ord, with a few riflemen of the 10th R.B., reached the enemy wire, where they were all killed in making a gallant attempt to get through.   Most of the troops, coming under overwhelming machine-gun fire from the front and flanks, were unable to make much progress. In the end all three battalions had to retire to their original line with very heavy losses.

Captain Johnson, medical officer to the 10th R.B., was awarded the M.C. for attending the wounded for many hours after he had been severely wounded himself.

This attack resulted in the only failure sustained by the Division during the battle of the Somme.

On the 18th the 6th Division made another attack on the Quadrilateral and succeeded in breaking down the very determined resistance of the defenders and in capturing the position.   A patrol of the 12th R.B. under Lieut. Breckon and 2nd Lieut. Ruddle was sent out to assist on the left flank of the attack, and was most successful.   About 300 yards from the 12th R.B. trenches was the head of the valley which runs north from Combles.   Here the patrol cut off several parties of the enemy as they retired from their trenches, and captured a machine gun and 26 prisoners (one party alone, under Cpl. Chitty, took 14 of them), besides accounting for some 50 more who tried to get away down the valley. One of the 12th R.B. bombing sections, which had been lent to the 12th K.R.R.C., was at this time holding an advanced bombing post. A man of this section, Rifleman Yates, went out by himself against a party of Germans who had been seen collecting for a counter attack behind a barricade in their trench. Bombing the Germans as he went he inflicted considerable loss upon them and broke up the attack. In the meantime a bombing attack had been made against the 6th K.S.L.I., and had been defeated.

The 7th K.O.Y.L.I. were moved up in the early hours of the 19th to the support of the 59th Brigade. They arrived at their position forty minutes after dawn, having suffered 60 casualties in passing through a very heavy barrage and in advancing across ground swept by machine-gun fire. Here they remained till they were relieved on the 21st, having lost 30 more men on the 20th from enemy shelling. The 12th King's also came up on the 19th to reinforce the 59th Brigade, and the 10th and 11th R.B. were withdrawn from the line.

Between the 17th and the 21st, when the Division was relieved, the nights were largely spent in digging a new line of trenches. The battalions of both brigades, the 84th Field Company R.E. and the 11th D.L.I., were employed on this work, which was carried through in spite of bad weather and a good deal of hostile fire.

Meanwhile the 92nd and 93rd Field Artillery Brigades had taken their part in the operations. The 93rd moved to Guillemont on the 19th, coming

G

under the Guards Divisional Artillery, and the 92nd
came into action on the 20th in support of the
18th Infantry Brigade of the 6th Division. The
91st Field Artillery Brigade remained with the 56th
Division, which was working towards Combles. All
three brigades were engaged in a general attack which
was made on the 25th of September. In this action
Morval and Lesbœufs were taken ; Combles was
practically surrounded, and was entered by British
and French troops simultaneously on the 26th, when
Gueudecourt also fell. This success was then extended
to the left flank by the capture on the 27th of
Thiepval.

After a few days' rest in the neighbourhood of Treux
the Division again moved forward on the 26th into
the line near Morval, only to be relieved next day
by the 2nd French Division, which took over that
part of the line in preparation for an attack on Sailly-
Saillisel. The 20th then took over from the 21st
Division of the XVth Corps a line extending from the
cross-roads half-way between Gueudecourt and Lesbœufs to a point 250 yards east of Gueudecourt.

All these constant changes of headquarters meant
necessarily very hard work for all the personnel of
the Signal Service, made more difficult by the continual rain and appalling mud. In spite of these
difficulties, communications were most successfully
maintained throughout this period.

The new sector was held for the first week by one
brigade—the 61st—which went in on the night of the
29th/30th. The 60th Brigade was in support near
Trônes Wood, the 59th remaining at Carnoy in reserve,
and Divisional Headquarters returned to Bernafay
Wood. Here also the headquarters of the Divisional
Artillery was established on the 29th, when Brig.-

General Hotham took command of the artillery covering the 20th Division, composed of his own three brigades and certain others which varied for the first few days, but which after the 4th of October consisted of the Guards Divisional Artillery and the 24th Field Artillery Brigade of the 6th Division.

The batteries were in a valley about 800 yards north-east of Delville Wood, known from its map reference as Toc 7 Valley. It was a most unpleasant place. Within a length of a mile all the guns of the whole of the artillery covering the 20th Division were crowded together, being in many places only ten yards apart. The gun-pits were very rough at first, consisting of a sandbag parapet with a tarpaulin or matting over the gun. The men lived in slits in the ground, with a sheet of corrugated iron over the top and a great deal of water at the bottom. The Germans knew well enough that our guns were concentrated in this valley—the only place in the neighbourhood that gave any flash cover—and shelled the positions continually. There was great difficulty at this time in getting up ammunition, all of which had to come by night over the exposed ridge east of Delville Wood. Owing to wet weather and the many shell craters the ground was so bad that it was impossible to get wagons up to the gun positions. After a few days it was arranged that all ammunition should be brought up by pack; and this became the regular way of supplying the guns as long as they remained in this valley.

It will be seen from the map that the line which the Division held ran north-west and south-east. It lay in low ground, facing a ridge beyond which were the villages of Le Transloy and Beaulencourt. The object of the operations which followed—the

last fighting to be demanded of the Division for some
time—was to gain possession of the crest of this ridge
and bring under observation the country on its north
east side.

As a preparatory measure, advantage was taken
of operations which were being carried out on the
left on the 1st of October to advance the line of the
61st Brigade. It was desired to get a good jumping-
off place from which to assault the enemy's position
on the crest of the ridge, and also to observe where
his barrages were placed and where they might be
expected in the course of the attack. At 3.15 P.M.
on the 1st of October the 7th Somerset L.I. on the
right and the 7th D.C.L.I. on the left pushed forward
small parties at an interval of 150 yards under an
intense artillery barrage. They gained ground to
an average depth of 400 yards and established strong
points within 200 yards of the German trenches.
While they were digging in on what was dead ground
from the enemy's trench the Germans made several
counter attacks. As soon as they appeared over the
top our men downed tools and drove them back with
rifle fire, " standing in the open." After dark, and
during the next night, these strong points were connected by the 84th Field Company R.E. and the
11th D.L.I. into a continuous line. The position of
the enemy's barrage was observed, and this was of
great assistance in the attack on the 7th of October,
when troops were kept away from the dangerous
areas and many casualties thereby saved. The
whole operation was carried out well and in a very
determined manner, but not without considerable
loss.

On the night of the 3rd/4th the 60th Brigade came
up into the line and took over the right sub-sector

from the 61st Brigade ; the latter continued to hold the left sub-sector, so that there were then two brigades holding the Divisional front.

The attack was put off for two days—that is, until the 7th—owing to a break in the weather. Between the 3rd and 6th the preparations were completed. Further supplies of bombs and ammunition were brought up, communications were improved, and assembly trenches dug with the help of the R.E. field companies and the 11th D.L.I. Most of the troops detailed to make the assault moved back for two days' rest, but by the 7th all had taken up their places in readiness for the attack. The 60th Brigade was on the right, with the 6th Oxford and Bucks L.I. and the 12th R.B. in the front line, the 12th K.R.R.C. in support, and the 6th K.S.L.I. in reserve. The 61st Brigade was on the left, with the 7th K.O.Y.L.I. (in touch with the 12th R.B.) and the 12th King's in front, each supported by two companies of the 7th Somerset L.I. The 7th D.C.L.I. were in reserve. The 59th Brigade was in Divisional reserve west of Trônes Wood. On the right of the 20th Division the 56th Division, also belonging to the XIVth Corps, carried on the line, and on the left the 12th Division of the XVth Corps. The strength of the brigades was as follows :—

59th Brigade	.	.	2075
60th Brigade	.	.	2087
61st Brigade	.	.	2317
			6479

The object of the operation was to establish a position on the top of the ridge overlooking Le Transloy and Beaulencourt, which might serve as a line of

departure for a further advance against these places.
With this end in view the attack was made along
the whole front of the Fourth Army, the objective
being a " Brown Line " which was taken to be the
crest of the ridge. For the 20th Division the first
objective was Rainbow Trench, on the near side
of the crest; the second objective, which included
Cloudy Trench, was about 1200 yards of the Brown
Line facing the original Divisional front. The direction of the advance, therefore, was north-east.

At 11.30 on the morning of the 7th a German aeroplane flew low over the lines. In spite of the men
lying quite still the observer probably noticed the
concentration of the troops, for the German guns,
which had been quiet up till then, opened a heavy
fire on and behind the assembly trenches, causing
a certain number of casualties in the Oxford and
Bucks L.I.

The formation of the ground hid the opposing
trenches from view—a factor of great importance,
for it made the task of cutting the enemy wire a most
difficult one for the artillery. The only point from
which a little wire could be seen was close behind
our front trenches. The F.O.O.'s and signallers had
therefore to lay out and maintain very long telephone
wires over fire-swept ground, which owing to the
heavy rain of the last few days was little better than
a morass. These difficulties were nevertheless overcome and the wire cutting was steadily carried out.

On the morning of the 7th patrols found that there
was still wire in front of the German lines, so the guns
again opened fire on it.

At zero—1.45 P.M.—the stationary barrage was
put down, and at 1.47 it began to creep forward.
In these two minutes three Stokes mortars with the

60th Brigade (the fourth had just been buried by a shell) fired 180 rounds on the German front line. The assaulting battalions moved forward close under the barrage with two companies in front and two in support, and with each company in two lines, thus forming four waves. With the fourth wave of each battalion were four machine guns from the 60th and 61st M.G. Companies.

The leading companies, advancing, according to a report from an officer in an observation post, " as though on Salisbury Plain," came under heavy fire as soon as they reached the crest of the slope, which was about twenty yards short of the enemy wire. Some of the wire was still standing, at least on the front of the 60th Brigade, and for a short time held up the first two waves. The casualties here were heavy. Of the five company officers in the two leading companies of the 12th R.B., four were killed between this point and the wire, and one was severely wounded; of the rank and file about half were casualties. The 6th Oxford and Bucks L.I. suffered almost as much. Many of their losses were caused by a machine gun in a sap close to the wire. The third and fourth waves were following close behind, and as they came up they carried the first and second waves with them and together they captured Rainbow Trench. The 61st Brigade had less trouble with the enemy's wire, but suffered from very severe rifle and machine-gun fire from the left flank, where a heavy barrage had prevented the 12th Division from reaching its objective. As the troops came up to Rainbow Trench the enemy surrendered in large numbers. At one point in the attack of the 61st Brigade the two op-posing lines were seen to meet; then there was a moment's pause, followed by the advance of our

line and the return of a large number of prisoners.
On the left of this brigade more resistance was met
and a hand-to-hand fight ensued before the Germans—
or such of them as were able to get away—were driven
out of the position.

On the capture of the objective the first and second
waves entered and held the trench, while the third
and fourth formed up beyond it ready for the next
advance.

When, at 2.5 P.M., the barrage again began to creep
forward the attack was continued in three waves, the
third being composed of the original first and second,
less some machine guns and a few parties of men left
behind to form posts in Rainbow Trench. The losses
in this advance were comparatively slight, although
the Germans, for the most part, remained in the
position throwing bombs until the attacking lines
were close upon them. Many of the enemy were
killed at the second objective, which was captured
about 2.15 P.M. Cloudy Trench was found to be
little more than a line of disturbed earth, and all
along the line the troops had to dig themselves in.

At the time the second objective was occupied
the position of the flanks was a very dangerous one.
The battalions in support had moved forward as the
attack progressed, and had kept in touch with the
leading units, but the divisions on the right and left
had not captured their objectives, and so both flanks
were in the air and under enfilade fire. Defensive
flanks had therefore to be thrown back, leaving the
Division occupying a pronounced salient. The heavy
casualties in the Oxford and Bucks L.I. and the 12th
R.B. have been mentioned; in the 61st Brigade
also the leading battalions had suffered severely,
especially in officers. The 12th King's had only

Capt. Milligan up in the second objective; the front line of the K.O.Y.L.I. was commanded by Lieut. Wright. Both these officers found their flank exposed, as there was a gap of three to four hundred yards between the two brigades, and they showed great initiative and judgment in siting their trenches and organising their defences so as to deal with any counter attacks that might develop. The situation on the left was especially difficult, as the troops were under a perfect hail of machine-gun and rifle fire, and casualties were becoming serious. The Somersets were called on for assistance and sent up two platoons under Sgt. W. E. Parker to strengthen the left flank, and a company to fill up the gap between the two brigades.

The enemy made several counter attacks in the course of the day, but all failed. Sgt. Parker was awarded the M.M. for his gallantry and good leadership in beating off one of these attacks. At 4 P.M. a company of the D.C.L.I. was sent as a further reinforcement to the left flank, arriving just in time to help to drive back a counter attack at this point. A working party of 200 men of the 11th R.B. came up to finish a communication trench in the 61st Brigade area, and to act as reinforcements if necessary. The 83rd and 84th Field Companies R.E. and 200 men of the 6th K.S.L.I. assisted the front line troops to consolidate their positions during the night; in spite of considerable casualties from the enemy's heavy shell-fire this work was successfully completed. Behind the line a section of the 96th Field Company and three companies of the 11th D.L.I. dug a communication trench for the use of both brigades.

At 9 P.M. Brig.-General Banbury ordered Major Simcox, commanding the 7th D.C.L.I., to go forward

with the rest of his battalion and take over and
reorganise the front line system.

The casualties were 626 in the 60th Brigade, 469 in
the 61st and 17 in the 59th. 192 prisoners, including
five officers, and four machine guns and two mortars
were taken.

The casualties of the last month are evidence in
themselves of the enormous work thrown upon the
R.A.M.C. and the regimental stretcher-bearers. It
is difficult to praise too highly the unselfish and un-
obtrusive work of these men.

The state of the trenches and the conditions under
which the battle was fought made the task of supplying
and replenishing the various wants of the Division a
most difficult one. Major J. M'Gown, the D.A.D.O.S.,
and the supply officers nevertheless overcame all difficulties and earned the deep gratitude of all ranks.

The 60th and 61st Brigades held the positions they
had won on the 7th until the night of the 8th/9th
of October, when the 20th Division was relieved by
the 6th and moved back to the neighbourhood of
Treux for a well-earned rest.

Here on the 13th the Corps Commander, Lord
Cavan, inspected each of the three brigades in turn
on a ceremonial parade, and addressed the troops.

" I have come here to-day," he said, " to thank
you from the bottom of my heart for the magnificent
work you have done for the Army and for the Corps.
The capture of Guillemont was chiefly due to you "
(the 59th Brigade). He praised all brigades for the
part they had taken in the Somme battle, and referred
to the vigorous action by which the 60th had assisted
the 6th Division in its successful attack on the Quadrilateral. After congratulating the 61st Brigade on
the part it had taken in the capture of Guillemont,

he said: "The Brigade was attached to the Guards
Division from the 15th to the 17th of September and
attacked on the 16th, when it gained the whole of its
objectives, in spite of the fact that the units attacking
on the two flanks were held up." " On October the
7th the Brigade attacked with the 60th Brigade and
once more gained the whole of its objectives." He
said how pleased he was with the extremely smart
and soldier-like manner in which the troops had
turned out on parade, and added: " I have asked the
Army Commander and the Commander-in-Chief not
to take away the 20th Division if they can help it,
and they have promised to do their best. I would
not lose the 20th Division for crowns and crowns."

CHAPTER VI

WINTER IN THE SOMME AREA

9th October 1916 *to* 16th *March* 1917

Divisional Artillery in Toc 7 Valley—Remainder of the Division
at rest—The Division in the line opposite Le Transloy—
The 93rd Field Artillery Brigade made an Army Brigade—
The Sailly-Saillisel Line—The sector between Sailly-
Saillisel and Le Transloy—Signs of the coming German
retreat.

(*Vide* Map II.)

WHILE the rest of the Division was out of the
line the artillery remained in action, covering
in succession the 6th, 8th, 17th and Guards
Divisions, and supporting a number of attacks on the
trenches which crowned the ridge facing Le Transloy.
The first of these was made on the 12th of October by
the 4th, 6th and 12th Divisions. The enemy put up
a barrage thirty seconds after the advance had begun
and brought very heavy machine-gun fire on to the
assaulting troops, who were able to make little progress.
The 20th Divisional Artillery supported also a minor
operation carried out by the 6th Division on the 15th,
and a further attack by the 4th, 6th and 12th Divisions
launched at 3.40 P.M. on the 18th. In spite of the
hopeless state of the ground and the difficulty of
moving over it in the dark, the line was advanced and
some of the enemy trenches were taken. The French
on the right captured Sailly-Saillisel.

On the following day the 6th Division was relieved

by the 8th, and the 12th Division on its left by the 29th. At the same time Brig.-General Hotham handed over the Left Artillery of the XIVth Corps to the C.R.A. Guards Division and took command of the Left Group, consisting of the three brigades of the 20th Divisional Artillery and the 24th Field Artillery Brigade of the 6th Division.

The 21st, 22nd and 23rd of October were spent in a bombardment of the enemy's trenches as a preparation for another attack. This was launched on the 23rd at 2.30 P.M. and was very successful. The infantry of the 8th Division, which by 9.55 P.M. had gained all its objectives, reported that the artillery barrage was excellent. At the end of the month this Division was relieved by the 17th.

On the 24th Brig.-General Hotham, who had done so much to create the excellent *esprit-de-corps* which existed in the 20th Divisional Artillery, was invalided home and handed over command temporarily to Lieut.-Colonel F. A. Wilson, D.S.O.

In the last week of October heavy rain made further operations impossible. Toc 7 Valley had been heavily shelled throughout the past month; the ground was worse than ever and the trenches waist deep in water, making the life of an artilleryman at this time a most unpleasant one. In this sector, too, the German aeroplanes seemed to have very much their own way, and several times flew unmolested low over the battery positions.

The Guards Artillery withdrew to rest on November the 10th. Lieut.-Colonel Wilson then took command of the Left Artillery of the Corps, consisting of the 91st, 92nd and 93rd Brigades and a brigade and two batteries from the artillery of the 4th Division. Three days later he handed over to Brig.-General

W. B. Browell, C.M.G., who came from the 14th Division to the 20th to take up the duties of C.R.A.

At this time the British line was extended on the right, where the Sailly-Saillisel area was taken over from the French. In the consequent rearrangement the Guards, who had taken the place of the 17th Division, were relieved by a division of Australians. Headquarters of the 20th Divisional Artillery and the 91st Brigade went back to Corbie to rest on the 26th, and the 92nd and 93rd Brigades moved to positions north of Combles, where they came under the C.R.A. of the 17th Division. The 92nd Brigade went back on the 10th of December to the Citadel, about a mile and a half south of Fricourt, sending C/92 and D/92 Batteries to Corbie to take the place of C/91 and D/91, which went as instructional batteries to the Corps artillery school at Daours.

For two months, from the 9th of October to the 9th of December, the Division was out of the line resting, training and bringing the much reduced units up to strength again. The necessary refitting threw considerable work on the D.A.D.O.S. and his staff. On the 14th of October Brig.-General Shute was promoted temp. Major-General in command of the Naval Division, and the 59th Brigade was taken over by Brig.-General R. C. Browne-Clayton, D.S.O.

On the 15th of October, Headquarters moved to Corbie, on the 19th to Vignacourt, on the 22nd to Belloy-sur-Somme, and on the 1st of November to Cavillon, west of Amiens in the area of the XVth Corps, with the various units billeted in the villages around. Here much time was given up to recreation of all kinds. Divisional and brigade football, tug-of-war, cross-country and boxing competitions were organised, and several very successful race meetings were held.

During this period of rest, under the ægis of Lieut.-Colonel Dundas, the A.A. and Q.M.G., the famous Divisional troupe of Pierrots, known as the " Verey Lights," was started. Thanks to the energies of Capt. Henson, Capt. Gilbey and Bandmaster Eldridge, and with the able assistance of Cpl. Fletcher's paint brush, performers and scenery were quickly produced. Thus began the career of the " Verey Lights," which from now onwards till 1919 continued, without a break, to do so much to make the lot of all ranks a happier one. Although space forbids to mention the long list of names of those officers and men who helped to make the name of the " Verey Lights " a household word, it is felt that special mention should be made of Capt. Gilbey, M.C., whose talent and unbounded enthusiasm did so much to guarantee the continuous success of their efforts.

The R.E. and the 11th D.L.I. were ordered on the 18th of October to the Citadel for work in the forward area under XIVth Corps. The R.E. Headquarters and the 84th Field Company rejoined the Division on the 25th of October ; the D.L.I. returned on the 2nd, and the 83rd and 96th Field Companies on the 11th of November.

After a fortnight at Cavillon the Division returned to XIVth Corps with headquarters once more at Corbie, where it remained for some three weeks, while battalions went at intervals to work under the C.E., and the 61st Brigade spent ten days in the XVth Corps area west of Amiens.

On the 9th of December units began moving forward again to relieve the 29th Division in the left sector of the XIVth Corps front. On the 12th Major-General Douglas Smith took over this sector, with

headquarters near the Briqueterie south-east of Montauban. The front line ran in a curve on the south
and south-west of Le Transloy and from 2000 to 1400
yards distant from the town. It was held by two
groups of six battalions each, the right group consisting of the 61st Brigade with the 10th K.R.R.C.
and the 10th R.B., the left group of the 60th Brigade
with the 11th K.R.R.C. and the 11th R.B. At the
same time the C.R.A. took command of the artillery
covering the Division. The 91st and 92nd Field
Artillery Brigades remained at the Citadel and at
Corbie till the 14th, when they both moved to Morlancourt, so that the only brigade of the 20th Divisional
Artillery under Brig.-General Browell's orders was
the 93rd.

The fortnight that followed was comparatively uneventful. On the 13th four prisoners were captured by
the 7th Somerset L.I.; on the 14th the right group
was heavily shelled, and an attempt of the enemy to
leave his trenches was stopped by the artillery, which
carried out a very successful shoot on the following day.
It was, however, one of the most disagreeable times that
the Division ever spent in the line. The weather was
cold and wet; rain and snow turned the ground into
bog which swallowed up all signs of roads and tracks.
The only communication trench to the front line was
impassable, so that rations and material were got up to
the trenches with the greatest difficulty. At first it
took as long as nine hours to complete one of the reliefs,
and one stretcher party took seven and a half hours to
get from company to battalion headquarters. The
trenches were very bad and kept falling in, especially
in the first few days spent in this sector, and frequently
men had to be dug out of the mud. The 11th D.L.I.,
composed chiefly of miners and well known for their

good work under the worst conditions, improved matters so that before the Division was relieved communication trenches could be used up to a certain distance. The conditions were so trying that after a week the period which a battalion spent in the front line was reduced from three days to two.

On Christmas Day the Division was relieved by the 17th and went back to Corbie. Divisional Artillery Headquarters moved to Morlancourt, where the 91st and 92nd Brigades were resting, leaving the 93rd in action until the 28th, when the 91st relieved it.

About this time the 93rd Brigade became one of the (Army) Field Artillery. Brigades which were then being formed, and No. 3 Section of the Divisional Ammunition Column consequently became the 93rd Brigade Ammunition Column. D/93 was split up, one section going to each of the other howitzer batteries. The 93rd Brigade remained for some time longer in the XIVth Corps, but ceased to belong to the 20th Divisional Artillery, which henceforth consisted of only the 91st and 92nd Brigades.

By the 4th of January 1917 the Division had taken over from the Guards a line running from south of Saillisel to north of Sailly-Saillisel. Half of the former village and the whole of the latter were in our hands. For the first week this was the right sector of the XIVth Corps front, but after a readjustment on the 10th it became the centre sector, with the 17th Division on the left and the Guards on the right.

The 91st Field Artillery Brigade was in the line. The 92nd came in on the 10th, when Brig.-General Browell took command of the artillery covering this sector, and consisting of the 20th and 29th Divisional Artilleries, two batteries of R.H.A., and a Heavy Artillery Group.

H

Little occurred to mark the month spent in this sector. The front covered by the XIVth Corps, however, was most important, and the Sailly-Saillisel sector was the key of the position. The ridge along which the front trenches ran not only flanked the enemy's position at Le Transloy, but also commanded all the approaches from Combles to the front line system. The valleys on the north and east of the ridge, as well as the large wood of St Pierre Vaast, gave the enemy covered approaches in which he might collect his troops in order to assault our line.

The front was held in two brigade groups, the 61st Brigade with the 10th K.R.R.C. and the 10th R.B. on the right ; the 60th Brigade with the 11th K.R.R.C. and 11th R.B. on the left. Divisional Headquarters was at Arrow Head Copse. The front line trenches consisted of a series of isolated posts, in some cases within 30 feet of the enemy, but they were much better than the trenches in front of Le Transloy ; nearly every man had a shelter of some sort, and the number of sick was very small.

Early in January a long list of New Year's honours for the Division was published, headed by Major-General Douglas Smith, who was promoted to the substantive rank of Major-General. On the 6th, Lieut-Colonel Maddocks, G.S.O.I., with several others who lived in the deep tunnel dug-outs at Divisional Head-quarters taken over from the French, was suddenly taken ill with a severe form of influenza and invalided to a base hospital. He was succeeded on the 10th by Lieut.-Colonel J. M'D. Haskard, D.S.O., Royal Dublin Fusiliers.

In the early morning of the 17th, during a heavy bombardment, a small party of the enemy advanced towards a post held by the D.C.L.I., at that time the right battalion of the right brigade group. A bomb falling into the post killed one man and wounded eight others, but the garrison of the neighbouring post by bombing and the fire of Lewis guns forced the enemy to retire in great disorder, leaving a number of dead and wounded on the ground.

A long spell of very severe cold set in at this time. On the night of the 16th/17th four inches of snow fell; on the 22nd, and again on the 26th, there were 20 degrees of frost. The front line was approached by a line of duckboards which became so slippery that one unit coming up for its tour in the trenches considered itself extremely lucky in having only two or three casualties from men falling off. Snow fell again on the 31st, and the hard frost lasted without a break until the middle of February.

On the 22nd of January a raid was attempted against the 6th Oxford and Bucks L.I.— the left battalion of the left group. The raiding party was dressed in white so as not to show up against the snow, but was nevertheless driven back with loss and in disorder.

The only other action in which troops of the Division were involved at this time took place on the 27th. On that day the 29th Division, then on the left of the 20th, made a very successful attack on the enemy's positions south of Le Transloy, taking all its objectives and about 400 prisoners. The 20th Divisional Artillery fired in support, and earned the congratulations of the 29th Division for its valuable assistance. The 60th M.G. Company with seven guns, reinforced by five guns from the 61st M.G. Company in reserve, put a barrage on the flank of the attack. In spite of the intense cold these twelve guns fired an average of 2500 rounds per gun, doing most useful work, for which the company was congratulated by the Corps, Division and Brigade, and by the 29th Division.

The next day the 17th Division took over this sector and the 20th moved back to rest, with headquarters at Heilly. The C.R.A. handed over to the C.R.A. 17th Division, under whose command the 20th Divisional Artillery remained in action. During February the batteries supported two successful attacks by the 17th Division on the 8th and by the 29th Division on the 28th. The result of these operations was to drive the Germans from the last bit of high ground which they had held on the Sailly—Sailly-Saillisel ridge.

By the 10th of February the Division was once more in the line, this time in the left sector of the XIVth Corps front. The right flank rested at the point which had marked the left of the line in January, a little north of Sailly-Saillisel; the left was 1400 yards south-west of Le Transloy. Again the front was held by two brigade groups, the right group consisting of the battalions of the 61st Brigade with the 6th Oxford and Bucks L.I. and the 6th K.S.L.I., the left group of the battalions of the 59th Brigade with the 12th K.R.R.C. and 12th R.B. The 83rd Field Company R.E. was in the right group and the 96th in the left; two machine-gun companies were in the line and one in reserve. Brigade headquarters, which relieved each other in a regular sequence, each spent sixteen days in the line and eight at Carnoy. The Divisional reserve, under the command of the Brigadier at Carnoy, consisted of two battalions from each group, the 11th D.L.I., the 84th Field Company R.E., and a machine-gun company. The C.R.A. commanded the 78th and 79th Field Artillery Brigades and the 28th Heavy Group, as the brigades of the 20th Divisional Artillery were still covering the centre sector of the Corps front.

A few days after the Division came into this line German aeroplanes dropped about 200 bombs around Maricourt and Carnoy. The chief damage they did was to set on fire the Plateau ammunition dump. Two very big explosions were heard by troops in the front line some hours afterwards, and the fire, which began at 5.30 A.M., continued till nightfall, some undetonated shells being thrown a distance of a mile and a half.

As part of the front line defences taken over by the left brigade group there was a very isolated post, known as " B " post, some 300 yards in front of the trenches and out of sight from anywhere in the line. This was a very difficult place to hold, and even to approach. Owing to the constant fire of the enemy's machine guns throughout the night, the only way in which reliefs could be carried out was by sending up two or three men at a time. Even then the men had to crawl on their hands and knees for the last seventy or eighty yards, finally entering the post through a gap in the wire at the rear. All reliefs sustained many casualties.

A request was therefore sent back for authority to give it up. On the night of the 17th/18th the 10th R.B. relieved the 11th R.B. in this part of the line. In order to reduce the casualties Sgt. L. Tatt of the 11th R.B. volunteered to lay a tape to guide the relieving party. Although he had to crawl about for several hours over ground which was being swept by machine-gun fire and shelled by trench mortars, he successfully carried out his task, for which he was awarded the M.M. The next day at 4.30 P.M. the enemy put down an intense barrage on this post, firing high-explosive and gas shells, trench mortar bombs and rifle grenades. The bombardment caused a good many casualties and did considerable damage; eventually all Lewis guns, rifles and ammunition became clogged with mud. This put the garrison at a great disadvantage when, between 5 and 5.30 P.M., the enemy attacked in three parties, one from the front and one on each flank working round to the rear, using two flammenwerfer and a large number of chemical and smoke grenades. All telephone communication was broken, the S.O.S. rockets failed to work, and the first four men sent back with messages were killed. When eventually information did get back to battalion headquarters the post had been lost. The garrison fought to the end and when for a short time the Lewis guns were got into action killed many of the enemy before being finally overpowered.

Permission to evacuate the post had in fact been granted, but the attack took place before the orders had time to get through.

Having taken " B " post the enemy tried to gain a footing in the front line. The attack was driven back by a company of the 10th R.B., under Capt. J. E. Trevor Jones, who was awarded the M.C.

About the middle of February the long frost broke and once more the ground became a mass of mud, trenches began to fall in, and movement was everywhere difficult.

The general situation had meanwhile undergone an important change. One result of the battle of the Somme had been to leave the enemy in a pronounced salient between Le Transloy and Arras, and during the winter 1916/1917 operations were carried out against the southern face and the south-east corner of this salient. In November an advance on the Ancre ended in the capture of St Pierre Divion, Beaucourt and Beaumont Hamel, and of commanding positions south of the river. Operations were continued early in 1917, and by the 17th of February we had gained the high ground overlooking Miraumont from the south and from the west. This gave us command of a further stretch of the Ancre valley and threatened the enemy's line north of the river, where he still held a sharp salient at Serre. On the 24th the enemy began to evacuate his forward positions, and by the evening of the following day the Fifth Army had occupied a line from the north-east of Gueudecourt through Warlen-court-Eaucourt and Miraumont to Serre and was established in the enemy's first defensive system. In the following fortnight the line was pushed forward to Grévillers, Puisieux and Gommecourt.[1]

Prisoners taken in these operations stated that the Germans were contemplating a retirement on a still larger scale to the newly-constructed Hindenburg Line, which ran from St Quentin through Havrincourt, eight miles south-west of Cambrai, and Quéant to the original defensive system east of Arras. They said that this line was to be reached by the 25th of March, that the water supply was being cut off, and that all possible dug-outs were being mined in the area which it was intended to evacuate.

Meanwhile British troops had taken over a consider-able length of line from the French ; by the end of February the British right flank rested at a point four miles west of Roye.[2]

On the 3rd of March the Divisional front was extended to the right some 750 yards to include the village of Sailly-Saillisel. This was due to the withdrawal from the line of the 29th Division, whose front the Guards and 20th Divisions took over between them. The

---

[1] Sir Douglas Haig's Despatches, pp. 49 to 71.
[2] *Ibid.*, p. 64.

XIVth Corps front was then held by two divisions instead of three, the Guards on the right and the 20th on the left. On the left of the 20th was the 5th Australian Division of the 1st Anzac Corps, belonging to the Fifth Army.

At this time the 91st and 92nd Field Artillery Brigades relieved the 17th Divisional Artillery, and came again under the orders of their own division. The 91st Brigade, with two batteries R.H.A., formed the right group, the 92nd Brigade, with one battery R.H.A., formed the left group, and the 460th (How.) battery of the 29th Division was in reserve.

On the 7th the regular brigade organisation was resumed, with the 61st Brigade on the right, the 59th on the left, and the 60th at Carnoy in reserve. Each of the forward brigades kept two battalions in the line and two at Guillemont.

On the 12th the 61st Brigade was relieved by the 60th and went back to Carnoy. Here on the afternoon of the 15th the whole camp of the 12th King's was wrecked by an explosion between the officers' huts and the men's camp. It is unknown what caused the disaster, but apparently some explosives which had long been buried were detonated by accident. Fortunately many of the officers and men were away at the time, either at a football match or at the Carnoy Coliseum, where the " Verey Lights " had been performing since the 20th of February. This must have saved many lives. Nevertheless, three officers were killed and one wounded, and nine men killed, 52 wounded, and one reported missing.

Since the beginning of March there had been increasing signs that the enemy was preparing to withdraw along the whole of his front in the Somme area. Arrangements were therefore made for an early advance.

Orders were issued for the formation of advanced guards; the lines on which the operations should be carried out were laid down, and patrols were kept constantly at work to give immediate information of any retirement from the German positions along the Divisional front.

CHAPTER VII

THE GERMAN RETREAT

17th March to 1st July 1917

The German retreat to the Hindenburg Line—Arrival of the Divisional Machine Gun Company—Actions at Neuville and Ruyaulcourt, at Metz-en-Couture, at Trescault and at Bilhem—The Division in the line facing Quéant under IVth Corps of Fifth Army.

(Vide Maps II and III.)

AT dawn on the 17th of March the German retreat on the 20th Divisional front began. The enemy withdrew from his positions very rapidly and with great secrecy. On the 14th the Guards on the right had occupied the western edge of St Pierre Vaast Wood and the south-east end of Saillisel ; on the 15th they had advanced to the east side of the wood ; patrols of the 20th Division, however, found the enemy still holding his front line up to 5 A.M. on the 17th. The Australians on the left then reported that they had advanced ; immediately patrols were sent out again, in broad daylight, up to the German line. This time they found it unoccupied.

The enemy was at once followed up. Along the whole British line from Monchy au Bois, ten miles south-west of Arras, to the right an important advance was made. The French took Roye, meeting with little opposition. British troops on the right of our line entered Chaulnes ; XIVth Corps occupied the Le Transloy trench system, and troops of the Fifth Army were in Bapaume. The 20th Division established a line of outposts 600 yards east of the Peronne-Bapaume road and parallel to it, including the town of Le Transloy; on the right the Guards were east of St Pierre Vaast Wood; on the left the Australians were in Beaulencourt and Villers au Flos.

Throughout the ensuing operations advanced guards followed up the enemy and drove in his rearguards. When halted they formed an outpost line, keeping touch with the enemy by patrols. As soon as sufficient ground had been gained in this way the main bodies moved forward to form a new main line of resistance, co-ordinated with those of the flank divisions. The advanced guards then made good a further tract of country to the front.

In order that the rapid retirement of the enemy might be closely followed up, it was necessary to push signal communications through the shelled area with all possible speed. This was most successfully performed by the Divisional Signal Company, which, as soon as Rocquigny was occupied, laid a 12-wire open route across "No man's land."

When the forward movement began the 96th Field Company, the 11th D.L.I., the 10th R.B., and the 7th K.O.Y.L.I. were detached for work on roads and railways under the orders of the Corps. They returned to the Division between the 24th and 29th of March,

By the evening of the 18th, Nesle, Péronne, Moislains, Rocquigny, Baupame and Ervillers were in our hands, and the French were advancing with their left directed on Ham. The outpost line of the Division ran from 500 yards west of Le Mesnil, past the east of Rocquigny to Lubda Copse, 500 yards south of Villers au Flos, with cavalry in touch with the enemy rearguards further east. Divisional Headquarters moved up on this day to Guillemont, and the 61st Brigade relieved the 59th on the left of the line.

On the 19th the 5th Australian Division entered Haplincourt. The outposts of the 20th Division were established on the line Le Mesnil-Rocquigny-Barastre, which was occupied on the 21st as the main line of resistance. The Corps Cavalry Regiment held Lechelle and Bus, and the following day occupied Bertincourt.

Once they had crossed a line running south-east from Le Transloy the troops had left the shelled area behind them; movement then became easier, as the roads were as a rule good and the ground had been little damaged. The enemy however had burned the villages, blown craters at cross-roads, set booby traps, and generally done everything he could to hinder the advance. One of these traps with a charge of about 50 bombs and a slab of ammonal was discovered by the headquarters of the 61st Brigade in some cellars at Le Transloy, and several others were found both there and at Rocquigny, but they were all destroyed. Troops entered all buildings with great care, and suffered no casualties from devices of this kind. Many of the dug-outs had been blown in or gassed, but enough were left to give shelter for most of the troops. At Rocquigny it was found that the village crucifix, which had been plainly visible from our original line, had been used by the Germans as an observation post.

On the 19th Major-General Douglas Smith left the Division for a time and returned to England. He was succeeded by Major-General T. G. Matheson, C.B.

The difficulty of getting the guns across the shelled area was great. At first it took as long as five and six hours to move the guns a mile. The roads were as bad as the open country, and had to be repaired before they could be used. On the 20th a section of C/91 Battery

MAJOR-GENERAL T. G. MATHESON, C.B., C.M.G.

[*To face p.* 124.

was ordered to support the cavalry at Rocquigny; not only was this section unable to get through, but one gun disappeared into a shell-hole full of water, where it was left with only the end of the trail to be seen. Next day the remaining gun did good work in support of the cavalry, firing 120 rounds on Ytres. On the 22nd C/92 went forward to Rocquigny by a track which had been made between Les Bœufs and Le Transloy, and was attached to the Corps cavalry. This battery and the gun of C/91 came into action on the 23rd, C/92 north-east of Rocquigny and at Bus, the gun of C/91 at Le Mesnil. On the 24th these guns were withdrawn to take up the defence of the main line of resistance.·

Between the 22nd and the 25th this part of the front was reorganised. XIVth Corps, reduced to two divisions (the Guards and the 1st), was withdrawn into reserve. The 20th Division was transferred to XVth Corps (Lieut.-General Sir John Du Cane), and extended its right as far as the west angle of the Bois St Martin, where it was in touch with the VIIIth; this line was covered by the 91st and 92nd Field Artillery Brigades and a brigade of the 4th Divisional Artillery. The XIVth Corps Cavalry Regiment (two squadrons of King Edward's Horse and one of the 21st Lancers), came under the orders of Major-General Matheson and was directed to act as liaison between the infantry and the 5th Cavalry Division.

On the 26th the 60th Brigade on the right of the line was relieved by the 59th.

The next phase of the operations consisted in advancing the main line of resistance to Equancourt, Ytres and Bertincourt. Equancourt and Vallulart Wood were occupied by cavalry on the evening of the 26th; the former was then taken over by infantry of the 8th Division and the latter by a company of the 10th K.R.R.C. On the 29th the 59th Brigade obtained a footing in the enemy's position east of Vallulart Wood and the 61st occupied Ytres and trenches to the east of it. The 59th Brigade entered the north end of Equancourt on the night of the 27th/28th, and on the following day the line Equancourt—Ytres—Bertincourt was occupied as the main line of resistance. The headquarters of the 59th Brigade at this time was south of Le Mesnil and that of the 61st Brigade was at Bus. The 60th Brigade had moved forward to the area east of Le Transloy, with headquarters in the village. The enemy held the line Fins—Neuville-Bourjonval—Ruyaulcourt. Owing to the long distance between Divisional Headquarters at Guillemont and the forward troops, it was found necessary to establish between Division and brigades an advanced headquarters with which all brigades were in direct signal communication. For the first time since the Division came to France units used their cable carts.

Meanwhile on the 24th the 217th Machine Gun Company under Capt. C. G. Stephens arrived from England and joined the Division as Divisional Machine Gun Company.

The enemy's resistance at this time began to stiffen. On the 28th the following troops under Brig.-General Banbury were detached as advanced guard : One squadron XIVth Corps Cavalry Regiment, the 91st Field Artillery Brigade, the 84th Field Company R.E., and the 61st Infantry Brigade. This advanced guard was ordered to capture Neuville and Ruyaulcourt.

The plan of attack provided that the 12th King's should take Neuville and that the 7th D.C.L.I. should attack Ruyaulcourt from the south and south-east, while the 7th K.O.L.Y.I. made a demonstration on

the north and the north-west. Four guns of the 61st
Machine Gun Company were attached to the King's,
four to the D.C.L.I., and two to the K.O.Y.L.I.

The operations began at 8.15 P.M. on the 28th, shortly
after dusk. The 12th King's on the right advanced
from Ytres against Neuville, " B " and " D " Companies
and two sections of battalion bombers carrying out the
assault, with " C " Company in support and " D " in
reserve in front of Ytres. The leading companies
soon came under heavy fire from machine guns, and on
approaching the position had difficulty with the enemy's
wire, but by 1.55 A.M. on the 29th they were reported
to be holding the south-west half of the village. The
place was then systematically cleared by bombing
parties, and by 2.30 A.M. the whole village had been
taken and posts established 100 yards east of it. A
support line was then dug to consolidate the defences.

The D.C.L.I. on the left moved out from a position
500 yards north of Ytres, " C " and " D " Companies
assaulting, "A " Company in support and " B " in
reserve. They advanced steadily until they were
stopped by strong barbed wire about 3½ feet high,
which had not been previously located. At this moment
they came under rifle and machine-gun fire, in the face
of which they made several attempts to cut through
the wire, which was found to encircle the village.

As they could make no progress, the assaulting
companies retired under shell fire for 200 yards and
from this point made further attempts to get through.
The wire, however, proved too strong and the enemy
too alert, while the intense darkness of the night and
the drifting snow made the task more difficult still.
They therefore withdrew to a line 500 yards south-west
of the village.

The K.O.Y.L.I. carried out their demonstration

on the extreme left, and a patrol sent out by this battalion reported Ruyaulcourt strongly held. The next night the Somerset L.I., who had relieved the D.C.L.I., found the village empty and occupied it. At the same time the 59th Brigade established an outpost line along 2500 yards of the road between Neuville and Fins, while Fins and Sorel le Grand were captured by the 8th Division.

The 61st Brigade received the following message on the 29th of March: "The Divisional Commander congratulates the 61st Brigade on its excellent work last night, especially the King's Regiment. Whilst all concerned did well this battalion especially distinguished itself and showed great dash."

On the 30th an advanced guard, under Brig.-General Browne-Clayton, composed of the 59th Brigade, the 83rd Field Company R.E., one squadron of the XIVth Corps Cavalry Regiment, and three batteries of artillery, occupied the high ground which extends for some 3000 yards south-east of Neuville. An advanced guard of the 8th Division moved at the same time on Revelon (east of Hendecourt) and Dessart Wood. At 4 P.M. the two Rifle Brigade battalions attacked, the 10th on the right and the 11th on the left, each in two lines on a two company front. The men advanced admirably over 1500 yards of open ground, although they incurred a certain number of casualties. including Capt. G. White and Lieut. Ramsey of the 10th R.B., who had both just previously carried out a most valuable reconnaissance. At 5.40 P.M. both companies of the 10th R.B. were reported to be digging in on their objective with the 11th Battalion on their left. Touch was gained with the 8th Division at 9 P.M. Little opposition was met during the attack, most of the casualties—5 officers and about 90 men—being caused by shell fire while the new line was being dug and consolidated.

By the evening of the 30th the outpost line ran from the north of Dessart Wood (where it was in touch with the 8th Division) through Neuville and Ruyaulcourt; the main line of resistance remained unchanged. On the 1st of April the 60th Brigade relieved the 61st on the left of the line, and on the 2nd, Divisional Head-quarters moved from Guillemont to Rocquigny.

By the 1st of April reconnaissances had found the enemy rearguards holding a line covering Metz-en-Couture and the south-west corner of Havrincourt Wood. The object of the following operations was to capture this line. As a preparatory measure a small party of the 11th R.B. advancing over ground covered with snow tried to occupy Metz-en-Couture on the night 2nd/3rd, but found the village strongly held. A similar attempt made by the 10th R.B. on the following night met with the same result. The main line of resist-ance on the right was advanced during the night of the 2nd/3rd to a monument 1000 yards north of Fins, running thence west for 1000 yards and joining the Ytres—Bertincourt line half a mile north of Equancourt. On the 4th Brig.-General Browne-Clayton's advanced guard attacked the enemy in front of it, while the 8th Division on the right advanced against Gouzeaucourt Wood and a line running thence to the south-east. A heavy snowstorm on the night before the attack added to the difficulties of the operation, but by 2.30 P.M. on the 4th, although the slush underfoot made the going very bad, the weather had to some extent improved.

The advanced guard as constituted for this operation consisted of the 59th Brigade, the 59th Machine Gun Company, one section of the 217th Machine Gun

I

Company, the whole of the Divisional Artillery, and two sections of the 83rd Field Company R.E.

The operation was divided into two phases :

1. At zero (2 P.M.) an advance on the right of two battalions (the 10th K.R.R.C. on the right and the 11th K.R.R.C. on the left) to capture and hold the first objective, Metz-en-Couture.

2. At 3.25 P.M. an advance on the left of one battalion (the 11th R.B., with one company of the 10th R.B.) to capture the second objective, the enemy's trench from the north-west corner of Metz to the south-west corner of Havrincourt Wood.

The 60th Brigade and one section of the 217th Machine Gun Company were to assist by bringing machine-gun fire to bear on the south-west corner and the west side of the wood from all available guns which could be assembled in Neuville.

The 12th King's moved up into the line on the 3rd to enable the whole of the 59th Brigade to attack. By the morning of the 4th, battalions were disposed as follows :

10th K.R.R.C. (Lieut.-Colonel Ley) in Dessart Wood.

11th K.R.R.C. (Lieut.-Colonel Priaulx) at Fins.

10th R.B. (Lieut.-Colonel Troughton) holding a line about 1500 yards south-west of Metz, facing the village.

11th R.B. (Lieut.-Colonel Cotton) prolonging this line to a point 400 yards south-east of Neuville.

At 2 P.M. the barrage opened and the 10th and 11th K.R.R.C. deployed from their positions and advanced in extended order. They met with little opposition for the first fifteen minutes, but when they came within 700 yards of Metz the enemy's rifle and machine-gun fire increased. At 2.30 the two companies of the 10th K.R.R.C. on the right flank suffered a good many casualties from the enemy's posts to the south-east of

the village; the two left companies and the 11th
Battalion had at this time reached the outskirts of
Metz, where they paused for a few moments till the
barrage lifted. They entered the village at 2.40 and
found it more strongly fortified than had been expected.
The left company of the 11th K.R.R.C. was at first held
up by a succession of trenches on the north-west of the
village, but after a good deal of fighting cleared them
all and established a line beyond them. In spite of
considerable fire from the houses and from Havrincourt
Wood, the centre companies of the attack soon cleared
most of Metz, leaving in the enemy's possession only
the northern part of it, where wire and covering fire
from the wood held them up for a time. Meanwhile
the two right companies of the 10th K.R.R.C. had
advanced in line with the rest of the battalion and were
just south-east of the village. Here no troops of the
8th Division could be seen, and the enemy counter
attacked from the south-east. A company of the 10th
R.B. in reserve was at once sent forward, but arriving
after the counter attack had been driven off, established
a defensive flank facing Gouzeaucourt Wood, and
eventually got into touch with the 8th Division. By
3.25 P.M. the whole of Metz was in our hands except
a few houses on the north; cellars and dug-outs had
been cleared and a number of prisoners taken.

The 11th R.B. then advanced on a two company
front, with a company of the 10th R.B. on their right.
On the left flank the attacking troops immediately
came under heavy fire from machine guns in the south-
west corner of Havrincourt Wood, and suffered many
casualties; they were reinforced by half a company
from the supporting line, but could not make much
progress. Capt. the Hon. A. M. Bertie, 11th R.B.,
was awarded the D.S.O. for a gallant effort to silence

these machine guns. The troops on the right were under cover of rising ground for the first hundred yards or so, and were able to advance to within a short distance of the first line of trenches, which they captured when the barrage lifted at 3.55 P.M. A fire fight then developed with the enemy, who had retired to the line of the wood, towards which the right companies continued to work forward. By 5 P.M. they had taken Mill Farm on the south edge and were in touch with the 11th K.R.R.C., though the left company was still held up by the machine guns in the south-west corner. These were eventually dislodged by a patrol from the right which worked round their flank, and by 7 P.M. the whole of the objective had been gained.

The 10th and 11th K.R.R.C. meanwhile had pushed through Metz and at 4 P.M. began to dig in on the further side. The village was heavily shelled by the enemy from 6.30 P.M. onwards, but as the battalions were on the far side consolidating the new line, little loss was caused. The advance, however, had cost heavy casualties—more than a quarter of all the troops engaged. The two remaining companies of the 10th R.B. and four guns from the 59th Machine Gun Company were therefore sent forward to reinforce the front line. The 10th K.R.R.C. in particular had suffered severely ; of the nine officers hit some had served with this unit since 1914, among them Capt. Egerton Leigh, one of the most gallant officers the battalion had known, who was killed. Lieut.-Colonel Ley, commanding the 10th K.R.R.C., received the D.S.O. The ridge captured on this day was afterwards known as " Greenjacket Ridge."

The operations were very well carried out by troops who had already held the front line for eight days and of whom half had been engaged in the advance on the

30th of March.   Twenty-five per cent. of the infantry consisted of newly arrived drafts, whose behaviour was very highly praised by their commanding officers.

It appears from prisoners' statements that the Germans did not expect to be attacked until the 7th; they certainly left behind many signs of a hurried retreat, including the remains of a meal in the middle of which some of their officers had evidently been disturbed, and which consisted of hot coffee and English potted meat.

Little mention of the artillery and machine gun companies has been made in the account of this fighting, but that they, as well as the infantry, did excellent work, is shown in the following message which was received two days later from the Fourth Army Commander: " Please convey to the 20th Division my hearty congratulations on their well-deserved success.   The co-operation of artillery, machine guns and infantry in the hard fighting of the last few days is most creditable to all ranks, and I offer them my warmest thanks."

On the night of the 5th/6th the 61st Brigade relieved the 59th, and next day the new main line of resistance, Metz—Neuville—Ruyaulcourt—Bertincourt, was occupied.   That night the 40th Division came into the line between the 8th and the 20th, taking over 500 yards of front from the latter, whose right flank then rested just in front of the south-east corner of Metz.   On the 9th the 60th Machine Gun Company co-operated with the 1st Australian Division, which made a successful attack on Hermies.

On the 10th of April (Easter Monday) the 61st Brigade was holding the near edge of Havrincourt Wood.   At 4 P.M. the 7th Somerset L.I. and 7th D.C.L.I. made an attack which took the Germans by surprise while having their evening meal.   The outpost line was advanced some 300 to 400 yards into the wood with very slight casualties, and the troops enjoyed an excellent meal which Fritz had kindly prepared for them.

The 83rd Field Company R.E. did excellent work during the first fortnight of April under the 60th Brigade, and was congratulated by the Brigade Commander. Sgt. W. Bee, Lance-Cpl. E. Reed and Cpl. J. Hamilton of this company were awarded the Military Medal at the end of the month, the two former for capturing a machine gun in the attack on Metz-en-Couture.

On the 13th the main line of resistance was again advanced, pivoting on Metz, to pass through the south-west part of Havrincourt Wood and along the west edge of it. Patrols penetrated as far as the north-east arm of the wood in daylight without seeing any of the enemy.

Further north, British troops got into the Hindenburg Line opposite Riencourt and Hendecourt on the 11th, and on the 15th repulsed a German counter attack on a six-mile front from Hermies to Noreuil.

On the 14th the 59th Brigade relieved the 60th in the left sub-sector, and on the 20th the 60th relieved the 61st on the right. Meanwhile the outpost line had been established well inside Havrincourt Wood.

On the 21st the 40th Division, assisted by the fire of the 91st Field Artillery Brigade, advanced its line to within 1000 yards of Villers Plouich and Beaucamp, while on its left the 60th Brigade advanced its right flank so as to keep touch. This operation was completed in the early morning, and shortly afterwards the enemy was reported to be shelling the south end of Trescault on the front of the 60th Brigade. Operations were at once begun for the occupation of this place. It was a somewhat awkward position to attack, as the village, standing on the north-west slope of a ridge, was under full observation from the enemy's position in Havrincourt, and machine guns guarded the low ground in front of it. It was important, therefore, to hold both the high ground south-east of the village and the spur which faced it on the north-west. The 12th K.R.R.C. were ordered to reconnoitre. 2nd Lieut. A. D. Thornton Smith, the intelligence officer of this battalion, crawled forward with three scouts in broad daylight into the village of Trescault and found the enemy holding the north and west outskirts of the village, and also working on a trench about Bilhem, a group of buildings 800 yards further east. North of Trescault he found enemy machine guns. By nightfall the 12th K.R.R.C. had established a line of posts on the ridge from a point 600 yards south-east of Trescault through the village to a bridge at its north-west corner. The right of this line was in touch with the 40th Division.

On the 22nd, 2nd Lieut. Thornton Smith continued to patrol. In the words of the official report, " his control of these operations was so decisive that by 9.30 A.M. . . . the village was cleared of the enemy." For his work on these two days he was awarded the D.S.O.

It then remained to occupy the high ground facing Trescault from the north-west.

This was carried out on the night of the 22nd. The 91st Field Artillery Brigade had done good work during the day in shelling the enemy's positions, and at 8 P.M. the barrage began. Half an hour later the 12th R.B. and the 6th K.S.L.I. advanced and occupied the objective against slight resistance and with little loss. The line was then held, from right to left, by the 12th K.R.R.C., the 12th R.B., and the 6th K.S.L.I.

The outpost line of the 59th Brigade was again pushed

forward on the 22nd, when it included the greater part of Havrincourt Wood.

The enemy remained in possession of Bilhem and was thus able to prevent the 40th Division from holding Beaucamp, which it had entered on the 24th. That night, therefore, at 11 p.m., the 60th Brigade attacked Bilhem with three companies of the 12th K.R.R.C., supported by the 91st Field Artillery Brigade, three 18-pr. batteries of the 92nd Brigade, and a heavy battery. Two guns of the 60th T.M.B. in the first five minutes after zero fired 120 rounds on the enemy's position. As a preliminary measure a patrol of the Oxfords cleared a cemetery on the north-east of Trescault; the left company of the 12th K.R.R.C., " D " Company, then deployed just south of this cemetery. " A " Company formed up just south-east of Trescault in front of the road, with " C " Company in support on the road behind. " B " Company was in reserve in Havrincourt Wood. When, in the course of the advance, " A " Company went too far to the right, 2nd Lieut. J. M. M'Donald, commanding " C " Company, on his own initiative took his company forward and filled the gap. " D " Company entered the Bilhem grounds on the north-west, turning the flank of the Germans who were holding the south-west wall, just at the time when " A " and " C " Companies attacked in front. All three companies then moved on to the far side of the buildings, having taken their objective and 14 prisoners at a cost of 9 men wounded.

The next day the 40th Division entered and held Beaucamp, and the 20th Divisional Headquarters moved forward from Rocquigny to Little Wood, south of Ytres. On the 26th the 59th Brigade was relieved by the 61st in the left sub-sector of the line.

With the capture of Bilhem the Division had finally

THE MILL HOUSE, HAVRINCOURT WOOD

[To face p. 156.

driven the enemy on its front into the Hindenburg defences. It then became necessary to organise the line
as a defensive position in order to safeguard the ground
which had been gained. The front line, after a certain
amount of readjustment, ran from the south-east of
Bilhem in a general north-westerly direction as far as
the right flank of the 11th Division on the canal, and
included the whole of Havrincourt Wood except a
part of the north-eastern area just south of the village
of Havrincourt. The guns were placed just west of
the wood.

The three weeks spent here were quiet and very
pleasant. After all the discomfort and hardships of
fighting through a wet and very cold winter, the warm
spring weather of May came as an intense relief.

It was a time, however, of hard work ; completely
new lines of trenches had to be dug. In the right
sub-sector, where the line resulting from the capture
of Trescault and Bilhem had to be re-sited, the battalions
of the 60th Brigade, with the help of the 83rd Field
Company R.E., dug and wired in twelve days a good
trench 5 feet deep and 6 feet wide throughout the
whole brigade' front—a distance of about 3000 yards.
Similar work was done by the 61st Brigade on the left,
and behind the front line support and communication
trenches were made.

During this month a considerable addition to the
direct responsibility of the Divisional Signal Company
occurred. The signal personnel of the field artillery
brigades was transferred to the R.E. and formed
into sub-sections of the Divisional Signal Company,
from which additional N.C.O.'s and men were posted
to complete the establishment.

A few weeks later the Wireless section, previously
attached, as occasion demanded, from the Corps

Signal Company, was also included in the establishment of the Divisional Signal Company.

Between the 12th and 14th of May the XVth Corps front was reorganised, the 8th Division being withdrawn from the line, which was then held by the 40th on the right and the 20th on the left. The 60th Brigade, which had been relieved by the 59th on the 4th of May, came up and extended the 20th Division line to the right, taking in Beaucamp and Villers Pluich.

The only break in the fine weather happened at this time. There was a very bad thunderstorm for about half an hour on the 14th. Dug-outs were flooded— those of the 12th K.R.R.C. to a depth of 6 feet— trenches began to fall in, and sunken roads became torrents. Water poured into a deep dug-out which formed the headquarters of the 60th Brigade and soaked the documents. By means of pumps and drains the dug-outs were cleared and kits and papers rescued, and as the weather became dry and warm again little damage was done.

On the 19th units began moving out of the line as the Division was leaving the Fourth Army to go further north, and on the 23rd General Matheson handed over the sector to the G.O.C. 42nd Division.

On the 20th the Corps Commander, Lieut.-General Sir John Du Cane, addressed the 12th King's and the 7th D.C.L.I. as representatives of the Division. He said that the 20th Division had driven back the enemy from the trenches in front of Morval and Lesbœufs to the Hindenburg Line, a greater distance than that achieved by any other division on that front. The 20th had seen much hard fighting and had never failed to gain its objectives. It had distinguished itself not only in fighting but also in the fine amount of hard work it had done during the advance and digging in before the Hindenburg Line.

Sir Henry Rawlinson, commanding the Fourth Army, wrote as follows :

" It is now nine months since the Division joined the Fourth Army, and I cannot allow them to leave without expressing to all ranks my gratitude for the excellent services they have rendered. Throughout the heavy fighting in October and November last at Guillemont, Lesbœufs, the Quadrilateral, and east of Gueudecourt, they displayed a gallantry and fighting spirit which was beyond praise.

" Throughout an exceptionally trying winter they had to hold one of the wettest and muddiest parts of the line, yet when it came to the advance in March and April they carried out the successful attacks on Neuville, Metz-en-Couture, Trescault, and Bilhem with a gallantry and dash which was wholly admirable, and for which I offer them my warmest thanks.

" I much regret that the Division is now leaving the Fourth Army, but I trust that at some future date I may again have the good fortune of finding them under my command."

On the 23rd, Divisional Headquarters moved to the monument north of Bapaume, and brigades went into the line facing Quéant during the following three days. The Division was now in the Fifth Army (General Sir Hubert Gough) and in the IVth Corps, which took over from the Ist Anzac Corps just at this time. The front of the IVth Corps (Lieut.-General Sir C. L. Woollcombe) was held by the 48th Division on the right and the 20th on the left; on the left of the 20th was the 58th Division of the Vth Corps. The Divisional line was held by the 61st Brigade on the right and the 60th on the left, with the 59th in reserve. In the right sub-sector a line of outposts was held some 500 yards in advance of the main line of resistance, which ran from just east of Lagnicourt to a point 1000 yards east of Bullecourt, the left flank being actually in the Hindenburg Line. In the severe fighting that had taken place in this sector the front line trenches had been blown to bits, and could be held only in a series of isolated posts. Most of the battery positions were very exposed. The only places for them lay in the Noreuil, Lagnicourt and Morchies valleys, which throughout their whole length ran towards the enemy. They could thus easily be observed not only from kite balloons, but also from the high ground in the enemy's lines.

The Divisional Machine Gun Company was disposed so as to cover the front with half the guns and the flanks and certain special points with others, keeping one gun for anti-aircraft work. The company established observation posts which gave a view of over a considerable part of the Hindenburg Line.

Three weeks of active trench warfare followed. The enemy shelled this sector heavily almost every day. On the night of the 1st of June the trenches of the 12th R.B. were badly blown in, but fortunately the casualties were few. A/92 Battery during a severe shelling on the 3rd had three guns damaged, and by the 8th seven 18-prs. and six howitzers in the Divisional Artillery were out of action, most of them knocked out by the enemy's fire. The 59th Brigade, coming into the line on the 6th of June, was heavily bombarded both that day and the next, and Noreuil and Lagnicourt were persistently shelled. At the same time the line had to be strengthened as much as possible, active patrolling maintained, and raids on the enemy's trenches carried out.

A very successful raid was carried out on the night of the 12th/13th of June by a platoon of the 7th Somerset L.I. under 2nd Lieut. C. J. Lewin. The barrage on the enemy's trench was so good that the raiding party was able to advance close up to it ; as soon as it lifted the Somersets attacked, fought their way through the wire, and charged with the bayonet. Then the enemy bolted. Nine men were seen to fall, nine others were left dead in the trench, and the rest ran into the barrage, leaving in our hands a prisoner belonging to a unit which had not been identified before on the Divisional front. Our casualties were three men slightly wounded. 2nd Lieut. Lewin was awarded the M.C. and Lance-Sgt. A. Harley and Pte. A. J. Gibbs the M.M. for this raid.

The 12th King's sent three patrols up to the enemy's line on the night of the 23rd/24th. They met with a good deal of opposition and all three had fights with parties of the enemy, but they obtained very useful information. The next night " B " Company of this battalion raided a sunken road south-west of Riencourt, eight guns of the 61st Machine Gun Company assisting with indirect fire. The wire was found to be very strong—thick and treble fenced—but some of the party got through, securing a useful identification from a few of the enemy dead who were left in the trench and who had evidently been killed by the barrage.

During this period there were two changes at Divisional Headquarters. Lieut.-Colonel E. M. Newell succeeded Lieut.-Colonel Rolland as C.R.E., and Major Stratton, who had commanded the Divisional Signal Company since it had been formed in England, was transferred to the IXth Corps. The latter was succeeded by Capt. A. G. Brace, M.C., who commanded the company until the end of the war.

Between the 20th and 22nd the Divisional Artillery was relieved and on the 23rd marched to the neighbourhood of Fricourt, with headquarters at Meaulte, to refit. The rest of the Division moved out in the following days, and on the 29th this sector was taken over by the G.O.C. 62nd Division.

In a special order issued at this time Major-General Matheson commended all units for their work in the last seven months, and for the way in which, after withstanding the hardships of a most inclement winter in perhaps the worst part of the old Somme battlefield, they pursued the enemy relentlessly, adapting themselves to the conditions of open warfare. He also praised the work done in digging the elements of an excellent trench system in the line near Havrincourt Wood, and in greatly improving the defences in front of Noreuil and Lagnicourt.

On the 29th, Divisional Headquarters moved to Bernaville, and on July the 1st to Domart. In this area the Division, less the artillery, concentrated for training and rest.

CHAPTER VIII

THE THIRD BATTLE OF YPRES

2nd July to 18th October 1917

The third battle of Ypres—Divisional Artillery in the attack
of 31st July—The crossing of the Steenbeek—The capture
of Langemarck—Capture of Eagle Trench—The 20th
Division (less Artillery) moved south—Artillery in support
of attacks towards Poelcappele and Houthoulst Forest.
(Vide Map I.)

DURING the first fortnight of July 1917 the
Divisional Artillery marched north into the
Ypres Salient. Headquarters was opened at
Elverdinghe on the 15th and batteries moved at once
into position between 1500 and 3000 yards further east.
The C.R.A. (Brig.-General Browell) took over command
of the Left Group of the Right Artillery, XIVth Corps,
consisting of the 91st and 92nd Brigades and the 93rd
(Army) Brigade, which again fought under its old
Divisional Artillery. Immediately after coming into
the line preparations were begun for an attack which
was to be made on the Allied front between the river
Lys, south-east of Messines, and Bixschoete.
    The plan underlying the operations of 1917 consisted
in striking a series of blows in different parts of the front,
so that each of the succeeding attacks might fall on the
enemy before he had recovered from the last. After
the German retirement to the Hindenburg Line,
operations were begun on the 9th of April at Arras.
At the end of the first six days' fighting our lines had

been pushed forward four miles on this front, and included the important Vimy Ridge, which gave to us and denied to the enemy most valuable observation. The 93rd (Army) Field Artillery Brigade (Lieut.-Colonel W. D. Stillwell) took part in this battle.

As the French were preparing to launch an attack on the Aisne, the Arras operations were continued in order to hold as many as possible of the German reserves from moving south. The French opened their offensive on the 16th of April, and on the 5th of May carried the Chemin des Dames. The fighting on the Arras front had then fulfilled its rôle, but activity in this area was still maintained until preparations for an offensive in the Ypres Salient were complete.[1]

The whole of the country round Ypres is overlooked by the ridge which runs up from Messines and Wytschaete, passing east of Hooge and Zonnebeke to Passchendaele. The British line until the 7th of June lay in a semicircle round Ypres at a general distance of 4000 yards from the town, following the foot of the high ground as far as Sanctuary Wood south of Hooge. From this point, while the main ridge continues north-east, the line curved in a general north-westerly direction past Wieltje to Boesinghe, but was still overlooked by the German positions on the long spur which extends as far as Pilckem.

On the 7th of June the very successful battle of Messines gained the whole of the southern part of the ridge as far as a point about a mile south of Hooge. The object of the operations which began at the end of July was to extend this success and to push forward our lines east and north of Ypres so as to embrace the whole of the high ground which at present dominated our position in the salient. On the front of the

[1] Sir Douglas Haig's Despatches, pp. 81–102.

XIVth Corps this meant an advance north-east, of which the first stage was to be the capture of Pilckem Ridge and the ground as far as the Steenbeek.

The Divisional Artillery covered the right sector of the XIVth Corps front, occupied till the beginning of July by the 29th Division, and after that by the 38th. The line, which extended from a point opposite Krupp Farm to the canal bank just short of the railway, was little changed since the 20th Division had held it in the spring of 1916. It had been pushed forward and straightened at certain points, and to the left of this sector the British had taken over a further stretch of 1500 yards along the canal, but the general situation of the trenches remained the same.

The conditions, on the other hand, had been very greatly improved. Many miles of new tram lines had been laid, so that nearly every battery had a line running to within a hundred yards of the gun positions, and a large number of ammunition dumps had been formed. The flatness of the country made it impossible to get complete flash cover for all guns. Camouflage screens, however, had been erected all along the front, and with the natural cover afforded by numerous small copses and farms, most batteries were able to obtain fair flash cover.

The Divisional Artillery had to occupy entirely new positions; these were reconnoitred on the 13th; work was begun on them that night, and on the 14th, 15th and 16th the batteries came into action and took their part in the preliminary bombardment.

The divisions detailed to carry out the attack in the XIVth Corps were the 38th on the right and the Guards on the left; the 29th Division was in reserve behind the Guards, and the 20th was to arrive in this area in time to come into reserve behind the 38th.

K

The bombardment continued throughout the rest of July, for the operations originally planned to begin on the 25th were put off till the 31st. A marked feature of this period was the silence of the German guns by day, a great contrast to the continual shelling of 1916. This was the result of the very thorough counter-battery work which had been carried out in the salient by the heavy artillery, assisted by our aeroplanes. It is known that the Germans withdrew their guns by day and brought them up each night, when they shelled the whole area heavily, especially with gas. They had been engaged, when the 20th Divisional Artillery came into the line, in moving back their battery positions across the Steenbeek, and the increased activity which they showed after the 21st of July pointed to the completion of this manœuvre.

The enemy's night firing, by killing and wounding many of the drivers and horses as well as by continually breaking the Decauville railway, made the supply of ammunition exceedingly difficult, especially for the Divisional Ammunition Column, which was working day and night forming dumps in the forward area for future operations. There were considerable losses, too, among the gunners ; B/92 Battery had 24 casualties in two nights, and on the 22nd had to be withdrawn from the line for a short rest. The 93rd (Army) Brigade was in the most forward position, and it had been decided to keep this as a silent brigade. Owing to the casualties incurred in the Divisional Artillery, this plan had to be abandoned on the 22nd in order to keep up the programme of night firing that had been laid down.

With the exception of a few raids on the enemy's lines, the only operation carried out before the battle began took place on the 27th, when information was received that the enemy had retired from his front line. Strong patrols sent out to verify this report crossed No Man's Land unopposed, entered the enemy's front line, and even pushed on beyond it. Later they met with strong resistance from numbers of the enemy concealed in large concrete dug-outs, and when reinforcements came up from the direction of Pilckem, the patrols were forced back to the original line. Prisoners stated that the enemy was much shaken by our bombardment, but had no intention of retiring on this front. Opposite Boesinghe, however, the enemy did retire, leaving in our hands both banks of the Yser Canal, which had formed till then a serious obstacle to the advance of the Allied left flank.

During this time the Divisional Ammunition Column worked very hard and earned the congratulations of the C.R.A. Between the 19th and the 26th the column delivered over 35,000 rounds to the batteries, besides sending out rations, water, and large quantities of camouflage and material. In the latter half of July the casualties in the column were 3 officers, 37 other ranks, and 113 animals.

Meanwhile the Division had entrained at Domart on the 20th of July and concentrated in the XIVth Corps area, with headquarters at Proven. For the rest of the month it remained in Corps reserve behind the 38th Division.

As the day of the attack drew near various units of the Division were attached for special work in connection with the operations. The 10th K.R.R.C. and the 10th R.B. went to the 38th Division on the 25th to provide carrying parties to the front line. They came under severe shelling, meeting for the first time the new German gas, in which it was possible to work for some hours before the effects of the gas were felt.

This gas, which could not be seen and could be detected only by the faint smell of sour apples, was very deadly, but few casualties were caused to these two battalions from this source owing to the efficiency of the gas helmet and the special rattles which had been provided to give warning. The 10th R.B. suffered heavy casualties from shell-fire.

During the operations both battalions were employed on reclaiming roads under the C.R.E., and the 11th K.R.R.C. did the same work under the 38th Division. The 59th and 217th Machine Gun Companies moved to forward positions on the 22nd to assist in the barrage on the 31st, when the 59th Machine Gun Company fired over 20,000 rounds on the S.O.S. lines. The 59th Brigade, the 83rd Field Company R.E., and the 11th D.L.I. moved to positions south and west of Elverdinghe on the 30th and 31st. During the operation the 83rd and 96th Field Companies and the D.L.I. constructed artillery tracks under the C.R.E.

The attack was launched at 3.50 A.M. on the 31st of July and went well. The infantry quickly gained the Pilckem Ridge, and by 11.35 A.M. both the 38th and the Guards Divisions were reported to be holding their final objective, the line of the Steenbeek. At 3.30 P.M. the S.O.S. went up from this line and the 92nd and 93rd Field Artillery Brigades opened fire; the barrage came down right on the attacking wave, which broke and ran.

During the advance the barrage, which had been practised daily during the preceding week, moved forward at the rate of 100 yards every four minutes, remaining stationary 200 yards beyond each objective. Whilst stationary on these " protectors " some batteries fired smoke shells to form a screen another 200 yards further on. In the 91st Brigade 2nd Lieut. G. C.

The Steenbeek

[To face p. 148.

Glossop, C/91 Battery, and Lieut. H. P. W. Humphreys, D/91, acted as F.O.O.'s, accompanied by twelve N.C.O.'s and men. A buried cable had been dug in up to the front line trenches. As the infantry advanced, a telephone line was run out from the cable head, one officer being responsible for the line and the other for obtaining information. Excellent reports were sent back, and 2nd Lieut. Glossop and Lieut. Humphreys were awarded the M.C. and four men the M.M. for their conspicuous success in maintaining communication to the foremost infantry positions for two days under heavy shell-fire. Lieut. A. Currie of the same brigade won the M.C. for carrying out under heavy shelling a most useful reconnaissance. In the 92nd Brigade Lieut. Pickard, D/92, and 2nd Lieut. Harrison, A/92, acted as F.O.O.'s, and advanced with the infantry. 2nd Lieut. Harrison and many of his party were killed during the action.

As the advance progressed the guns were moved forward. At 10 A.M., when the infantry had taken a line between Pilckem and the Steenbeek, the 92nd Brigade moved forward to positions already chosen just west of the canal. As soon as this brigade was reported in action, about 1.45 P.M., the 91st was ordered to the western slope of Pilckem Ridge. At this time it began to rain. The tracks forward were not yet completed; one road was passable, but only as far as the old German front line. As a result of our bombardment the ground was a mass of shell-holes, with pill-boxes blown upside down and débris scattered everywhere, difficult enough for infantry to move over and almost impossible for guns. As the planked track could not be finished till nearly dark, only one battery, C/91, was able to get to the forward position that day, with eight horses per gun team and all

ammunition by pack. The remaining batteries got to
the position by dawn the next day. The ground, however, was so swampy that the guns could not open fire
until platforms had been made. During the 1st of
August, in the efforts to get the guns into some sort of
line, one or two were completely bogged and could not
be got out for some days. There was great difficulty
in getting up ammunition; all had to come by pack
along a plank road, at the end of which it was dumped
and then brought up some distance to the gun
positions by hand. It was hard work for the men,
who had no cover of any kind, and who, when there
was time to rest, simply slept in the mud.

The rain continued for the next three days, making
any movement most difficult. On the 4th the weather
cleared and aeroplanes could go up, an opportunity of
which the Germans took full advantage, for they shelled
the wagon lines heavily that night, causing many
casualties among the men and horses.

The C.R.A. took over command of the Right Artillery
on the 5th, and the Left Group (91st. 92nd and 93rd
Brigades) came under Lieut.-Colonel Ricardo. The
next day the 20th Division relieved the 38th, with
headquarters at Dragon Camp, about three miles east
of Elverdinghe, the 61st Brigade taking over the
outpost line.

On the 7th of August Major-General Matheson went
to hospital, suffering from gas poisoning. Two days
later Major-General Douglas Smith returned to the
Division and took command. At the same time Brig.-
General Browell, the C.R.A., was invalided home. He
was succeeded on the 10th by Brig.-General H. W. A.
Christie, C.M.G.

The 61st Brigade was relieved that night by the
59th.

The task before the Division was to capture Langemarck. The line held, on taking over the right sector
of the XIVth Corps front, extended for 1000 yards
along the west bank of the Steenbeek, with the left
flank resting on the Ypres-Staden railway. As a
preliminary operation it was necessary to gain command
of the Steenbeek valley in order to obtain ground on
the far side of the stream, where the leading waves
might form up for the attack.

It was originally intended to do this by peaceful
penetration. This was a very difficult matter, not
only because the stream and the marshy ground on each
side of it formed a serious obstacle, but also because
the enemy, profiting by a week of bad weather which
had prevented any advance on our part, had thoroughly
organised his defences on the east bank.

Major J. W. Massie, 83rd Field Company R.E.,
made a remarkably fine reconnaissance of the Steenbeek
along the whole Divisional front—work which was
particularly valuable, as previous reports had been
misleading.

The 29th Division on the left and the 11th Division
on the right had already established a line of posts
on the far side. On the front of the 20th Division
there was a very strong work at Au Bon Gite, 300 yards
beyond the east bank on the Langemarck road. This
was an extremely well fortified place, containing many
concrete shelters. There were many other concrete
blockhouses at intervals on both sides of the stream,
commanding all approaches, but Au Bon Gite was the
key to the enemy's defences in this sector.

On the 8th, the 11th R.B. (Lieut.-Colonel Cotton),
who held the whole of the front line, were ordered to
send over three patrols to establish themselves by peaceful penetration. As one of these patrols went forward

to the stream the road was blown up; a bridge was blown up in front of another patrol; the third got across and established a post on the right flank in prolongation of the line of posts thrown out by the 11th Division. This patrol remained in its position until the night of the 10th/11th, when the 11th R.B. were relieved by the 10th K.R.R.C. (Lieut.-Colonel Lee), and the post was withdrawn.

During this week the Divisional Signal Company made great improvements in the signal communication with the front. The buried cable head was still in the original front line just east of the canal. It was impossible with the labour available to continue the bury to the two infantry brigade battle headquarters, so arrangements were made to establish a route from the cable head to each brigade and to bury each of these lines for a short distance over the worst shelled area on the Pilckem Ridge. This exceedingly unpleasant task was accomplished before the coming operation, thanks to the untiring energies of the infantry working parties and signal personnel. Forward of brigade headquarters one main route on each brigade front was laid. These were supplemented by visual wireless and amplifiers, so arranged as to form alternate routes as necessity arose. Breakdown parties were placed at intervals along all routes.

On the 11th of August the 59th Brigade was ordered to force the Steenbeek with artillery support. Two companies of the 10th K.R.R.C. were detailed to make the assault. Unfortunately a patrol of the enemy crossed the stream shortly before operations began. and fired on the troops as soon as they advanced. This disorganised the attack. The two companies, however. got across, but were overwhelmed by the enemy on the east bank.

Another attempt was made on the 14th, this time with six companies, two of the 11th R.B. on the right of the Langemarck road and the whole of the 10th R.B. on the left of it, all under Lieut.-Colonel L. H. W. Troughton, commanding the 10th R.B. The objective was a line about 300 yards east of the Steenbeek and included Au Bon Gite.

The joint headquarters of these two battalions was at this time at Stray Farm, an old farmhouse reinforced with concrete and in full view of the enemy. Here, under the filthiest and most unsanitary conditions, the staffs of both battalions and the signallers were crowded together. The Germans had the range exactly, and hit the place repeatedly.

Although they came under a good deal of shelling the assaulting companies were assembled by 3 A.M. on the 14th, under cover of detachments thrown forward to guard the line of the stream. At 4 A.M., under an artillery barrage which was described by Lieut.-Colonel Troughton as the best he had ever seen, the troops crossed, some by wading through the stream and others by light bridges which they themselves carried down. The 10th R.B. suffered heavily from machine-gun and rifle fire from Au Bon Gite and other pill-boxes, but after severe hand-to-hand fighting round the pill-boxes they established themselves 250 yards beyond the stream and consolidated the position. Lieut. Martin and Sgt.-Major Salter, D.C.M., were killed gallantly capturing a pill-box which was holding up the advance. Immediately afterwards, while attacking another pill-box Capt. Edwards and Capt. Irvine were killed. When information was urgently needed as to the situation, Lieut. E. Chapman, intelligence officer to this battalion, went forward with Rfm. Moore to the front line in full view of the enemy under a hail of bullets and made a most valuable reconnaissance of the position. Lieut. Chapman was killed but Rfm. Moore succeeded in bringing back the information which Lieut. Chapman had written.

The left company of the 11th R.B., after crossing with some difficulty the Steenbeek and the swampy ground on each side of it, had a hand-to-hand fight with the enemy on the east bank, and then carried straight on under heavy machine-gun fire to Au Bon Gite. The mill at this place and several smaller dug-outs were taken, but the main work, a solid structure scarcely damaged by the bombardment of our heavy guns, held out. Men were all round it and even on top of it, but the Germans inside had closed a strong iron door and could not be captured. At this point a counter attack developed, and the company of the 11th R.B., now short of ammunition and without bombs, had to fall back to a position some 200 yards west of Au Bon Gite and partially surrounding it. The company commander, Capt. H. A. Slade, greatly distinguished himself and was awarded the D.S.O.

The right company gained its objective, but then became involved in the counter attack on Au Bon Gite and had to withdraw, forming a defensive flank with one post practically in the objective.

In the early morning of the 15th a party of the enemy tried to work round the flank of the left company of the 11th R.B., but under the steady fire of this company the attack melted away. The two remaining companies were then sent up to reinforce the front line. They suffered heavily on the way, but succeeded in reaching the forward troops.

The casualties, especially in officers, were very heavy. By 6 A.M. on the 14th the only two officers remaining in the 10th R.B. were Capt. S. J. Pegler and Lieut.

Bidwell; they were awarded the D.S.O. and the M.C. respectively for their gallant actions on this day. The battalion lost altogether 11 officers killed, 4 officers wounded, and over 200 men.

Preparations were made for a company of the 10th K.R.R.C. and a company of the 11th K.R.R.C. to capture Au Bon Gite at 2 A.M. on the 15th, with the assistance of trench mortars, machine-gun fire from the 217th Machine Gun Company, and six R.E. detachments from the 83rd Field Company to blow in the doors. The artillery put down a barrage according to orders, but owing to the darkness of the night, the difficulties of communication, and the continuous shell and machine-gun fire, the troops could not reach their jumping-off ground in time. The attack was therefore cancelled by the senior officer on the spot.

Although the strong point at Au Bon Gite had not been reduced, the Steenbeek had been crossed and sufficient ground gained to enable the assaulting waves for the main attack to be formed up on the far side.

The way was now clear for the larger operation, which included the capture of Langemarck. This was fixed for the 16th of August, and was part of an attack carried out by the Allied armies on the east and north of Ypres.

The attack on the 20th Division front was made by the 60th Brigade on the right and the 61st on the left. These two brigades on the night of the 14th/15th relieved the 59th, which went back into reserve on the canal bank, leaving, however, the 10th and the 11th R.B. as covering troops on the east side of the Steenbeek. After the losses incurred in the operations of the last week this brigade was very weak, and two battalions of the 38th Division were attached to the 20th as Divisional reserve.

The first objective followed the road bounding the

west edge of Langemarck ; the second was clear of
the village on the east side of it ; the third and final
objective ran east of Schreiboom, and was part of the
German Gheluvelt-Langemarck line.

The direction of the attack was north-east, with the
left resting on the Ypres-Staden railway. The extent
of the front increased from 1000 yards on the Steenbeek
to 1400 on the final objective. The boundary between
brigades as far as the first objective was the Langemarck
road ; it then skirted the south of Langemarck and of
Schreiboom. It will be seen that this gave a wider
front to the 61st Brigade than to the 60th until the
final objective was reached. The reasons for this
were as follows :

(1) The 61st Brigade was thus made responsible
for the whole village of Langemarck.

(2) The 60th Brigade on a narrower front would
be able to keep one battalion in reserve ;
this brigade was more liable to be attacked
from the direction of Poelcapelle, where the
enemy was known to keep his reserves.

(3) If the 61st Brigade were held up at Langemarck,
the 60th, by working round to the south-
east, could partially surround the village.

The 60th Brigade was to attack the first and second
objectives on a one battalion front with the 6th Oxford
and Bucks L.I. ; the 6th K.S.L.I. and the 12th K.R.R.C.
were then to advance to the final objective. If all
went well this would leave one battalion (the 12th R.B.)
still in reserve.

The 61st Brigade was to advance throughout on a
two battalion front, two half battalions of the 7th
K.O.Y.L.I. and the 7th Somerset L.I. being allotted
to each of the first and second objectives ; the 12th

King's and the 7th D.C.L.I. being detailed to attack the third.

Special arrangements were made to deal with Au Bon Gite. The company of the 11th R.B. which had made the original assault on the 14th, and a party of the 83rd Field Company R.E., were to advance with the first wave of the Oxfords and reduce this place while the main attack pressed forward on either side.

The 11th Division was on the right of the 20th and the 29th Division on the left, and at certain fixed points during the advance touch was to be gained with these divisions.

The Right Artillery of the XIVth Corps (the 20th and 38th Divisional Artilleries) covered the attack with standing and creeping barrages, pausing on the first objective for twenty minutes and on the second for an hour, so that under cover of smoke shells the infantry might have time to re-form or to come up to the objective should the attack have been delayed. The Corps heavy guns co-operated in the barrage on areas further behind the enemy's lines. A machine-gun barrage was provided by the four machine gun companies with the exception of half of the 60th and half of the 61st, which accompanied their brigades.

The attacking troops formed up during the night of the 15th/16th. It was, of course, of the utmost importance that they should take up their position east of the Steenbeek without the knowledge of the enemy. As the enemy's posts opposite the 60th Brigade were at an average distance of 150 yards from the stream and only 80 yards opposite Au Bon Gite on the front of the 61st Brigade, this was an extremely difficult manœuvre. During the night the 83rd and 84th Field Companies R.E. placed bridges, covered with canvas, across the Steenbeek, Lieut. E. C. Delamain

of the 84th Field Company being awarded the M.C.
for his work during the night. Further, Major P. G.
Norman, commanding 84th Field Company, carried
out the very hazardous task of laying tapes under
severe fire to mark the forming-up places on the east
bank of the stream. It reflects great credit on all who
directed the operation and on the troops who carried
it out that in spite of the enemy's shelling, which was
at times severe, and of machine-gun fire from Au Bon
Gite, the leading battalions formed up in their positions
apparently without the enemy being aware of their
presence.

The disposition of the troops, when the assembly
was completed, was as follows :

On the right was the 60th Infantry Brigade (Brig.-
General Butler), with headquarters at Stray Farm.
The 6th Oxford and Bucks L.I. were formed up with
the first wave east of the Steenbeek, and the second
wave west of it. The 6th K.S.L.I. on the right and
the 12th K.R.R.C. on the left were a short distance
in rear of the Oxfords. The 12th R.B. were 800 yards
south-east of Pilckem.

On the left was the 61st Infantry Brigade (Brig.-
General Banbury), with headquarters on the railway
north of Pilckem. The 7th Somerset L.I. on the right
and the 7th K.O.Y.L.I. on the left were east of the
Steenbeek ; behind these battalions the 12th King's
on the right had crossed the stream, and the 7th D.C.L.I.
were crossing it at the time when the attack began.

The 60th and 61st Trench Mortar Batteries and half
of the 60th and 61st Machine Gun Companies were
close to the infantry of their brigades.

The guns of the 91st Field Artillery Brigade were
in action on the west slope of Pilckem Ridge, those of
the 92nd Brigade on the canal bank.

AU BON GITE

[To face p. 158]

At 4.45 A.M. the artillery barrage, accurate and beautifully timed, fell like a curtain, and close behimd it the leading waves of the infantry moved forward to the attack. It was then just light enough to see the country for about 300 yards ahead. Bombers of the 11th R.B. had crawled up during the night to within a few yards of Au Bon Gite, where they lay concealed in shell-holes. At zero these men threw smoke bombs on to the enemy, making a screen under cover of which the rest of " B " Company attacked. After a short fight the position was captured with its garrison of an officer and 50 men.

The first wave of the Oxfords had meanwhile passed Au Bon Gite, and the second wave had crossed the Steenbeek. This battalion met a certain amount of opposition from parties of the enemy in blockhouses, but by 5.20 A.M. had reached the first objective with trifling loss.

All movement, however, was very difficult. On the whole Divisional front the ground was nothing but a swampy crater field as far as the final objective. Up to the first objective it was particularly bad, and in many places the only possible formation for the troops was a series of small columns which wound their way in single file between the pools of mud and water.

The 61st Brigade came under enfilade fire from Au Bon Gite until that place was taken, but otherwise, although under fairly heavy rifle and machine-gun fire, met no serious opposition until the K.O.Y.L.I. on the left were held up by concrete blockhouses west of Langemarck and later at Langemarck station. At these two places great dash and initiative were shown by individual men, who, when practically all their officers had been lost, carried on, and with Lewis guns and bombs fought splendidly together. Here Pte. W.

Edwards of the 7th K.O.Y.L.I. won the Victoria Cross. The following is the official account of his valiant action :

" For most conspicuous bravery when under heavy machine-gun and rifle fire from a strong concrete fort. Having lost all his company officers, without hesitation he dashed forward at great personal risk, bombed through the loopholes, surmounted the fort, and waved to his company to advance. By his splendid example he saved a most critical situation at a time when the whole battalion was held up and a leader urgently needed. Three officers and thirty other ranks were taken prisoner by him in the fort. Later Pte. Edwards did most valuable work as a runner, and he eventually guided most of the battalion out through very difficult ground. Throughout he set a splendid personal example to all, and was utterly regardless of danger."

Lance-Cpl. Powel fired a Lewis gun through the enemy's loophole and so cleared a point which had held up the line. Altogether at this stage the battalion captured 5 officers, 70 other ranks and 12 machine guns, in addition to 3 guns, with a quantity of ammunition.

By 5.40 A.M. the whole of the first objective was in our hands.

At 5.45 A.M. the advance was continued. The original second wave of the Oxfords attacked and reached the second objective with little loss. In the meantime the 6th K.S.L.I. and 12th K.R.R.C. had crossed the Steenbeek. The former reached the line of the first objective without incident, but the latter came under machine-gun fire from a blockhouse near Langemarck and lost a good many men, including the commanding officer, Lieut.-Colonel Prioleau, who was wounded.

The situation was retrieved by Sgt. E. Cooper of the

12th K.R.R.C. The gallant action, for which he was awarded the Victoria Cross, is given as follows in the *London Gazette* :

" For most conspicuous bravery and initiative in attack. Enemy machine guns from a concrete blockhouse, 250 yards away, were holding up the advance of the battalion on his left, and were also causing heavy casualties to his own battalion. Sgt. Cooper, with four men, immediately rushed towards the blockhouse although heavily fired on. About a hundred yards distant he ordered his ' men to lie down and fire at the blockhouse. Finding this did not silence the machine guns, he immediately rushed forward straight at them and fired his revolver into an opening in the blockhouse. The machine guns ceased firing and the garrison surrendered. Seven machine guns and forty-six prisoners were captured in the blockhouse. By this magnificent act of courage he undoubtedly saved what might have been a serious check to the whole advance, at the same time saving a great number of lives."

After this the 6th K.S.L.I. and the 12th K.R.R.C. continued to advance ; they mopped up all shelters and dug-outs which they passed, and in this way killed many of the enemy and took a further 46 prisoners. They then formed up east of the second objective, ready to move forward to the attack.

On the left, once the station and the railway trucks had been cleared, comparatively little opposition was met. The losses, however, in the first stages of the battle had been heavy. Second-Lieut. Robinson was the only company officer of the K.O.Y.L.I. left after reaching the first objective ; he had a very trying time and set a splendid example throughout. Sgt. S. Goodman and Sgt. G. H. Jackson deserve great credit for the

L

way in which they took their companies to the second objective when all their officers had been hit.

The right of the 61st Brigade had some trouble with machine guns and snipers in the outskirts of Langemarck, but the mopping-up parties did their work thoroughly and accounted for any of the enemy who were left behind the leading wave. On this front, too, there had been heavy losses. One company of the Somersets had no officers left and lost touch with the rest of the battalion. Second-Lieut. J. R. Hill, M.C., of " D " Company, got these men together and then took his own company on to the objective. Although wounded in the face and leg, he remained in command until he was satisfied that the position was assured. He was awarded a bar to his M.C. The mopping-up parties for the village were twice the strength of the assaulting troops ; they worked from shell-hole to shell-hole under cover of Lewis gun fire and then bombed the enemy out of each concrete dug-out in turn. In one blockhouse the Somersets took 1 officer and 30 men ; in another 40 men and 4 machine guns.

The 12th King's and the 7th D.C.L.I., who had sustained a good many casualties in following close behind the leading battalions, formed up on the second objective.

Up to this time the enemy's barrage, which came down on the Steenbeek four minutes after zero, had been ineffective, and though he now began to shell the south-west of Langemarck, little damage was done.

At 7.20 A.M. the whole line advanced to the final objective, the 6th K.S.L.I. and 12th K.R.R.C. on the right, the 12th King's and the 7th D.C.L.I. on the left. The battalions of the 60th Brigade met with strong opposition from parties of the enemy concealed in hedges, ditches, concrete dug-outs and fortified houses, and came under intense machine-gun fire from the right flank. Many of the enemy were killed and 135 prisoners taken. By 7.45 A.M. the 60th Brigade held the final objective. The 61st Brigade had little difficulty except on the extreme left. Here it was possible to advance only in single file along the railway line. The left company of the D.C.L.I. had a certain number of casualties, chiefly from machine-gun fire from the left front, but cleared the line and took 60 prisoners. This brigade had gained the final objective by 8 A.M.

No sooner had this line been occupied than enemy aeroplanes appeared flying low, about 50 feet above the ground, firing machine guns on the infantry and apparently taking photographs.

The divisions on the flanks had meanwhile advanced. On the left the 61st Brigade was throughout in touch with the 29th Division. The co-operation of the 29th Division on the left of the 61st Brigade could not have been better. On the right of the 20th Division the situation was not so good. The divisions further south had not made much progress ; the 11th Division therefore had to form a defensive flank. Its left was in touch with the 60th Brigade on the third objective, but Rat House, south-east of Langemarck, remained in the possession of the enemy.

About 400 prisoners had been taken by the Division, including the officer commanding the battalion which had held Langemarck. A section of 4·2 howitzers, one 77 mm. field gun, and 20 or 30 machine guns had also fallen into our hands.

The artillery F.O.O.'s were excellent ; their reports were generally the first to be received and were accurate. The liaison, too, between the artillery and the infantry was all that could be desired. In this battle 2nd Lieut. Potter and Lieut. Green, of B/92 Battery, won the M.C.

The R.E. field companies did most valuable work, both in preparing for the crossing of the Steenbeek and in making strong points during the advance.

The bearers of the Division worked under the 61st Field Ambulance, commanded by Lieut.-Colonel W. J. S. Harvey, who also devised a most successful scheme for the organisation of the medical officers of battalions.

Walking wounded collecting posts had been established by the 60th Field Ambulance (Lieut.-Colonel A. C. Osburn) at Cheapside, and by the 62nd Field Ambulance (Lieut.-Colonel E. F. L'Estrange) at Mouton Farm near Elverdinghe.

Although the Decauville railway line was broken early in the day, the evacuation of wounded by hand, by wheeled stretcher, and by hand trolley went on smoothly and without congestion, but the long carry from the R.A.P.'s in the front line to the forward A.D.S. at Gallwitz Farm threw very heavy work on the bearers.

Gallwitz Farm was heavily shelled and had to be abandoned. Here Capt. G. Adam, 62nd Field Ambulance, won the M.C.—one of many honours awarded to the R.A.M.C. for this battle. Capt. Adam attended the wounded in the open under heavy shell fire until the dressing station was destroyed. He then got his cases safely away and went on with his work at another point until he was utterly exhausted.

Two hundred stretcher bearers, detailed by the Division for clearing the battlefield, were given a short training and organised as the Divisional Stretcher Company. They were an unqualified success and did valuable work on the afternoon of the 16th and that night.

After the capture of the second objective the rest of the morning was spent in consolidating the position, involving on the part of the 60th Brigade preparations to deal with a counter attack on the dangerous right flank. The line was held from right to left by the 6th K.S.L.I., the 12th K.R.R.C., the 12th King's, and the 7th D.C.L.I. The Oxfords were on the first and second objectives, and the 12th R.B., who had been employed during most of the fighting in carrying bombs and ammunition to the front line, occupied a position east of the Steenbeek. The Somersets and the K.O.Y.L.I. were on the second objective.

From mid-day onwards various reports were received stating that the enemy appeared to be crawling up along hedges in front of the position. At 4 p.m. he attacked the junction of the two brigades about Schreiboom and drove back the 12th K.R.R.C. and the 12th King's for a distance of 200 yards. The left company of the 12th K.R.R.C. was practically wiped out, and a company of the Oxfords was sent up as reinforcements. Nearly all the ammunition had been spent in fighting this attack, and a further supply was sent up by parties of the 12th R.B., two companies of which battalion moved forward to ensure the safety of the second objective.

At 7 p.m. the two battalions of the 38th Division were placed at the disposal of brigade commanders, the 10th Welch coming under the 60th Brigade and the 15th Welch under the 61st. They did invaluable work in bringing up water, rations, and ammunition, besides helping in the work of consolidation.

On the 17th an attempt was made to regain that part of the line which had been lost. In the 60th Brigade the attack was made by two and a half companies of the 12th R.B. ; in the 61st by the 12th King's, supported

by the remaining three companies of the Somersets
and one company of the D.C.I I. On the left the
objective was occupied without much trouble, but the
right of the 61st Brigade and the 12th R.B. were
enfiladed by heavy rifle and machine-gun fire from Rat
House, and suffered severely. It was therefore decided
to dig in on the original line.

That night, on relief by the 38th Division, infantry
units began to move back to Proven, where Divisional
Headquarters was opened on the morning of the 19th.
During the following three weeks the field companies
and some of the battalions were at intervals employed
in the forward area, but the time was devoted principally
to rest and training.

The headquarters of the Divisional Artillery went
back to rest, but the 91st and 92nd Field Artillery
Brigades remained in action under the C.R.A. of the
38th Division, the 92nd Brigade moving up on the
26th to the west slope of Pilckem Ridge.

During the following three weeks the general situation was little changed. The weather until the end of
August was wet and windy, and time was needed to
prepare for the next advance. Minor operations were
carried out against Eagle Trench, a part of the enemy's
line east of Schreiboom, but without much result. The
French had not lately been heavily engaged, and in
consequence the Germans turned most of their guns
in this area on to the British lines. The battery
positions of the 91st Brigade were heavily shelled on
the 2nd of September, and again on the 4th, when two
howitzers of D/91 were hit.

At this time the enemy, finding that his stronges
defences were unable to hold out against our attacks,
adopted a new system of defence by which he held his
front line only lightly, relying on large reserves kept

close at hand to regain any ground that might be lost.[1]
He devoted his time in this part of the battlefield
principally to organising shell-holes as posts and strong
points. In order that our guns might bring all these
posts under fire, the front was divided into a number of
areas, some of which were shelled each day ; barrages
were frequently carried out, not creeping regularly,
but lifting backwards and forwards at odd intervals,
so as to harass the enemy. These continual bombardments entailed very heavy work not only on the
batteries, but also on the Divisional Ammunition
Column. In September the weather improved, and,
except for occasional heavy bombardments, the
German artillery became less active ; aeroplanes, however, flew frequently over our lines, particularly
between the 11th and the 16th, when they bombed
the camps and wagon lines and killed a large number
of horses.

The 93rd (Army) Field Artillery Brigade pulled out
of action at this time and moved to another area.

On the 5th the headquarters of the Divisional Artillery
returned to the line, and on the 11th the 20th Division
again relieved the 38th, and prepared to launch an
attack on the 20th of the month, when the British
offensive was being resumed on a front of eight miles,
from the Ypres-Staden railway to the south. By the
day of the attack the front line, which ran from a point
on the road 1000 yards east of Langemarck in a north-
westerly direction to the railway, was held by the 60th
Brigade on the right and the 59th on the left ; the 61st
was in reserve. Divisional Headquarters was near
Elverdinghe. All units had been very weak since the
fighting at Langemarck, and even after they had had
three weeks out of the line to refit, the average fighting

[1] Sir Douglas Haig's Despatches, p. 120

strength of the battalions was only 350. The 51st Division of the XVIIIth Corps was on the right of the 20th, and the Guards on the left.

The signal communications taken over from the 38th Division included a new buried cable in the much-shelled area between Langemarck and Au Bon Gite, but there was no buried line back to Stray Farm. The task of completing this bury across a mile of sodden and difficult ground was at once undertaken by the Signal Company, and successfully accomplished in time. The value of this work was proved in the course of the day's fighting, when not only was signal communication maintained, but in addition to continual telephone calls, one thousand and ten telegrams were dealt with at the Divisional Signal Office.

The objective in the forthcoming attack included 't Goed ter Vesten Farm and the enemy trenches south-east of it ; from the farm it ran west to the railway, involving on this flank only a short advance. On the right the attack was to be made in two bounds, but on the left there was an intricate network of trenches, which it was considered better to capture without any pause.

The attack was preceded by a twenty-four hours' hurricane bombardment, which started about 4 A.M. on the 19th, and during the action the usual creeping, standing, and smoke barrages were carried out, covering altogether a depth of 2500 yards. Half of the machine gun companies of the 60th and 59th Brigades were under their brigade commanders, the remaining two half companies being kept back as a reserve until the objective had been taken. The 61st and 217th Machine Gun Companies worked under the orders of the Divisional Machine Gun Officer.

The night before the attack a direct hit on the headquarters of the 10th K.R.R.C. killed Lieut-Colonel Rixon, Capt. Wallington, and several others. Major Cockburn took over the command of the battalion.

The operations began at 5.40 a.m. on the 20th of September.

East of Schreiboom the enemy held a defensive position known as Eagle Trench. It was a curiously constructed work, in which the actual trench ran between two solid embankments about 8 feet high. These details were not known at the time of the attack, as owing to the formation of the ground it was an extremely difficult place to see. As, however, it was known to be strongly held, 290 oil drums were fired on to it at zero; they seem to have fallen beyond the trench, and to have done little more than light up the surroundings and show the enemy our advancing lines.

On the left flank all went well; the enemy's trench system was carried and the line pushed forward to 't Goed ter Vesten Farm, but in the centre the right of the 59th Brigade and the left of the 60th, owing to the enemy's excellent field of fire, could make no headway against Eagle Trench. The right gained some ground, but, coming under machine-gun fire from houses and strong points on its right, was unable to advance very far. This was the situation at 8 a.m. Owing to this delay the infantry ceased to gain any immediate advantage from the pre-arranged artillery barrage, which, after a short pause on the first objective, continued to sweep forward. During the next hour the left flank reached the objective and the right moved forward some distance, but the centre remained held up. The 51st Division on the right had advanced successfully, and was in touch with the 60th Brigade.

Orders were then issued for the attack to be continued at 6.30 p.m., when the situation had been cleared up. The artillery barrage, which was reported from all sides to be perfect, was in the main a repetition of that of the morning, but smoke shells were fired at Eagle Trench to mask the machine guns there while the infantry moved into position. This proved to be a wise precaution, in view of the high command which this trench was afterwards found to possess. On the front of the 11th R.B. the smoke screen was ineffective. The companies of this battalion, having been widely separated to support other battalions in the morning, had to form up in daylight in view of the enemy. This daylight assembly was the signal for a tremendous barrage on Langemarck, while machine guns in Eagle Trench simply raked the plain.

The 60th Brigade advanced on the right, and by 9.15 P.M. had taken between 60 and 70 prisoners, but the north part of Eagle Trench, immediately east of Schrei-boom, resisted all efforts to take it. The 59th Brigade, while holding the objective on the left, had its right thrown back to pass a little east of the Schreiboom cross-roads. The 11th R.B. in gaining a footing in Eagle Trench, just north of the cross-roads, had lost 66 per cent. casualties and 11 out of 16 officers. The result of the day's fighting left the enemy holding a salient in the centre of the Divisional line. On the general front the advance had been successful, and had gained ground to an average depth of 500 yards.

The remaining part of Eagle Trench had still to be captured. With this object an attack, in which two tanks were to precede a party of infantry, was ordered to be carried out on the 22nd. The tanks stuck in Langemarck, so the operation was postponed till the morning of the 23rd. At the same time an alternative plan was prepared to be carried out in the event of the tanks remaining derelict. As the tanks were unable to

move forward in time to take part in the attack at
5.30 A.M., the alternative plan was put into operation
at the last moment, and zero put forward to 7 A.M.
These orders provided for a three-minute bombardment
by Stokes guns and a smoke barrage, followed by a
bombing attack up the trenches from the south and
north covered by a barrage of rifle grenades, and an
assault above ground from the west. Detachments of
the 12th K.R.R.C. and the 10th R.B. were to carry out
this operation.

The Stokes bombardment was timed to begin at
7 A.M.   At 6.25 the enemy attacked the 60th Brigade,
but was driven off by rifle and machine-gun fire,
leaving 23 prisoners behind. This in no way disorganised the preparations for the attack, which started
punctually at 7 o'clock.   After a very effective bombardment by the Stokes mortars, the bombing parties
worked their way inwards from the flanks, the 12th
K.R.R.C. from the south, the 10th R.B. from the
north, covered by a rifle grenade barrage. While the
enemy was engaged with these parties, one company
of the 10th R.B. assaulted Eagle Trench from the west,
and after a short and sharp fight, carried it. The
attack took place practically in broad daylight, and
came as a complete surprise to the enemy, who had just
" stood down." The bombers did their work well, and
the frontal attack was splendidly carried out by Capt.
T. G. L. Ashwell, who won the M.C. Our casualties
were not heavy, but the enemy left 94 prisoners and
10 machine guns in our hands.

In the fighting for Eagle Trench 2nd Lieut. Allan,
A/91 Battery, gained a bar to his M.C., and 2nd
Lieut. Robinson, C/91, won the M.C. The latter was
very badly wounded, and completely lost his sight.

The stretcher bearers, working under the 60th Field

Ambulance, had more casualties in this action than in the battle of Langemarck. Again, their task was a severe one, as the Decauville line was broken too often to be of much use, but by their untiring efforts all the wounded were cleared without a hitch. As an example of what was done, 24 bearers at Gallwitz Farm carried back 142 stretcher cases in 24 hours.

Prisoners stated that a concerted attack against the Divisional front had been arranged, and it is evident that our success here completely upset the enemy's plans. By the evening the total number of prisoners had risen to 1 officer and 102 other ranks. The successful issue of this fighting is all the more creditable since between the 18th and the 23rd the troops had little or no cover and during the whole time were exposed to heavy shelling day and night. From prisoners' statements it appears that since the 11th of September the regiments opposed to the 20th Division had lost over 60 per cent. of their strength, largely from artillery fire, and that their morale had been much shaken.

By the evening of the 23rd the 60th and 59th Brigades were well established east of Eagle Trench. They were relieved that night by the 61st Brigade, which during the next few days straightened the line to give a good jumping-off place for the relieving division in the subsequent operations. The total number of prisoners was brought up to 2 officers and 156 other ranks.

So gallant had been the fighting and so important had been the result of the capture of Eagle Trench that the following message was sent by the Army Commander, General Sir Hubert Gough :

" The tenacity, gallantry and skill which your Division showed over the operations round Eagle

Trench are very fine. Please accept my congratulations and expressions of admiration to you and all
ranks of your gallant Division."

Throughout the period spent in this sector the
11th D.L.I. (Major G. Hayes) were constantly at
work; they carried up material, dug and wired new
lines of trenches, repaired tramways and constructed
a duckboard track from Langemarck to the front
line. On the 20th of September the Lewis gunners
of the battalion were employed on anti-aircraft work
and assisted the attack on Eagle Trench. That night
two companies working with the R.E. constructed
strong points in the captured area. For his work at
this time Capt. W. G. L. Sear was awarded the M.C.
The continual shelling, particularly on the line of
the Steenbeek, made the journey to and from work
always difficult.

In the last days of September the 20th Division
was relieved by the 14th, and on the 1st of October
entrained for Bapaume.

Before leaving, another congratulatory message was
received from General Sir Hubert Gough :

" The Army Commander wishes to thank all ranks
20th Division for the part they have played in the
third battle of Ypres. The Division may well be
proud of the capture of Langemarck on August 16th
and the taking of Eagle Trench on September the 23rd.
While holding the line of the Steenbeek during a prolonged spell of bad weather the Division showed a
good soldierly spirit under difficult conditions. The
Army Commander is sorry to lose such a good fighting
Division."

Once more the Divisional Artillery was left in action,
although all ranks were well-nigh exhausted after two
and a half months' continuous fighting in the battle.

The C.R.A. and headquarters moved out of the line on the 28th, when the artillery brigades came under the 4th Division, commanded by Major-General T. G. Matheson. The gunners of both brigades were immediately employed in preparing gun positions on the Steenbeek. The line of the Steenbeek was continually being shelled, especially at night, when all ammunition had to be carried down to the positions; and as the usual artillery programme had to be carried out in addition to this work, the strain was very great.

Since the capture of Langemarck the German possession of Poelcapelle had prevented the advance on this part of the battle front from being pushed to any great depth. A successful advance further to the south gained Polygon Wood and Zonnebeke on the 26th of September, thus establishing a footing on the main ridge at these places, and the line was advanced to within striking distance of the high ground as far north as a point east of St Julien.[1] In the XIVth Corps area there was no infantry action, though both the 91st and 92nd Field Artillery Brigades took part in an artillery bombardment. On the 4th of October an attack between the Menin road and the Ypres-Staden railway included Poelcapelle as an objective of the 11th Division, which was at this time on the right of the 4th. The 4th Division advanced at 6 A.M. parallel to the railway, with its left flank some 600 yards south-east of it, and by 10 o'clock, when the protective barrage was reported to be most effective, had gained the final objective, the right of which touched the northern outskirts of Poelcapelle. The town itself was entered by the 11th Division.

The fighting on the general battle front since the 20th of September had been remarkable for the many

[1] Sir Douglas Haig's Despatches, p. 123.

heavy counter attacks launched against our troops
when the objectives had been taken. These attacks
were repulsed with great loss to the enemy, and Sir
Douglas Haig states in his despatch [1] that documents
captured on the 4th of October showed that the
Germans, recognising the failure of these methods,
were endeavouring to return to their old practice of
holding their forward position in strength.

After this attack the 92nd Field Artillery Brigade
moved to positions on the eastern slope of Pilckem
Ridge completely open to the enemy's view. The 91st
Brigade was transferred to the sector north of the
railway, to cover the Guards Division, and was ordered
to take up a position on the Steenbeek (Hannebeek)
during the night of the 6/7th. Batteries worked
all through the 6th, trying to make a track round the
shell-holes towards the positions, which were in a
swamp on both banks of the stream. They began to
move forward at 7 P.M. along the road which follows
the crest of the ridge as far as the cross-roads at
Pilckem, then down the Langemarck road for a mile,
after which they branched off to the north.

This was the only available road in the neighbourhood for all traffic. It was constantly shelled, and
on the evening of the 6th it was crowded with infantry
units, ration parties and troops of all kinds when
the German guns opened fire. In the confusion that
ensued the batteries were a good deal delayed, but
in spite of the awful state of the ground they reached
a road close to the position during the night and
actually got four guns and two howitzers into action.
All the next day they struggled to get ammunition
down to the position by pack, skirting the northern
edge of the Pilckem Ridge. It rained heavily, and

[1] Sir Douglas Haig's Despatches, p. 127.

the mud was so deep that it was found to be impossible to get the remaining guns into action that night.

On the 8th, at dawn, Lieut.-Colonel Erskine, commanding the brigade, borrowed a hundred men under Lieut. Hoare from the 4th Battalion of the Grenadier Guards to assist in moving the remaining guns. This battalion was at the time in reserve, and the men showed extraordinary goodwill and keenness to do all they could, and worked with the greatest determination. Each man carried down with him two rounds of ammunition besides his own rifle and equipment. Then, with fifty men on each gun besides the men of the batteries and one team of horses, the whole brigade was got into action by mid-day, with the exception of one gun which was badly stuck upside down in a shell-hole. It was a fine piece of work, which earned the congratulations of the XIVth Corps and of Brig.-General F. A. Wilson, the C.R.A., Guards Division. Major Balfour, commanding C/91, a first-rate battery commander, was killed while actually man-handling one of the guns.

The last two actions in this battle in which the Divisional Artillery took part were fought on the 9th and 12th October, when attacks were launched on the British front from Zonnebeke to the left flank, and on part of the French front further north. The Guards on the extreme left of the British line attacked at 5.20 A.M. on the 9th. They made a brilliant advance in cold, wet weather and over sodden ground to a line close to the south-east end of Houthulst Forest. Further south the eastern outskirts of Poelcapelle were cleared and progress was made up the main ridge towards Passchendaele.[1] On the 12th, attack-

---

[1] Sir Douglas Haig's Despatches. p. 129.

ing again in rain and a high wind, the Guards reached the edge of the forest.

Forward positions for one brigade of the 20th Divisional Artillery were reconnoitered on the 14th, but the continued bad weather made the movement of guns impossible. Four days later the batteries were at last relieved.

For three whole months the 20th Divisional Artillery had been in the battle without any relief. Throughout this time, over ground sodden with rain, the men had fought continuously, practically without protection of any sort and under a continuous bombardment of gas and high-explosive shell. Casualties had been exceptionally heavy and the strain abnormal. It was the hardest time in the line that the Divisional Artillery ever spent, and the men were absolutely played out when on the 18th of October they moved out of action to entrain two days later for Peronne.

M

CHAPTER IX

THE BATTLE OF CAMBRAI

1st October to 16th December 1917

The Battle of Cambrai and the German counter attack.
(*Vide* Map III.)

AFTER three days in the Bapaume area the Division moved east to face the Hindenburg Line south-west of Cambrai. By the 10th of October, when this sector had been taken over from the 40th Division, headquarters was at Sorel, about 1000 yards south of Fins. All three brigades were in the line, the 61st on the right, east of Villers Guislains and Gonnelieu, the 59th in the centre from the outskirts of Gonnelieu to a line passing through Villers Plouich, and the 60th on the left, with its left flank between Beaucamp and Bilhem. Except for ten days towards the end of the month the Division was in the IIIrd Corps of the Third Army.

October passed quietly. By the 25th the Divisional Artillery had returned from the Ypres Salient and was in action, covering the Divisional front; the battery positions of the 91st Field Artillery Brigade lay in the area Villers Guislain - Gonnelieu - Gouzeaucourt, those of the 92nd Brigade about Gouzeaucourt and in the country to the north.

On the 27th Brig.-General Butler left to command an infantry brigade in the Guards Division and handed over command of the 60th Brigade to Brig.-General F. J. Duncan, C.M.G., D.S.O.

178

On the 29th the 55th Division took over from the
61st Brigade the ground up to Villers Guislains
inclusive. The front occupied by the 20th Division
was even then a long one, but the formation of
the ground made it po;sible to defend it without
holding a continuous system of trenches. It will be
seen from Map III that the line crossed several spurs
and valleys. The spurs were held as defended
localities, fortified for all-round defence and each
occupied by one battalion; places of tactical importance in the position were held by a number of
small strong points. At the heads of the valleys
machine guns were so placed as to cover both the low
ground and the slopes of the spurs on each side.

Preparations for an attack to be launched on the
20th of November were then begun, but with the
greatest secrecy, as the success of the operation
depended on the Germans being surprised. The
scheme was revealed to brigade commanders and
their staffs early in the month, but no other officers
in the brigades were told until a week before the
battle, and then only under a strict pledge of silence,
which was faithfully kept. Not until the day before
the attack were the details generally disclosed. It
was, of course, impossible in the later stages to conceal
these preparations from the troops. When battalions
were withdrawn to the rear to train with tanks, gun
positions reconnoitered close to the German line,
new ammunition dumps formed in forward positions
and all the familiar measures carried out, it became
clear that an operation of some magnitude was at
hand. Among the many arrangements made to
facilitate the advance of the artillery, bridges were
constructed and carried forward to enable the guns
to cross the trenches. During the four nights before

the attack the guns were moved up to positions in the open close behind the front line, camouflaged and left there. By the night of the 19th/20th only two guns remained in the original line to cover the front of the Division.

The task of providing signal communication for the three attacking divisions on the Divisional front fell almost entirely on the 20th Divisional Signal Company. 137 miles of armoured cable were laid out to the front line and to the various battle headquarters of all arms. As the day of attack drew nearer the normal five to seven hundred messages per day received at the Divisional Headquarter office at Sorel grew to two thousand a day, which severely taxed the powers of the Signal Company.

A thick mist which hung over the position for several days before the attack assisted the preparations incalculably, as it prevented the enemy's aeroplanes from obtaining any information. On the 17th and 18th of November the 61st and 60th Brigades, which were to deliver the assault on the Divisional front, were relieved by troops of the 12th and 6th Divisions; outposts belonging to the 20th Division were left, however, covering the original front. On the 19th the 61st on the right and the 60th on the left took over the new Divisional line, which then extended only from a thousand yards north-west of Gonnelieu to the north-east of Villers Plouich. At the same time the 59th Brigade, to which a special rôle had been assigned, moved back to Gouzeaucourt in reserve. The concentration was a very complicated and difficult one, especially for the 20th Division, which was manning the trenches up to the last moment. Concentration camps for the 20th and for three other divisions had been made and completely camouflaged by the 83rd, 84th and 96th

Field Companies R.E. and the 11th D.L.I. under
the orders of Lieut.-Colonel Newell, the C.R.E.

The essence of the plan was to surprise the enemy,
overwhelm him with a sudden rush of tanks followed
by infantry, and break his line before he had time to
realise the nature or the locality of the attack. There
was therefore no preliminary bombardment, nor even
was any registration of the guns allowed. The infantry
lines were to be preceded by waves of tanks and the
attack covered by standing barrages, which were to
lift from objective to objective as the assaulting troops
advanced. Of the 60 tanks at the disposal of the
Division 36 were allotted to the 61st Brigade and 24 to
the 60th.

The general direction of the attack was north-east,
across the Hindenburg and Hindenburg Support
Lines on the front of La Vacquerie and Welsh Ridge.
The left boundary was the Villers Plouich—Marcoing
railway ; the right boundary an approximately parallel
line about 2500 yards to the south-east. The first
objective followed the general line of a track from
Banteux to Ribécourt, between the road from La
Vacquerie to Bonavis and the railway. La Vacquerie,
a particularly strong point, was the key position of the
enemy's first line of defence on the right. This village
and the trenches north-west of it formed an initial
objective in the area of the 61st Brigade. The second
and final objective included the whole of Welsh Ridge,
from a point in the sunken road nearly 3000 yards
north-east of La Vacquerie to the railway 1200 yards
south-west of the railway junction at Marcoing.

The 12th Division on the right and the 6th Division
on the left were to attack objectives prolonging those
of the 61st and 60th Brigades.

After this line had been taken the 29th Division

was to pass through the 20th to a line north of Masnières and Marcoing. To prepare the way for this advance and to secure the right flank of the 29th Division the 59th Brigade was to move forward as soon as the second objective had been occupied in order both to seize the crossings of the canal between Masnières and Marcoing and to form a defensive flank by holding a line from Les Rues Vertes to the south for a distance of 2000 yards. For this purpose sixteen tanks from those allotted to the 61st Brigade were to be placed at the disposal of the 59th. Defensive flanks were to be formed by the 12th Division from the right of the 59th Brigade as far as Lateau Wood (inclusive) and by the 6th Division from the left flank of the 29th towards the south-west. During the night of the 19th/20th the infantry and tanks formed up about 1000 yards from the enemy's wire. To help to drown the noise of the advancing tanks intermittent bursts of machine-gun fire were kept up throughout the night.

By zero, 6.20 A.M. on the 20th, the dispositions were as follows :

The 61st Brigade, under Brig.-General Banbury, held the right of the line, with the 7th Somerset L.I. (Lieut.-Colonel Troyte-Bullock) on the right and the 7th D.C.L.I. (Lieut.-Colonel Burges Short) on the left. The 12th King's (Lieut.-Colonel Vince) on the right and the 7th K.O.Y.L.I. (Major Storr) on the left were in support.

The 60th Brigade, under Brig.-General Duncan, held the left of the line with the 6th Oxford and Bucks L.I. (Lieut.-Colonel Boyle), in touch with the D.C.L.I. and the 12th K.R.R.C. (Lieut.-Colonel Moore), with their left on the railway just north-east of Villers Plouich. In support were the 6th K.S.L.I. (Lieut.-Colonel Welch) and the 12th R.B. (Lieut.-Colonel Riley).

The 59th Brigade, under Brig.-General Hyslop, was concentrated in and about Gouzeaucourt.

The Division was covered by two artillery groups. The Right Group, under Lieut.-Colonel Ricardo, consisted of the 92nd Brigade, the 232nd Brigade, and the 3rd Brigade R.H.A. The Left Group, under Lieut.-Colonel Erskine, consisted of the 91st Brigade, the 178th Brigade, and the 15th Brigade R.H.A.

The first wave of tanks moved forward at 6.10 A.M., and at 6.20 the barrage opened along the whole front. The attack went exactly as planned from beginning to end. The Somersets and two companies of the D.C.L.I. advanced on La Vacquerie and the trenches north-west of it. The garrison at these places offered little opposition and, apparently demoralised by the tanks, ran towards the Hindenburg Line. La Vacquerie was taken by the Somersets about 7.30 A.M., and had been mopped up by 9 o'clock, when 80 prisoners, 6 machine guns and 2 trench mortars had been taken. Two companies of the King's, with the two remaining companies of the D.C.L.I., carried on the advance to the first objective. The enemy offered a certain amount of opposition in the Hindenburg Line and the King's on the right suffered rather heavily, but before 10 A.M. this line was taken, with 200 prisoners and many machine guns.

On the front of the 60th Brigade the 6th Oxford and Bucks L.I. and the 12th K.R.R.C. carried the defences of Welsh Ridge. The reserve company of the 12th K.R.R.C. —" B " Company, under Captain Hoare—lost heavily in attacking a strong point which held up the advance, for when this point had been taken, out of 3 officers and 96 men in the company only 34 men remained. ˙That this company reached its objective was largely due to Rfm. A. E. Shepherd, K.R.R.C., whose gallantry was

rewarded with the Victoria Cross. The following is
the official account of his action : " For most conspicuous bravery as a company runner. When his
company was held up by a machine gun at point blank
range he volunteered to rush the gun, and, though ordered
not to, rushed forward and threw a Mills bomb, killing
two gunners and capturing the gun. The company,
on continuing its advance, came under heavy enfilade
machine-gun fire. When the last officer and the last
N.C.O. had become casualties he took command of
the company, ordered the men to lie down, and himself
went back some seventy yards under severe fire to
obtain the help of a tank. He then returned to his
company and finally led them to their last objective.
He showed throughout conspicuous determination and
resource."

On the whole, however, the casualties of the 60th
Brigade were few. and the first objective was occupied
at 9.25 A.M.

The advance to the final objective was more
vigorously opposed. The remaining two companies
of the King's and the K.O.Y.L.I., attacking on the
61st Brigade front, encountered a good deal of resistance in the Hindenburg Support Line, a good natural
position, well fortified and strongly held. Behind the
line there were many gun-pits, some of which the enemy
defended to the last. The K.O.Y.L.I. on the left
fought with great dash, and in spite of severe losses
carried all before them. Second-Lieut. Joffe, Sgt. Roberts
and about a dozen men of this battalion distinguished
themselves by rushing a 77 mm. gun which continued
to fire point-blank till they were within fifty yards of
it. The King's also forced their way forward by hard
fighting and took a number of prisoners.

The 60th Brigade attacked the second objective

with the 6th K.S.L.I. and the 12th R.B.   The enemy
gave little trouble except on the right of the R.B.,
where " A " Company found him defending his positions throughout with determination.   A particularly
difficult point to carry was a nest of five machine guns
and a trench mortar in the Hindenburg Support Line.
Capt. Fraser, commanding " A " Company, obtained
the assistance of a tank, which advanced straight on
the post while a party of the R.B. worked round it.
When the tank came within fifty yards of the enemy
a direct hit from the trench mortar killed two of the
crew and severely wounded the rest.   The tank section
commander, Capt. R. W. L. Wain, got out and rushed
at the enemy with a Lewis gun, while " B " Company
on the left turned the flank.   In the fighting that
ensued Capt. Wain was killed, but the post was taken,
and the only gun of the five which could be used
was turned on to those of the enemy who were able to
get away.   " A " Company took over 130 prisoners, a
trench mortar, and 6 machine guns during the day.

About eleven o'clock the final objective was taken,
and the 59th Brigade and the 29th Division were
passing through the lines.

Arrangements had been carefully made by the
Divisional Signal Company to establish signal communication as the attack progressed.   The tanks,
however, made small work of the ground lines as
they were laid, and recourse had to be made to a poled
cable route on each brigade front, which was successfully established in due course.

Meanwhile at 10.30 A.M. the 91st Field Artillery
Brigade was ordered forward to the north-east of
La Vacquerie.   Good positions were found along the
track from Banteux to Ribécourt between the roads
leading from La Vacquerie to Bonavis and Masnières.

Batteries were held up by tanks which had stuck in the sunken road, but managed to come into action during the afternoon.

Starting from Gouzeaucourt at zero the 59th Brigade moved forward, and led by the 10th and 11th R.B., with a troop of the 1/1st Northumberland Yeomanry under Captain the Hon. C. F. M. Ramsay, left the old front line at 9.10 A.M. to follow the assaulting battalions.

By 11 A.M. this advanced guard was passing through the second objective. The 11th R.B. (Lieut.-Colonel Cotton) advanced in open order along the north-west slope of the La Vacquerie valley to seize the crossings over the canal; the 10th R.B. (Lieut.-Colonel Troughton), to whom the two troops of yeomanry were attached, deployed on the south-east slope before moving on to form the defensive flank. In rear of these two battalions the 10th K.R.R.C. (Lieut.-Colonel Sheepshanks) formed up in the valley on either side of the sunken road and the 11th K.R.R.C. (Lieut.-Colonel Priaulx) took up a position about the crossing of the sunken road and the track from Banteux to Ribécourt.

The 11th R.B. advanced on a two company front. They came under a certain amount of shelling, but parties of the enemy who tried to hold them back by long-range fire, seeing the tanks and infantry coming on, either withdrew or gave themselves up. " B " Company on the left, moving towards a bridge east of Marcoing, encountered an enemy strong point about 800 yards south of the canal, but an outflanking movement by Lewis guns and bombers soon brought about the surrender of the garrison, which was estimated at 150 men. The bridge-head was then occupied and troops of the 29th Division crossed

THE BROKEN BRIDGE, MASNIÈRES

[To face p. 186.

unopposed. " C " Company on the right had little difficulty, except from a machine gun which for a time delayed its progress ; the gun was silenced by a tank, and the company then entered Les Rues Vertes. Here between 12 and 1 o'clock a certain amount of street fighting took place, but the village was cleared as far as the canal.

About 12.40 P.M., when the 11th R.B. were held up at the main bridge in Masnières, a tank arrived on the scene and prepared to move across, carrying a small party of the 11th R.B. to bomb the houses on the opposite side. Owing to a mechanical break-down the tank was unable to move for an hour, by which time two more tanks had arrived and began to fire their 6-prs. into the houses across the canal. It is probable that the bridge, though apparently intact, had been partially destroyed, for when the tank eventually moved across, the centre of the bridge collapsed and the tank became wedged between the two ends, effectually blocking the crossing at this point. The Canadian Cavalry Brigade arrived in Les Rues Vertes about 2 P.M., but finding the bridge broken retired, although Lieut.-Colonel Cotton pointed out several other bridges close by, one of which was not marked on the map. Lieut.-Colonel Troughton, 10th R.B., who was holding two bridges intact to the south of Masnières, gave the same information. Only one squadron passed over, and in a brilliant engagement captured a battery of the enemy's guns.

The town of Masnières, where the arrival of British troops was naturally most unexpected, was full of civilians, mostly women and children. It was an amazing and a most pathetic sight to see women with babies in perambulators in the streets under the fire of the enemy. Many of them were evacuated at once, and good work was done by Lieut. Duval, the interpreter of the brigade. The civilians showed great courage under shell-fire.

By 4.30 the 11th R.B. had handed over the canal crossings to the 29th Division and were established in the northern part of the defensive flank.

Meanwhile the 10th R.B. on the right had deployed on the line south of Les Rues Vertes ; their right flank was exposed, as the 12th Division was still behind the Bonavis-Masnières road and the two troops of the Northumberland Yeomanry filled up this gap. Later, touch was gained with the 12th Division.

The 10th K.R.R.C. moved forward along the La Vacquerie valley, with two companies on each side of the road. All went well on the right, but the left companies were troubled by machine-gun fire from the north. A patrol sent out in this direction discovered the enemy holding a strong point, which was vigorously attacked and captured with some 200 prisoners. The battalion then took up a position in a sunken road 1500 yards south-west of Les Rues Vertes, sending one company in the afternoon to relieve the yeomanry on the right of the 10th R.B.

The 11th K.R.R.C. in reserve moved forward to a position close in rear of the 10th K.R.R.C.

The 61st and 60th Brigades were consolidating their objective across the north-eastern end of Welsh Ridge, and the 59th Brigade occupied the line running south from Les Rues Vertes. The 12th Division held the second objective from the right of the 61st Brigade to Lateau Wood inclusive, with a line running forward from there to the right of the 59th Brigade. The 6th Division, on the left of the 60th Brigade, had pushed through Ribécourt and thrown out a defensive flank

along the high ground north and north-west of
Marcoing, where it was in touch with the left of the
29th Division. The right flank of the 29th was then
working through Masnières. The 51st Division was
on the outskirts of Flesquières and the 62nd and 36th
Divisions were advancing further to the north and
north-west. Divisional Headquarters moved forward
at this time to Villers Plouich.

By 9 P.M. the 10th R.B. on the right and the 11th
R.B. on the left had pushed forward along the spur
and were established between Les Rues des Vignes
and the canal south of Mon Plaisir Farm. One company, under Capt. Ashwell, occupied part of the village
of Les Rues des Vignes after severe opposition.

During the afternoon considerable advance was
made on the left, where the 52nd Division penetrated
as far as Anneux, over two miles north of Flesquières,
although the latter still remained in the hands of the
enemy. The British line, therefore, formed a salient
between Lateau Wood and Marcoing, divided from
the very sharp salient at Anneux by the re-entrant
at Flesquières. It had been impossible to get the
guns forward along the sunken roads quickly enough
to support the infantry fighting at Masnières and
Marcoing, but the two factors which most limited
the results of the battle as a whole on this day were
the check at Flesquières and the absence of a large
force of cavalry on the far side of the canal. These
factors, and the consequent inability of the 29th
Division to push forward north and east of Masnières,
allowed the Germans to occupy the Beaurevoir-
Masnières line which ran in front of Rumilly and
Crèvecœur. From this position the Germans were
able to command the line of the 59th Brigade. On
the 21st Flesquières was captured and the line

straightened, and further advance was made towards the north.

On the night of the 20th/21st the 11th R.B. were ordered to seize the crossings at Crèvecœur to allow French cavalry to pass through at dawn. The night was pitch dark, the men were exhausted, and Crèvecœur was found by then to have been occupied by the enemy. The battalion captured an enemy machine gun complete with team, but was unable to take the bridges. That night IIIrd Corps issued orders that every effort must be made to gain possession of the Beaurevoir-Masnières line and to capture Crèvecœur. The rôle of the Division was to push on to Crèvecœur in conjunction with the 29th Division on the left. The 59th Brigade was detailed to carry out this operation, with the assistance of twelve tanks, and zero was fixed at 11 A.M. on the 21st. Later, the attack of the 29th Division was cancelled. The tanks ran out of petrol, and eventually at 2 P.M. the 11th K.R.R.C., the assaulting battalion of the 59th Brigade, had to attack alone. The battalion came under enfilade fire from Rumilly and the high ground north of the canal, so that in spite of several efforts to force a passage during the day, little progress was made. That night the 11th K.R.R.C. consolidated a position on the spur north-west of Les Rues Vignes, while a company of the 11th R.B. held the bridgehead below the village. This company, owing to heavy casualties and to the impossibility of obtaining reinforcements, was ordered to withdraw during the night. Before doing so, the remains of the company, assisted by the R.E., made four gallant but unsuccessful attempts to destroy the bridge.

The 11th R.B. formed a defensive left flank, covering the crossings south and south-east of Mon Plaisir Farm.

Two batteries of the 92nd Field Artillery Brigade moved forward at daybreak to positions north-west of Lateau Wood and supported this attack under considerable shell-fire. In the evening they withdrew to a small re-entrant between Lateau Wood and the La Vacquerie—Masnières road, where they were joined by the rest of the brigade.

The medical arrangements for the battle included an A.D.S. and a walking wounded collecting post at Gouzeaucourt, and advanced posts near Villers Plouich and on the Gouzeaucourt—Bonavis road just behind the front line. After the attack other posts were pushed forward to the La Vacquerie valley, towards Marcoing and later to Les Rues Vertes. Wounded from many different divisions passed through the A.D.S. at Gouzeaucourt. Excellent work was done by the bearers of the Division under Lieut.-Colonel A. C. Osburn, commanding the 60th Field Ambulance.

During the following days, while fierce fighting continued for the possession of an important ridge at Bourlon Wood, three miles north of Flesquières, the 20th Division was occupied in consolidating the position it had won. The main line ran from the left flank of the 12th Division, which was holding Lateau Wood, along the top of the spur and then north to the canal. In front of this an outpost line was held joining the main line on the right flank, passing forward on the spur about 500 yards north-west of Les Rues des Vignes, and turning back to the left flank south-east of Mon Plaisir Farm.

The position held by the Division at this time was most important. The line formed a deep salient, overlooked by the high ground which the enemy occupied. Not only did the enemy hold the bridges across the canal, but on the south-east face of this

salient the steep convex slope of the ridge left a strip
of dead ground along the front, so that even from the
outpost line the bottom of the valley and the village
of Les Rues des Vignes were out of sight. The
two artillery brigades west and north-west of Lateau
Wood covered an extent of front out of all proportion
to the number of guns, and while they fired at ranges
between 3000 and 6000 yards, the enemy had to
advance only a few hundred yards into Lateau Wood
to look straight down on their positions. A successful
attack by the enemy on Bonavis Ridge would then
completely cut off the whole of the infantry holding
the Les Rues des Vignes salient and take the artillery
positions in flank.

Between the 21st and the 24th the 7th Somerset L.I.
moved to Masnières in support of the 88th Brigade
of the 29th Division. The following is an extract
from a letter sent by the Brigade Commander of
the 88th Brigade to Brig.-General Banbury : " I wish
to tell you how much I appreciate the excellent
work done by the 7th Somerset L.I. in Masnières, in
clearing the houses of snipers and exploring the
many underground passages. The place is quite quiet
now, with a Somerset on guard at each hole."

By the morning of the 30th the Divisional front was
held by two brigades, the 59th, which after seven
days in reserve had just relieved the 60th, on the
right, and the 61st on the left. None of the battalions
had a fighting strength of over 400, and some of them
well under 300. The front line from right to left
was held by the 10th K.R.R.C., the 11th K.R.R.C.,
the 12th King's and the 7th Somerset L.I. In support
were the 10th R.B. in a ravine about 1500 yards south
of Les Rues Vertes and the 7th D.C.L.I. at the
northern end of the La Vacquerie valley, 1500 yards

south of the canal. The 11th R.B., 800 yards north-east of La Vacquerie, and the 7th K.O.Y.L.I., were in reserve. The commanding officers of some battalions were sent back for a rest, as it was considered a good opportunity for their seconds in command to get some useful experience. On the 29th the 61st Brigade was ordered to take over next day another 1000 yards of front on the right. This all points to the fact that no counter attack was expected at this time.

The relief of the 60th by the 59th Brigade Head-quarters was not complete when the Germans launched their great counter attack. Brig.-General Duncan therefore commanded the 59th Brigade throughout the operation, and the 60th Brigade fought under the orders of Lieut.-Colonel Troyte Bullock (7th Somerset L.I.), who was temporarily filling the place of Brig.-General Hyslop. The latter brigade was in reserve at Villers Plouich.

At 7 A.M. on the 30th the enemy opened a bombardment on the front of the 55th and 12th Divisions on the right. This spread to the 20th Division about 7.30, when three barrages, which included smoke and mustard-gas shells, fell simultaneously between the outpost line and the sunken road from La Vacquerie to Masnières. The infantry attack in the same manner developed from the south, the 55th and the 12th Divisions having been heavily engaged for some time, when at 8 A.M. the Germans advanced on the whole of the 20th Divisional front.

Covered by a thick mist the enemy moved forward with extraordinary rapidity. Although they put up an extremely good fight the outpost companies were soon overwhelmed; the majority were entirely cut off and were never heard of again. The right flank, which owing to the convex slope of the ground and the con-

N

sequent difficulty of observation was the most vulnerable
point, had already been turned by the successful attack
on the 55th and 12th Divisions. The companies in
the main line, therefore, at the moment when they had
to face an attack in great strength on their front,
found that the enemy had broken through to their
right rear. The German infantry advanced in a succession of from eight to twelve waves, preceded by a great
number of low-flying aeroplanes which rained machine-
gun fire on the troops and dropped smoke bombs to
screen the assaulting lines. The front line battalions
met the enemy with heavy rifle and Lewis gun fire,
but when the right companies had been taken in front
and rear and all had lost a large proportion of their
strength, the whole line was eventually overcome.

All communications had been cut, and battalion
headquarters and the supporting battalions had no
sooner become aware of the German advance than they
found the enemy upon them. The headquarters of the
10th R.B. with two companies put up a gallant fight
in a vain effort to stem the enemy's onslaught on their
flank and front. The few officers and men of the
battalion headquarters who survived were eventually
captured. Capt. T. H. Henderson, M.C., the adjutant,
was killed while bravely attempting with a few riflemen
to hold up the masses of the enemy. Capt. S. J. Pegler,
D.S.O., took command of the battalion, of which he
could find at that time only a party of 4 officers and 20
men. The remnants of these two brigades then fell
back fighting to the north-eastern and south-eastern
slopes of Welsh Ridge, where the reserve battalions had
taken up their position. Major Macmillan, commanding the 7th D.C.L.I., lost his life while gallantly
leading a party of men against the enemy, and many
other attempts were made to check the advance, but

wherever a stand was made the position was at once outflanked.

The machine gun companies fought valiantly but suffered great loss. Of the 217th, in the area north of Lateau Wood, only a few men got back. The 59th Machine Gun Company was on the ridge a little further east. As soon as the German aeroplanes came over, the twelve guns in the front line were mounted for anti-aircraft work and so had to be immediately remounted to engage the infantry attack. These guns then continued to fire, helping to cover the retirement of their own infantry, but the company was overcome, and such guns as still remained in action were destroyed before falling into the enemy's hands. The officer commanding the company took the headquarter party forward to a trench which except for one machine gun was empty; he then went to look for a better position and was not seen again. The sergeant-major took command, fired the gun until it was put out of action, and then held the trench with bombs for an hour. After that the party moved to another trench occupied by one man with two guns, and remained there till at 4 P.M. the sergeant-major reported to an officer of the 61st Machine Gun Company, under whom he worked for the next three days. The second in command at the transport lines brought his men forward with two guns and joined the 11th R.B., with whom he served until the following afternoon.

Twelve guns of the 61st Machine Gun Company near Les Rues Vertes were quickly overwhelmed. All the teams disappeared, but from the accounts of eye-witnesses it seems clear that they fought bravely to the last. Meanwhile, Lieut. J. Neil had got No. 2 Section into action about 2000 yards south-west of the village, and opened fire directly on to the enemy, who

was then on the spur east of his position. When he
had only two guns left, the pressure of the enemy, and
the fact that he was well in front of the infantry, forced
him to withdraw. Pte. Drummond showed great
courage at this time by firing his gun till the last
possible moment although surrounded by the enemy.
These two guns fired till 3 or 4 o'clock in the afternoon,
when they were moved to form a defensive flank to the
right.

Two sections of the 83rd Field Company R.E.
were resting after night work north of Lateau Wood
when the attack began, and became involved in the
fighting between Lateau Wood and La Vacquerie.
Their bivouacs were completely outflanked and they
lost 2 officers and 22 men. The rest of the company
manned a trench in front of Villers Plouich.

The 84th Field Company, under Major P. G. Norman,
was south of Marcoing, and under orders of the 61st
Brigade took up a position on Welsh Ridge, 2000 yards
south of the village. As he could see parties of the
enemy to the east and large numbers advancing down
the slope of Bonavis Ridge, Major Norman sent reinforcements to the D.C.L.I. and to an important
trench on the right, where they met the two sections
of the 83rd Field Company. Then, as both the brigade
major and the staff captain of the 61st Brigade had
become casualties, Major Norman took over the duties
of brigade major. Two sections of the company were
sent later to reinforce the K.O.Y.L.I., under whose
orders they remained until the brigade was relieved.

Two companies of the 11th D.L.I. took part in the
fighting on this flank. " D " Company was on Welsh
Ridge. On seeing the troops retiring Capt. Pemberton
in command took up a position facing north-east and
later advanced to reinforce the front line. At 5.30 P.M.

this company was ordered to gain touch with the 7th K.O.Y.L.I. " B " Company, under Capt. Jee, returning from work near Les Rues des Vignes, occupied a line on the north end of Welsh Ridge to bar the Marcoing valley, and during the afternoon joined " D " company further to the right.

The A.D.S. near Les Rues Vertes was kept open until the enemy came within a few hundred yards. Capt. Edmond, 60th Field Ambulance, who was in charge of the dressing station, then withdrew his bearers, but finding a man dangerously wounded he ran back under heavy fire to get a stretcher, and with the help of Private Barker, carried back the wounded man for 6000 yards. Later he went forward again under severe shell fire to attend to other casualties and then was unfortunately killed by a fragment of shell.

A bearer party of the 61st Field Ambulance with a party of infantry fell into the enemy's hands near Masnières. An officer broke away, collected some 20 men and fought for two days while the bearers, often at great risk, collected and treated the wounded. On the second night the few remaining men of the infantry party and the bearers returned to their own lines, bringing the wounded with them. The M.C. was awarded to Captain Rogerson, temporarily commanding the 61st Field Ambulance, for his excellent organisation, and to the bearer officer, Captain Jones.

At an early stage in the battle the situation of the artillery in the La Vacquerie valley became critical. The 92nd Brigade, in a fold of the ground on the slope of Bonavis Ridge, remained in action after the infantry had retired through the guns and drove back four attacks, firing at a range of 200 yards. Finally, with the enemy close in front and on both flanks, the gunners were overcome and the survivors were compelled to remove the sights and as many of the breech-blocks as possible and to withdraw. Part of the waggon lines of this Brigade, 2000 yards east of Fins, had been captured, but the rest got away with some loss, and the brigade collected at Metz-en-Couture.

The 91st Brigade was about a thousand yards in rear of the 92nd. When information was received that the enemy was advancing and had taken the valley in which the 92nd had been in action, Lieut.-Colonel Erskine turned all guns on to the spur just beyond this valley in order to prevent reinforcements coming up and to give room for a counter attack, sending officers forward to the crest just in front of the batteries. No counter attack, however, was possible with the few troops who were left. The trench which had formed the headquarters of the 61st Brigade and 91st Field Artillery Brigade was a short distance to the left front of the 91st battery positions. When the enemy had captured the 92nd Field Artillery Brigade and had advanced to a few hundred yards of Brigade Headquarters, Brig.-General Duncan moved his headquarters to a ravine north-east of Villers Plouich, the headquarters of the 91st Field Artillery Brigade joining the batteries in action.

Throughout the rest of the day the men continued to serve the guns with great coolness and gallantry under heavy fire and repeated aeroplane attacks, although the Germans were only a few hundred yards in front and completely overlooked the flank from the Bonavis Ridge. The steady fire of this brigade played no small part in checking the advance and in enabling the infantry to hold on.

The 11th R.B., the reserve battalion of the 59th Brigade, moved forward at 8.50 A.M. with the object of occupying a line below the north-east slope of Welsh

Ridge. It soon became evident, however, that the enemy had broken through on the front of the 20th Division. Major Morgan Owen, who was in command of the battalion on this day, therefore decided that the two most pressing duties were to endeavour to save the guns and to take up a defensive position and gain touch with the troops on each flank. A position in front of the guns of the 92nd Brigade was then impossible. The line chosen crossed the La Vacquerie valley about 1500 yards from the village, and followed the south-east slope of Welsh Ridge. A platoon of " C " Company, under 2nd Lieut. Crawford, drove the enemy back from a wireless station on the lower slopes of the ridge so that some secret papers might be removed and the destruction of the apparatus completed. This platoon, with some forty artillerymen, then took up a position commanding the dismantled guns of the 92nd Brigade. Half " B " Company was sent up as a reinforcement and the guns were temporarily retaken, enabling the artillery to remove the remaining breech-blocks, but heavy shelling and an encircling movement of the enemy afterwards compelled this party to with-draw. 2nd Lieut. Crawford was awarded the D.S.O. The battalion, with both flanks in the air, repulsed four attacks before the remains of the other three battalions of the brigade fell back on to this line.

At 6 P.M. Lieut.-Col. Priaulx, commanding the 11th K.R.R.C., was placed in command of the battalions of the 59th Brigade.

The 7th K.O.Y.L.I., in reserve to the 61st Brigade, manned the Hindenburg Support Line on Welsh Ridge and formed a valuable rallying-point.

While the remnants of the 59th and 60th Brigades had been fighting desperately to stem the enemy's advance and had finally established a line on the north-eastern and south-eastern slopes of Welsh Ridge, the 60th Brigade also had been hotly engaged.

The enemy's most dangerous advance developed on the right flank, where by 9.30 A.M. he had taken Bonavis, Villers-Guislain, Gonnelieu and Gouzeaucourt, and was on the southern outskirts of La Vacquerie. On the left the 29th Division was gallantly holding out in Masnières.

Communications with flank divisions having been broken and the wireless station put out of action by a hostile shell, Divisional Headquarters knew that the Germans had broken through on the south only when parties of men were seen retiring over the high ground at Gonnelieu. A staff officer who was sent out to ascertain the situation ordered these men to hold the bank of the Gouzeaucourt—Villers Plouich road.

At 9 A.M. the 60th Brigade at Villers Plouich was ordered forward, the 6th K.S.L.I. and the 6th Oxford and Bucks L.I. to the ridge running south-west from Gonnelieu, the 12th R.B. to the village itself, and the 12th K.R.R.C. to La Vacquerie. Shortly after these orders had been issued it was reported that the front of the 20th Division had been broken; they were immediately cancelled as far as they concerned the K.S.L.I. and the Oxford and Bucks L.I., who were then directed to take up a position in the Hindenburg Line north-east of La Vacquerie. But by the time these two battalions had received the new orders, the K.S.L.I. were engaged with the enemy south-west of Gonnelieu and could not be withdrawn. The Oxford and Bucks L.I. stood fast, reported the situation, and later were ordered to attack the ridge. Both battalions made some progress but were unable to gain the crest, and eventually dug in on the north-west slope. The 60th Machine Gun Company reinforced the line near Gouzeaucourt.

The 12th R.B. advanced at 9.30 A.M. on Gonnelieu, which was already in the enemy's hands. The leading companies worked up the valley north-west of the village, and by 10.30 were deployed south of the main road. For some time both flanks were exposed, but later the Oxford and Bucks L.I. moved forward on the right, and touch was gained in the afternoon with the 12th K.R.R.C. about 400 yards to the left. About 6 P.M. a patrol entered Gonnelieu and captured two German N.C.O.'s but found the village held in strength. Later patrols could get no further than the outlying buildings.

The 12th K.R.R.C. took up a position east and north-east of La Vacquerie, wisely putting no troops in the village, which during the day was heavily shelled. Some men of other divisions were collected about 10.30 A.M., and posted on the south-west side, and one company moved to the right to a position on the high ground to gain touch with the 12th R.B. and to watch the village of Gonnelieu.

At mid-day a very fine attack by the Guards drove the enemy out of Gouzeaucourt. At the same time the K.S.L.I. made a second attempt to clear the high ground south-west of Gonnelieu. Owing to heavy machine-gun fire and to the obscure situation on the right one company had to be sent towards Gouzeau-court ; the rest of the battalion was unable to gain the crest, but the right company fired into the flank of the Germans, mowing them down as they retired before the Guards.

Another attempt to seize Gonnelieu and the ridge was made that night. The K.S.L.I. were to work down the railway to a point east of Gouzeaucourt and then turn left-handed, while the Oxford and Bucks L.I. attacked in conjunction with the 12th R.B.

The battalions were met by very heavy machine-gun fire, and although the right pushed forward the left encountered a hostile attack launched simultaneously with our own and was unable to gain ground.

A party of the 11th D.L.I. had meanwhile fought a spirited action on the extreme right. " A " Company of this battalion near Villers Plouich took up a position to cover the approaches from the south and was not engaged, but the headquarters and " C " Company were in Gouzeaucourt at the time when the German attack was developing against the village.

Except for heavy gun-fire nothing very unusual was apparent until 9.15 A.M., when Lieut.-Colonel G. Hayes, commanding the battalion, noticed men coming back and horses galloping towards Fins. At that moment heavy machine-gun fire was heard close to the village and an artillery sergeant-major stated that the enemy was coming over in masses from the direction of Villers Guislain. Lieut.-Colonel Hayes immediately led the party out towards a small hill, known as Hill 135, some 700 yards south-west of the village. There he saw the Germans advancing in the most perfect order, entirely unopposed. The leading waves were by that time across the railway and the others were in force on the ridge behind, from which they swept the crest of Hill 135 with machine-gun fire. He ordered one platoon to defend the houses in the southern end of Gouzeaucourt, in order to cover the left flank, placed two along the road between Hill 135 and the village to check the advance from the ridge in front, and sent one to the southern end of the hill to protect the exposed right flank. The men were well led by the company commander, Lieut. Bushell, who showed great coolness and courage throughout the day. Three sections of

R.E. of another division then came up; two were
sent to reinforce the left flank and one to fill the
gap between the top of the hill and the right platoon.
The machine-gun fire was by this time extremely
heavy; the Germans had broken through Gouzeaucourt, where the left platoon had found them already
in possession. Lieut.-Colonel Hayes, therefore sent
Sgt.-Major M'Evoy and twenty men to a position a
little south of the main road 1500 yards west of
Gouzeaucourt, with orders to hold on to the last man
and cover the retirement of the others. The rest of
the company and the R.E. withdrew to this line under
heavy machine-gun fire both from the town and from
Hill 135, but with comparatively little loss. Later
the 20th Hussars reinforced the party and prolonged
the line to the right, and at noon the counter attack
of the Guards on Gouzeaucourt relieved the situation.
The adjutant of the 11th D.L.I., Captain Tollit, had
meanwhile returned to the old battalion headquarters
and succeeded in getting away with the confidential
papers; he was sent to Sorel for machine guns and
reinforcements, and then returned to the line. On
the following day " C " Company moved back to a
position near Villers Plouich.

In the A.D.S. at Gouzeaucourt between thirty and
forty wounded were lying when shell and machine-gun
fire gave the first warning of the enemy's approach.
A shell hit the dressing station, bringing down the wall
of the room in which the wounded were being dressed,
and soon afterwards the enemy appeared on the ridge
between Gouzeaucourt and Villers Guislain. The
wounded were immediately placed in the Decauville
train and got away and the A.D.S. was abandoned just
before the enemy surrounded the village. Lieut.-
Colonel Osburn, commanding the 60th Field Ambul-

ance, went back to his rear headquarters at Fins and
ordered all available bearers to march towards Gouzeaucourt. Captain R. V. C. Ash had meanwhile withdrawn
the unit. A provisional A.D.S. was formed half way
between Fins and Gouzeaucourt, and there three or
four hundred wounded were dressed. In the evening,
when Gouzeaucourt had been retaken, most of the stores
were rescued from the original dressing station.

When the enemy's attack was launched on the
morning of the 30th, Brig.-General Hyslop was at
rear Divisional Headquarters at Sorel on his way
home on sick leave, and he took command of the
headquarter details of the 20th and 29th Divisions,
and also of the details of the 20th Division at Nurlu.
Part of this force was rushed forward towards Gouzeaucourt and part took up a position near Revelon and
helped to repel an attack. All transport except the
mobile ammunition echelon was sent back to Moislains.
A line of straggler posts was formed, and all labour
units in the neighbourhood, as fast as they could be
collected, were employed either in digging or in
carrying forward ammunition and R.E. material.
Towards evening it was ascertained that the situation
was in hand.

Thanks to an alternative emergency ground line
which the 20th Divisional Signal Company had laid
to Corps through the outskirts of Gouzeaucourt, to
supplement the poled cable route erected by Corps,
signal communication between Divisional Headquarters
and Corps was successfully maintained throughout the
day, in spite of the fact that at one time a portion of
the line passed into German hands and out again.
This line also proved of inestimable value to the 6th,
12th and 29th Divisions, whose communications with
Corps had broken.

Constant and most strenuous efforts were made to maintain signal communication forward of Division. Cpl. Thompson gained the M.M. for conspicuous bravery in mending lines time after time under heavy shell-fire.

By the end of the day the line ran from Gouzeau-court, past the north-west outskirts of Gonnelieu to La Vacquerie; it then turned east round the cross-roads between La Vacquerie and Bonavis, thence north-west to the ravine, and along the eastern and north-eastern slopes of Welsh Ridge. There were gaps in the line, in particular north-east of La Vacquerie. As no troops were available to fill them, IIIrd Corps was asked for reinforcements and sent two battalions of the 6th Division—the 2/6th Sherwood Foresters, who were placed under the 59th Brigade, and the 1st Buffs, who went to the 60th. Between the 59th and 60th Brigades were elements of the 12th Division.

The 91st Field Artillery Brigade in action in the valley received orders from the C.R.A. during the afternoon to withdraw the batteries to Beaucamp that night. The limbers had been ordered up by the C.R.A., and they made their way by Metz and Beaucamp to Villers Plouich.

It was out of the question to withdraw the guns until after dark, as the enemy lay close up to the south-east edge of La Vacquerie, and through this village passed the only route to the battery positions. This was a deep sunken road, only wide enough for one team, and it had to be used to bring up the teams as well as to withdraw the guns. To ensure that no block should take place, arrangements had to be made for each battery to complete its withdrawal through the sunken road in turn.

Thanks to the thorough grasp of the situation and to the greatest coolness shown by all ranks the guns were successfully withdrawn with extraordinarily few casualties, in spite of the darkness of the night.

By 3 A.M. on the 1st of December the brigade was again in action just north of Beaucamp.

Among the many decorations awarded to the 91st Brigade for its successful action this day was the M.C. to Lieut. Ardagh, who was the sole remaining officer of C/91 Battery.

The same night Divisional Headquarters moved from Villers Plouich to a point half-way between Gouzeaucourt and Gouzeaucourt Wood.

Meanwhile the main German attack had been delivered with great determination on the north face of the salient. The divisions on this front inflicted enormous losses on the enemy, and against greatly superior numbers held their general line unbroken.

During the two following days the enemy's attacks on the Divisional front were directed against the centre and the right of the line ; the 61st Brigade on the left was not seriously threatened. Capt. Pegler, commanding the 10th R.B., who with a small party of his battalion had been fighting during the 30th under the 61st Brigade, reported at 2 A.M. on the 1st to Lieut.-Colonel Priaulx and took up a position on either side of the La Vacquerie—Masnières road. The enemy delivered two assaults against the 10th R.B. and the 11th R.B. at this point during the morning, but both were driven back, and the line was held under severe shelling throughout that day.

On the right the 60th Brigade was engaged more heavily. At dawn the Guards attacked along the ridge and entered Gonnelieu from the west, but at 8.30 A.M. the enemy put down a heavy barrage, followed by an attack on Gonnelieu and on the front of the 12th R.B. and the 12th K.R.R.C. to the north.

The Guards were forced out of the village, and a wedge was driven between the centre and left companies of the 12th R.B. The three front line companies of this battalion ("D," "A," and "B") had then only one unwounded officer among them. The company sergeant-major of "D" Company organised a counter attack with some of his men and a handful of "A" Company, and was last seen advancing against vastly superior numbers of the enemy near Gonnelieu. The right company of the 12th K.R.R.C. ("D" Company, under Capt. G. B. Loyd) meanwhile fired into the flank of the attack. At a critical moment Capt. Loyd was mortally wounded while directing the fire of his men, and this company, with twenty remaining men of "B" Company of the 12th R.B., fell back.

The situation at this point was saved by the right company of the 12th R.B. ("D" Company, under Capt. Williams, M.C.), which stood firm in the face of repeated attacks. Although wounded in the leg Capt. Williams remained in command and drove back the Germans on his front when they had broken through the gap on the left and were 200 yards to his rear. The men on the left used nearly all their ammunition, and three Lewis guns fired about twelve drums each into the enemy at ranges under 100 yards. The company suffered severely, only five men remaining unwounded in the left platoon, but the enemy was held and abandoned his efforts to break through.

At 10 A.M. the Guards delivered a counter attack with great steadiness under machine-gun fire and again entered Gonnelieu.

Meanwhile the 12th K.R.R.C. had been engaged at La Vacquerie. After very fierce fighting most of the day, they gallantly drove the enemy back and held the line unchanged. The battalion held a long line with no reserves, and the men were very exhausted. That night the 60th Brigade was relieved by the 183rd Brigade of the 61st Division.

The 29th Division at Masnières still held its ground, and during the day beat off a succession of determined attacks, withdrawing under orders during the night to the west bank of the canal. The gallant action of this division and of the 12th R.B. and 12th K.R.R.C. on each side of La Vacquerie went far to check the German advance.

During the 2nd of December the enemy confined his attacks to the La Vacquerie front, where he was repulsed three times by the 183rd Brigade. North-east of the village, after heavy shelling, he launched a bombing attack on the 10th and 11th R.B. under cover of heavy machine-gun fire, and gained a footing in the trench. Counter attacks were organised at once. Twice the trench was almost cleared, but eventually the supply of bombs gave out and a part of the line had to be withdrawn to the sunken road. " B " and " D " Companies of the 11th D.L.I. were sent from the 61st Brigade to reinforce the 11th R.B., and a new line on the slope just north-west of the road was established and held.

On the night of the 2nd/3rd the 59th and 61st Brigades were relieved, and on the morning of the 3rd the front was handed over to the 61st Division. Divisional Headquarters moved to Sorel, with the three brigades about Villers Plouich, Sorel and Fins.

The relief of the Divisional Artillery was out of the question, and the 91st Brigade remained for another fortnight in action north of Beaucamp. On the 3rd of December the enemy renewed his attack and succeeded in entering La Vacquerie and completed his capture of Gonnelieu. At Masnières and Marcoing he was again repulsed, but the line there was very exposed, and at night all troops who remained east of the canal were moved back to positions west of it.

Local attacks during the next few days gained little ground, and it was evident that the enemy was becoming exhausted. His success along the Bonavis Ridge, however, had left the divisions further north holding a dangerous salient, and made it necessary to withdraw that flank to the high ground at Flesquieres.[1] This was completed by the 7th, when our positions were finally established along the line shown in Map III.

The Headquarters of the Divisional Artillery was relieved on the 14th, and two days later the 91st Brigade pulled out of action.

[1] Sir Douglas Haig's Despatches, p. 169.

o

CHAPTER X

THE MENIN ROAD SECTOR.

12th December 1917 *to* *20th February* 1918

Relief of 30th Division by 20th Division in the Menin Road
Sector—Importance of this Line—Reorganisation of the
Division—Move of the Division to the Fifth Army area
south of the Somme.
(*Vide* Map I.)

A FTER the battle of Cambrai the Division went
back into Corps reserve for a few days, and
then moved north again into the area of
the Fourth Army (General Sir H. S. Rawlinson). By
the 12th of December units were concentrated some
twenty to twenty-five miles south-west of Ypres,
with Divisional Headquarters at Blaringhem. The
Divisional Artillery, after a most trying march over
roads coated with ice, arrived in this area on the
24th, when the Divisional Artillery Headquarters was
opened at Robecq and the batteries went into billets
in the neighbourhood of Haverskerque. On the 7th
of January 1918 the 20th Division, less the artillery,
relieved the 30th Division in the left sector of the
IXth Corps front (Lieut.-General Sir A. Hamilton
Gordon).

The front line, 2700 yards in length, ran north-east
and south-west for about an equal distance on either
side of the Menin road, which it crossed north-west of
Gheluvelt. The position lay on the forward slopes
of the long ridge which overlooks Ypres from the south

and east. From the high ground about Clapham Junction several marshy streams flow south and east, cutting the slopes of the ridge into a succession of spurs, on one of which the village of Gheluvelt stands.

The defensive system included a series of lines which at this time were still in course of construction. Behind an outpost line lightly held ran the main defensive position in which the reserves of battalions were generally posted. Behind this again ran an Intermediate Line just below the crest of the ridge, a Corps Line, and an Army Line which extended from the ramparts of Ypres to the south.

The ground along which the front trenches ran had been won as a result of the hard fighting in September and October 1917, since when British troops had twice attacked in the northern part of the sector with a view to improving their position. In the second attempt, on the 3rd of December, some progress was made in the face of heavy machine-gun fire, but only a temporary advantage was gained, as the Germans, attacking on the 14th under cover of a trench mortar barrage, recovered the greater part of their original line. In so doing they curtailed our observation and to a certain extent improved their own.

It was this problem of observation that made it essential for us to yield no further ground, for should the enemy capture the front line here his view of our position would be improved very greatly. An official memorandum issued by the Fourth Army at this time states : " The area of the Army Battle Zone about the Menin road is probably the most important on the whole Army front, and it rests with the IXth Corps to make it as nearly impregnable as possible." This, then, was one of the tasks which the Division had to undertake.

A boundary line running east and west cut the front trenches about three hundred yards south of the Menin road, dividing the front into two sub-sectors, the right held by one battalion in the front line, the left by two battalions. On the night of the 6th/7th of January the 61st Brigade took over the right sub-sector and the 60th Brigade took over the left. The 59th Brigade was in reserve in the area between Dickebusch and La Clytte, three to five miles south-west of Ypres. Divisional Headquarters was nearly seven miles south-west of Ypres at Westoutre. The 37th Division was on the right of the 20th, and the New Zealand Division on the left.

The front was covered by three brigades of artillery formed into two groups, one to support each of the infantry brigades in the line. The Southern Group consisted of the 242nd (Army) Field Artillery Brigade ; the Northern Group, when the 20th Division first took over this sector, consisted of the 37th Divisional Artillery. The whole was under the command of the C.R.A. 20th Division.

In spite of the advantages which the Germans would have obtained by penetrating the front line in the Menin road sector, the six weeks which the Division spent there were extremely quiet. The great trouble was the weather. The first half of January was cold, with hard frosts and heavy falls of snow ; occasionally there were warmer days when it poured with rain. About the middle of the month the thaw began with torrents of rain and a gale of wind. The trenches soon became feet deep in mud and water. Part of the front line was so deeply flooded that certain trenches had to be evacuated. Posts were established behind them, and the line was constantly patrolled at night to prevent the enemy from occupying these positions.

THE MENIN ROAD, YPRES

[To face p. 212.

Being on the forward slope of the ridge, a great deal
of the position was in full view of the enemy. The
whole of the ground was a mass of shell-holes, and the
only approaches to the front line lay along a few duckboard tracks, which the Germans regularly shelled.
The journey to the front line and back along these
slippery tracks was a very unpleasant and dangerous
business, and as a brigade relief took place every six
days and battalions remained in the front trenches
only forty-eight hours, and sometimes only twenty-four,
it had to be made very often.

Along the top of the ridge were several " tunnels,"
which gave cover to a large number of troops. Just
south of Sanctuary Wood, Tor Top Tunnels, a huge
underground cavern lit by electric light, held the
whole of the battalion in reserve to the left brigade.
As there were only four exits from this place, so that
very few men might have escaped if a fire had broken
out, great precautions were taken, and nobody was
allowed even to strike a match. These orders were
the outcome of a disastrous fire which had occurred
in Hedge Street Tunnels the night before the 61st
Brigade went into the line, when several officers and
men were burnt to death, including some of the advanced party of the 61st Brigade.

The swampy ground along the banks of the various
streams which crossed the line was generally impassable,
so that it was sufficient to organise the spurs for defence,
and to wire the gaps in the line where the streams
flowed through. For the first half of January, however,
the hard frost made it possible to move across these
marshes, and constant patrolling was necessary to
ensure the safety of the line.

Almost the only events which involved any fighting
occurred on the night of the 9th/10th of January. In

order to assist some operations of the 37th Division, the 20th carried out a demonstration in which artillery. Stokes mortars, machine guns, Lewis guns and rifle grenades all played a part. The 37th Division raided the enemy's trenches twice during the night, and on both occasions the enemy put down a heavy barrage for an hour on the front and support lines of the 20th Division.

At 4.45 A.M. on 10th of January a party of the enemy, estimated at 30 to 50 strong, attempted to raid the left company of the 6th K.S.L.I. in the left sub-sector. The forward posts were temporarily driven in, but the positions were quickly retaken, and though the Germans failed to capture any of the K.S.L.I., they left two of their own party prisoners in our hands. About this time the 37th Division on the right was relieved by the 4th Australian Division.

On the 22nd of January the artillery of the 37th Division was relieved by that of the 20th, which from that date formed the Northern Group, under Major H. Price Williams, M.C. The battery positions extended between Zillebeke and Hooge. It was laid down that the policy of the artillery in this sector should be defensive and not aggressive, as it was not desired to stir the enemy into activity without good cause. Accordingly, while no favourable opportunity of inflicting loss on the enemy was missed, no harassing fire or fire without a definite object was carried out.

Throughout this period our patrols were active, as it was considered important that we should keep command of " No Man's Land." This was successfully done. A number of patrols went out from each brigade every night, and although they kept the enemy's trenches and posts constantly under observation, as a rule no parties of the enemy were met. One patrol of the 7th D.C.L.I. had an unpleasant experience and was forced to spend a considerably longer time in front of the line than was expected. A liaison patrol of one N.C.O. and one man of this battalion had been sent out on the night of the 24th/25th to the battalion on the left. The patrol had encountered an enemy machine gun and the N.C.O. had been killed. An officer and one man of the D.C.L.I. went out at 4 A.M. on the 25th to investigate. They also found the machine gun, which opened fire on them at fifteen yards' range. Fortunately they escaped, and they crawled away eastwards. At daybreak they found themselves between the enemy's posts, and there they had to remain concealed in a shell-hole all day. As soon as it became dark they moved towards their own trenches, coming across a post of the enemy on the way, and then being driven back by Lewis gun fire from our line. Having thus had to spend another night out, they eventually rejoined their battalion at daybreak on the 26th.

Good work was done also by the machine gun companies. Between the 23rd and the 29th the 59th Machine Gun Company fired 36,000 rounds in indirect fire, and in conjunction with trench mortars silenced all the enemy's forward machine guns near the Menin road, making the reliefs much easier to carry out.

On the 31st the Division was transferred from the IXth to the XXIInd Corps, under Lieut.-General Sir A. Godley, but as the XXIInd Corps took over the Menin road sector, this involved no change in the dispositions. On the night of the 7th/8th February the Divisional line was extended to the left as far as a point 600 yards east of the south-east corner of Polygon Wood. A readjustment of the inter-brigade boundary then became necessary, so that after this time each brigade had two battalions in the front line.

Meanwhile, the organisation of the Division had been changed. It had been decided to reduce all infantry brigades to three battalions each. On the 3rd of February three battalions—the 6th Oxford and Bucks L.I. (Lieut.-Colonel Boyle), the 10th K.R.R.C. (Lieut.-Colonel Sheepshanks), and the 10th R.B. (Lieut.-Colonel Morgan-Owen)—were told that they were to be broken up at once. The 7th K.O.Y.L.I. (Lieut.-Colonel Janson) were to leave the Division. The preparation of rolls and the many details which had to be settled in a short time involved a great deal of work, but it was quickly carried out. A certain number of the 10th K.R.R.C. and the 10th R.B. joined the 11th K.R.R.C. and the 11th R.B. and so remained in the Division, and in all units officers were given, as far as possible, their choice of various battalions to which they might go. In general, complete companies were posted to other battalions of their own regiments.

The order came as a great shock to battalions all of which had a fine record and in which *esprit de corps* stood high, and both officers and men felt the disbandment keenly.

By the 8th of February only a few headquarter details were left. Lieut.-Colonel Morgan Owen, commanding the 10th R.B., returned on the 12th from a conference to find that his battalion no longer existed. About the middle of the month the last few details went to the Divisional Wing of the Corps Reinforcement Camp.

The 7th K.O.Y.L.I. remained with the Division until the 15th, when they came under the O.C. Reinforcements XXIInd Corps ; on the 20th they became the 14th Entrenching Battalion.

The 2nd Scottish Rifles, a very fine battalion over 1000 strong, under Lieut.-Col. H. C. H. Smith, D.S.O., came from the 8th Division to the 20th on the 3rd of February, and from that time formed part of the 59th Brigade.

In the Trench Mortar Batteries the personnel of V/20 Battery was transferred to the XXIInd Corps (H) T.M.B. ; X, Y, and Z/20 were then reorganised to form the new X and Y/20 Batteries. At the same time, twelve mortars were handed over in exchange for ten six-inch Newtons.

After this the 20th Division was relieved by the 37th. All units were out of the line by the 19th, and on the following day began to entrain for the area of the Fifth Army south of the Somme.

CHAPTER XI

THE GERMAN OFFENSIVE ON THE SOMME

21st February to 25th March 1918

Occupation of the rear zone defences—Retreat to the Somme—
Defence of the Libermont Canal—Actions of the 61st
Infantry Brigade and 91st Field Artillery Brigade under
the 36th Division.

(Vide Map IV.)

ON the 23rd of February 1918 Divisional Headquarters was opened at Ercheu in the area
of the Fifth Army. The 60th Brigade was
billeted in the Ham area ; the 59th near Beaulieu,
three miles south of Ercheu ; the 61st near Freniches,
three miles south-east of Ercheu ; the 91st Field
Artillery Brigade at Esmery-Hallon ; the 92nd Field
Artillery Brigade at Rouy-le-Grand, two and a half
miles north-east of Nesle. The Division was in
G.H.Q. reserve but was to be placed at the disposal
of the XVIIIth Corps, commanded by Lieut.-Gen.
Sir F. I. Maxse, in the event of a German attack on
the Corps front. During the rest of February and
the first three weeks of March all units worked from
time to time on the defences behind the battle zone
and reconnoitred the positions which they would have
to occupy in accordance with various schemes which
had been prepared to meet a German offensive. All
these schemes entailed considerable work for the 20th
Divisional Signal Company. The Divisional Artillery,
under Brig.-General Christie, took full advantage of

the unique experience of being out of the line for a whole month to train batteries in open warfare, the ground lending itself admirably to this kind of work.

At the end of February the four machine gun companies of the Division were formed into the 20th Battalion, Machine Gun Corps, under Lieut.-Colonel H. L. Riley, D.S.O. The 59th, 60th, 61st and 217th Companies became " A," " B," " C," and " D " Companies of the battalion respectively. In the middle of March Brig.-General Banbury, commanding the 61st Infantry Brigade, went home for six months' rest. He was succeeded by Brig.-General J. K. Cochrane, C.M.G.

It soon became clear that the expected German offensive would not be long delayed. On arrival in this area troops had been ordered to be ready to move at twenty-four hours' notice; this was reduced to twelve hours on the 10th of March, and on the 20th to one hour. Just after 5 A.M. on the 21st, XVIIIth Corps issued the order " Man Battle Stations."

The Fifth Army, under General Sir Hubert Gough, consisting of the IIIrd, XVIIIth, XIXth and VIIth Corps, held an extended front of some forty-two miles from the Oise to Gouzeaucourt, where the Third Army, under General the Hon. Sir Julian Byng, continued the line to the Scarpe. The XVIIIth Corps held a line facing St Quentin from Urvillers to Gricourt, with the 36th Division on the right, the 30th opposite St Quentin, and the 61st on the left. On the right of the 36th Division was the 14th Division of the IIIrd Corps. On the left of the 61st Division was the XIXth Corps. The 20th Division, if called upon to support this line, was to move forward ready to man the rear zone defences between the Somme and the Omignon river from St Simon to Trefcon, sending a brigade of artillery to each of the 36th and 30th Divisions.

At 4.40 A.M. on the 21st of March the enemy opened an intense bombardment along practically the whole front of the Fifth and Third Armies, using a great quantity of gas shells. The infantry attack, launched in a thick fog after several hours of this bombardment, developed on the XVIIIth Corps front about 10.30 A.M.

By noon the line had been penetrated at various points, although on all parts of the front isolated detachments held out most gallantly. The infantry of the 20th Division was ordered at 1 P.M. to concentrate behind the rear zone defences, and the artillery brigades moved forward to their allotted divisions, the 91st (Lieut.-Colonel Erskine) to the 36th Division and the 92nd (Lieut.-Colonel Balston) to the 30th.

In the course of the day the enemy pushed forward, particularly on the right of the Corps line, where by 3 P.M. the situation had become critical. The 61st Brigade (Brig.-General Cochrane) was ordered therefore to man the bridge-heads at St Simon and Tugny immediately on arrival in that area. Pressed on the front and outflanked on the right, the 36th Division retired during the night south of the Somme. The 61st Infantry Brigade and the 91st Field Artillery Brigade covered this retirement, and from that time came under the orders of the 36th Division. Here we will leave them for the moment in order to trace the movements of the rest of the 20th Division during the following four days.

On the left the Germans had penetrated the line at the junction of the XVIIIth and XIXth Corps and at Roupy, and had gained a footing in Grand Seraucourt. The 60th Brigade (Brig.-General Duncan) therefore pushed out covering troops on the defensive line from

the Somme to Vaux, and as troops of the 30th Division
were retiring on the left, the 59th Brigade (Brig.-
General Hyslop) manned the defences between Vaux
and the Corps left boundary at Trefcon. The 92nd
Field Artillery Brigade under the 30th Division was in
action south of Fluquières, covering a line between
Roupy and Savy.

All details were formed into a Divisional Reinforcement Battalion under Major Storr, second in command
of the 12th King's, and moved to a position between
Matigny and Douilly. The 11th D.L.I. concentrated
at Golancourt and sent " D " Company to reinforce the
61st Brigade. Divisional Headquarters came forward
to Ham.

This was the situation on the night of the 21st, when
the enemy had advanced west and south-west of
St Quentin for a distance of about three miles. Although
he had made an important advance along the whole
front, he had not yet broken through the battle zone.

Taking advantage of the thick mist which still
hung over the country, the enemy worked down the
St Quentin Canal on the 22nd towards Happencourt.
This threatened the right flank of the 60th Brigade.
The 59th was therefore withdrawn from the rear zone
defences ·between Vaux and Trefcon, leaving there
only a skeleton force, and assembled in the Germaine—
Foreste area, ready to launch a counter attack, if
necessary, towards the south-east. But at 5.50 P.M.
the enemy turned the left flank of the Corps north of
Holnon Wood, driving back the 61st Division, which
retired towards the Somme. To meet this new situation the 59th Brigade occupied a previously sited
rearguard position between Douilly and Lanchy.

The 60th Brigade was attacked after heavy shelling
at 3.50 P.M. Although their front line was driven

back for a short distance, all battalions withstood the attack until they were ordered to withdraw. The 6th K.S.L.I. (Lieut.-Colonel Welch) on the right made a fine stand west of Happencourt with the enemy on both flanks; two companies of the 12th R.B. (Lieut.-Colonel MacLachlan) in the centre were surrounded, but fought their way back; and the 12th K.R.R.C. (Lieut.-Colonel Moore) on the left were heavily engaged with the enemy, who penetrated through Vaux and Fluquières. "A" Company of the 12th K.R.R.C. was practically cut off, but gallantly held on. In front of this company there was a gap in the wire through which the Germans tried to force their way four times, but two Lewis guns so successfully covered the gap that all efforts failed. Eventually, when all officers and many N.C.O.'s had been wounded or killed, the company was forced to fall back.

The pressure on the Corps front continued, and in view of the general situation the forward divisions were ordered to retire across the Somme during the night through the 59th and 60th Brigades, which after covering the withdrawal were to move back, fighting rearguard actions, to a position between Canizy and Béthencourt, and blow up all bridges on their front. At 8 P.M., before this movement was timed to take place, the enemy was reported to have broken through Vaux with a force of all arms, and the 20th Division was ordered to prolong the rearguard position held by the 59th Brigade to the right. The 60th Brigade accordingly occupied the line Bray—Douilly. Just before the troops moved back the Germans were heard advancing down a sunken road from Happencourt, singing for all they were worth. They had probably seen men of other divisions retiring and thought that the whole line had gone, and they were very much surprised and completely scattered when they suddenly came under Lewis gun fire from the 6th K.S.L.I.

During the night the 20th covered the withdrawal of the 30th and 61st Divisions, and then fell back in close contact with the enemy across the Somme Canal. Most of the fighting occurred on the front of the 60th Brigade. Brig.-General Duncan received the orders for this retirement at 10.45 P.M., and made repeated efforts to send them on to battalions, but, owing to the heavy fighting which was going on, none of the orderlies got through. All units, however, had been told what the plans were, and they successfully carried them out. At 11 P.M. the Germans, who had crept up close to the position under cover of a dense mist, drove a wedge between two companies of the 12th K.R.R.C. and got into the line of the 6th K.S.L.I., cutting off practically the whole of one company. Lieut.-Colonel Welch, commanding the 6th K.S.L.I., led the battalion head-quarters forward to counter attack, but the enemy was found to be too strong. The companies of the K.S.L.I. were driven back in various directions, and the headquarters and most of the men became separated from the brigade until the afternoon of the 24th. The 12th R.B. particularly distinguished themselves; they inflicted very heavy casualties on the enemy and caused a stampede among his transport, which was moving down the main St Quentin—Ham road, but they lost their commanding officer, Lieut.-Colonel MacLachlan, who was killed while gallantly leading his men.

" D " Company of the 11th D.L.I. (Lieut.-Colonel Hayes) had been sent to reinforce the 61st Brigade. The rest of the battalion had come under the orders of the 60th during the afternoon, and by 8 P.M. had taken up a position between Tugny and Bray to fill a gap between the 61st and 60th Brigades. Soon afterwards the 12th King's, on the left of the 61st Brigade, were forced back, leaving the right flank of the D.L.I. exposed. The enemy could be heard in Tugny shouting in English and making a lot of noise, and patrols sent out by the battalion found that he had worked round the right flank in the fog. About midnight " B " Company on the left was rushed from the right rear. A strong party of " A " Company on the right, under Capt. Endean, however, held out until the battalion was ordered to retire through Ham and hold the bridge-head at Offoy. By this time the enemy had broken through the line and the casualties were heavy; but leaving twenty men under 2nd Lieut. English as a rearguard with two Vickers guns on the main road, the remains of the battalion withdrew. Capt. Endean, two other officers, and forty men of " A " Company, although surrounded, fought their way through, and a small party of " B " Company, under C.S.M. Craggs, who was afterwards awarded the D.C.M., got back with the 12th R.B. and took part in the rearguard actions fought by that battalion. In the early hours of the 23rd, 97 men of " A " and " B " Companies were formed into one company under Lieut. Bushell and occupied the Offoy bridge-head.

The bridges over the Somme Canal were reported to have been prepared for demolition. The 83rd Field Company R.E. (Major Massie) and the 96th Field Company R.E. (Major Story), on arrival at the canal found that this work had been most inadequately done. In many cases the charges were far too small, the main girder at one bridge had been ignored, and some bridges had not been prepared at all. This, of course, threw a great deal of extra work on the field companies, as many new charges had to be laid. Where the existing charges were fired they failed to make complete gaps in the bridges; extra charges had to be laid afterwards, and by this means the work was satisfactorily completed.

By dawn on the 23rd the Division had successfully crossed the canal, the 83rd and 96th Field Companies R.E. had blown up the bridges, and the 60th Brigade on the right and the 59th on the left had occupied the line from Canizy to Béthencourt. At the same time the 92nd Field Artillery Brigade, which had helped to beat off heavy attacks on Roupy on the 22nd, rejoined the Division temporarily and came into action about one and a half miles south-east of Nesle, covering the crossings of the Somme opposite the front of the 60th Infantry Brigade. Divisional Headquarters was opened at Nesle, and the 20th Divisional Signal Company (Major Brace), whose signal lorry had been the last vehicle to cross at Ham, quickly established communications with brigades.

The 12th K.R.R.C. took over the defences opposite Offoy from the D.L.I., who then prolonged the line to the right as far as Canizy, where they were joined by 34 more men of " A " Company, under Capt. Endean. About 26 men of the K.S.L.I. and parties from various divisions joined the 60th Brigade on this flank. On the left were the 12th R.B. Brig.-General Duncan found a large number of men of the 30th Division holding the canal, and these he took under his command and placed in support on the railway. On the 59th Brigade front the 11th K.R.R.C. (Lieut.-Colonel Priaulx) held the line about Voyennes, with the Scottish Rifles (Lieut.-Colonel H. C. H. Smith) in the centre and the 11th R.B. (Lieut.-Colonel Cotton) on the left at Béthencourt.

P

The work of the R.E. was made particularly difficult at this time, as someone had set fire to the R.E. park at Chaulnes long before the enemy got anywhere near it. In consequence, for two or three days hardly any shovels or R.E. stores could be obtained. Parties went to the park with lorries but were unable to do very much good, owing to the great heat and to the impossibility of getting at much of the most necessary material. The 83rd and 96th Field Companies now joined their respective brigades, to which they had already sent two sections each, the 83rd going to the 60th Brigade and the 96th to the 59th Brigade.

The 60th, 61st and 62nd Field Ambulances had been attached respectively to the 59th, 60th and 61st Brigades, but during the successive retirements they had to deal with the casualties of many different units. Their work was splendid. Many times when communication was difficult and the situation uncertain, advanced dressing stations were established close to the front line and the wounded carried back, often under heavy fire, with great perseverance and courage.

On the 22nd, between 2000 and 3000 cases passed through a temporary aid post of the 60th Field Ambulance established at Matigny by Major C. A. Boyd before the post was abandoned at the last possible moment that night when the enemy was entering the village. Major Boyd and his party crossed at Voyennes just before the bridges were destroyed.

At 8 A.M. on the 23rd the enemy was reported to have broken through at Ham and to be advancing on Esmery Hallon, through which the 30th Division was retiring towards the Libermont Canal. Brig.-General Duncan was ordered to counter attack, and elements of the 182nd Brigade (61st Division) were placed at his disposal to assist this operation.

Lieut.-Colonel Bilton, of the 61st Division, was placed in command of the counter attack, and was assisted by Major A. E. Sanderson, the Brigade Major of the 60th Brigade. Lieut.-Colonel Bilton moved off with about 800 men and at 4 P.M. launched the attack from the main Ham—Nesle road, about 1500 yards west of Eppeville. The attack, delivered with great dash, drove back the enemy, captured Verlaines, and restored the situation.

The Division held the canal crossings throughout the day in spite of many attempts by the enemy to force them. Fighting was heavy at Offoy on the front of the 12th K.R.R.C.; at Béthencourt the 11th R.B. drove back with considerable loss several parties which tried to cross the canal.

In the evening the 182nd Brigade (61st Division), which had been under the orders of Major-General Douglas Smith since the morning, was transferred to the 30th Division, and the 183rd and 184th Brigades (61st Division) came under the 20th Division for counter-attack purposes and moved to Nesle. The Division was further reinforced by two batteries of a Canadian Motor Machine Gun Battalion under Capt. Merling. " In all subsequent operations," the official report states, " up to the 31st March, these batteries performed yeoman service, and on account of their mobility were of inestimable service in holding the extended fronts allotted to the Division."

As soon as night came on, a great noise of traffic and shouting was heard in Offoy, where " C " Company of the 12th K.R.R.C. guarded the crossing. Under the fire of Vickers and Lewis guns the Germans became quieter, but at various points along the canal they could be heard driving in stakes, moving planks, and making evident preparations to throw out bridges.

They planked what remained of the Offoy bridge
during the night and made several attempts to cross
it, but the 12th K.R.R.C. held on with great courage
and complete success.

All through the 24th the Division was repeatedly
attacked, particularly on the flanks, and the whole
line was severely shelled. At 5 A.M. it was reported
that the enemy had crossed the canal at Pargny,
forcing a gap between the 20th and 8th Divisions,
and was moving south along the west bank. Dispositions to meet this were made by the 11th R.B. and
by battalions of the East Lancashire Regiment and
the Royal Berkshire Regiment, who prolonged the flank
to the left. Under cover of a thick mist the Germans
shortly afterwards worked their way into Béthencourt,
where their machine guns caused many casualties
among the headquarters of the 11th R.B. At 8 A.M.
an attempt to cross the canal on the front of the 11th
R.B. was frustrated. "C" Company counter attacked
the enemy in Béthencourt about 10 A.M., but was hope-
lessly outnumbered, and only a few men returned.

In spite of the flanks being in the air, the line held
until 11.30 A.M., when a heavy trench mortar bombardment, directed by low-flying aeroplanes, forced
the left flank to withdraw to a ridge 200 yards in
rear. In making a further counter attack another
company of the 11th R.B. was almost wiped out
by artillery and machine-gun fire.

Shortly after mid-day the 183rd Brigade, reinforced
by eight motor machine guns, counter attacked, and
temporarily relieved the pressure. Later, as the
enemy was getting further and further round the
left flank, these three battalions retired to a better
position in rear. Here Lieut.-Colonel Cotton was
wounded, and was succeeded by Major the Hon. A. M.

Bertie, D.S.O., M.C. By 4 P.M. " A " Company consisted of 1 officer and 25 men ; " D " Company had
1 officer, and " B " and " C " Companies none at all.

About 2 P.M. the 11th K.R.R.C. at Voyennes lost
their commanding officer, Lieut.-Colonel Prialux, who
was killed by a shell, with most of the battalion headquarters. He was succeeded by Major M. S. Ormrod.
Soon afterwards the enemy crossed the canal and
turned the line, forcing the battalion back to the
high ground west of the village. The Scottish Rifles
were then attacked from the rear. " B " Company,
under Capt. Steward, made a fine stand, and eventually withdrew from a difficult position only 24 men
strong.

Meanwhile a critical situation had developed on the
right. At 8 A.M. the enemy, advancing from Ham,
forced our troops out of Canizy and back to the railway. Lieut.-Colonel Moore, commanding the 12th
K.R.R.C., immediately led " B " and " D " Companies
of his battalion forward to counter attack. It was a
great charge, and the bayonet was used with wonderful
effect, but when it was over, Lieut.-Colonel Moore
was missing. The Germans were driven back into the
village, but later they came on again in greater numbers
than before, and under very strong pressure the
right of the 12th K.R.R.C. swung back to the railway
again. In the course of this fighting our aeroplanes
gave invaluable help. At one time, when " C "
Company of the 12th K.R.R.C. was holding on to
its position with great difficulty under heavy trench
mortar fire, they nose-dived to a height of 200 feet
and dropped bomb after bomb on to the German
trench mortars until they put them completely out
of action.

At 9.30 A.M. Major Massie, commanding the 83rd

Field Company R.E., with about thirty of his men, reported to Brig.-General Duncan, who ordered him to take up a position south of Canizy on the main Ham road. Moving forward behind cyclist scouts and an advanced guard Major Massie took up the allotted position, keeping one section in reserve. He collected a considerable number of stragglers of various units and took them under his command. He was in touch with the 12th K.R.R.C. on his left, but had no troops on his right.

During the morning, repeated attempts of the enemy to advance were held up by the rifle fire of this party, with the help of one Lewis gun of the 30th Division. At 1.15 P.M. the pressure on the right increased, and half an hour later the reserve section was sent up to reinforce this flank with about thirty men of other divisions and some two or three hundred rounds of ammunition which had been collected. By 3 P.M. the right flank was being very heavily pressed and ammunition was running out, and at 3.30 the enemy made a heavy and determined attack against the whole company front. The losses from enfilade machine-gun fire were severe, but although the right was forced back the company held on until the troops on the left had retired. Then, having made a very gallant stand, Major Massie gradually withdrew his party while heavily engaged with the enemy, and eventually reported to the 60th Brigade at 7 o'clock that evening.

By 1.20 P.M. the 30th Division had been forced back to the line of the Libermont Canal, leaving the right flank of the 60th Brigade exposed. At Pargny the enemy had increased the gap between the 20th and the 8th Divisions, while he maintained great pressure along the whole Divisional front. There was no course, then, but to fall back to the line Buverchy—Mesnil-St Nicaise.

Major Boyd, 60th Field Ambulance, made two attempts on the 23rd to establish an A.D.S. at Béthencourt, but in the afternoon the shelling was so heavy that the party could not get through, and at night the danger of the enemy turning the flank was too great to make this a suitable place. An A.D.S. was therefore formed between Béthencourt and Mesnil-St Nicaise, where many casualties were brought in. Severe shelling forced Major Boyd and his party to evacuate this dressing station on the 24th and to take shelter wherever possible. The stretcher cases were collected in a cowshed, but as the shelling showed no signs of abating and the enemy was pressing forward, this A.D.S. was definitely abandoned and the wounded carried back by repeated journeys through the barrage to a place on the side of the road. Here, fortunately, a motor lorry came up, steering an erratic course between the shell-holes. All cases were crowded into it and got away, while the party moved off to Nesle, picking up and carrying back many more wounded men on the way.

Lieut.-General Sir F. I. Maxse, the Corps Commander, states in his report on these operations: " Throughout the 23rd March and until the afternoon of the 24th the 20th Division not only held their own new line, but also counter attacked with the 60th Brigade to restore the situation south of Ham. The 12th Battalion K.R.R.C. particularly distinguished themselves on this date, as did also the 11th Battalion of the Rifle Brigade at Béthencourt in the area of an adjoining Corps."

The following extract from Sir Douglas Haig's despatches [1] deals with the situation on the 24th:

[1] Sir Douglas Haig's Despatches, p. 201.

" At nightfall the line of the river north of Epenan-
court was still held by us, but the gap opposite Pargny
had been enlarged, and the enemy had reached Morchain.
South of that point the 20th Division, with its left
flank in the air and having exhausted all reserves in a
series of gallant and successful counter attacks, fell
back during the afternoon to the line of the Libermont
Canal, to which position the great weight of the enemy's
attacks from Ham had already pressed back the troops
on its right."

On the Libermont Canal, on the afternoon of the 24th,
the right of the 60th Brigade rested about Buverchy ;
the 83rd Field Company R.E., the 11th D.L.I., and
the 6th K.S.L.I., who had rejoined the brigade, held
this flank ; the 12th K.R.R.C. were opposite Bacquen-
court, and the 12th R.B. continued the line to Quicquery.
The troops of the 59th Brigade had become rather
mixed, but generally the Scottish Rifles held the right
from Quicquery to the railway, and the 11th R.B.,
with elements of the 61st and 8th Divisions, the left
as far as Mesnil-St Nicaise.

The 11th K.R.R.C. had not received the orders to
retire, but having been forced out of their line at
Voyennes, had fallen back to Quicquery and had taken
up a position on the high ground west of the village
under the 184th Brigade. The 183rd Brigade formed
a defensive flank to the north, as touch with the 8th
Division had not been gained. Divisional Headquarters
moved to Réthonvillers.

At this time French troops began to arrive on the
British front. Four companies from the 22nd French
Division and a mitrailleuse company were sent to
reinforce the Divisional right flank, and were placed
under the 60th Brigade.

By the evening of the 24th the situation on the left

flank had become serious. The gap betweeen the 20th and the 8th Divisions had still further increased, as the 8th had retired due west. The enemy was in Morchain. It soon became evident that the 59th Brigade, already weakened by heavy attacks during the day, would be called upon for further resistance during the night. The brigade was therefore reinforced by four motor machine guns, the 25th Entrenching Battalion, which had been placed under the orders of Major-General Douglas Smith, and the Divisional Reinforcement Battalion. The 183rd Brigade extended the left flank as far as Potte, but could not obtain touch with the 8th Division.

At night, on the left of the 59th Brigade, the 11th R.B., the Divisional Reinforcement Battalion and the 25th Entrenching Battalion were forced back by strong attacks to positions about half-way between Mesnil and Nesle, facing north-east. This new position was then held by a most mixed force composed of the above three battalions and elements of the 61st and 8th Divisions.

During the morning of the 25th, while the right of the line between Buverchy and Quicquery stood firm, the left was continually outflanked and was gradually pressed back.

Soon after dawn on the 25th the Germans, attacking down the Mesnil—Nesle road, drove in the front line at this point. Later they got round the flank, and these troops were forced to fall back to a line south of Nesle, where the Lewis gunners of the 11th R.B. did excellent work and captured three German machine guns.

The Scottish Rifles on the right of the 59th Brigade found the enemy working round their left early in the morning, and formed a defensive flank with " A " Company, under 2nd Lieut. H. Grant. About 11 A.M.

the French mitrailleuse company came up, and firing over the heads of the infantry on to the Nesle road, gave invaluable help. By mid-day " A " Company, after a very gallant fight, was driven back to a sunken road which ran at a distance of 150 yards behind the front line, and the whole battalion came under intense machine-gun fire from the left flank. The Nesle road was swarming with Germans, who by 2 P.M. were firing straight down the sunken road, making the position untenable. The only way of escape lay along a marshy stream with thickly wooded banks, which ran through the line towards Nesle. By this way small parties were sent back, and by 2.30 P.M. the last man was out of the sunken road. Many were caught by shell and machine-gun fire on their way, and most of those who survived appear to have gone into Nesle, where they must have fallen into the hands of the enemy. After making a fine stand, only 7 officers and 55 men got back to the brigade.

The line of the 59th Brigade then ran from Quicquery back to the high ground north of Billancourt.

At Quicquery the 11th R.B. beat off a determined attack, and on the whole front south of this the troops of the 60th Brigade held their line with very little artillery support and under fire from German field guns which had been brought up close to the front line. Once more, however, they were left with their right flank in the air, for by 6 o'clock the 30th Division was back at Moyencourt. At the same time the out-flanking movement on the left of the 59th Brigade became more dangerous, and the two brigades were therefore ordered to retire to the line Cressy (two miles north-west of Ercheu)—Billancourt—Réthonvillers.

Just as the 12th K.R.R.C. were moving out of their position the enemy broke across the canal, led by an officer dressed in British uniform, who called on the K.R.R.C. to halt. The officer was bayoneted at once, but his men pushed on and captured the battalion headquarters. On the whole of the 60th Brigade front, in spite of a good deal of fighting, the retirement was successfully carried out. Divisional Headquarters moved at 9.45 P.M. to Roye.

The 92nd Field Artillery Brigade had been fighting meanwhile with the 30th Division, coming under the orders of the 20th only for a short time on the 23rd of March. At 11 A.M. on that day the brigade marched south to positions of observation to cover the crossings at Libermont and at Ramecourt, a mile and a half further north. Between 3 and 4 P.M. it was decided that guns were wanted just north of Esmery Hallon, so four 18-pdrs. and four howitzers, from A/92 and D/92 Batteries respectively, were pushed forward. By the time these had come into action it was getting dark, and, beyond the fact that the enemy was shelling Esmery Hallon, the situation was obscure. It was a bad bit of country, low-lying, marshy, and full of irrigation cuts, and observation was made difficult by small scattered osier beds.

The early morning of the 24th was misty. Under cover of darkness the enemy had worked his way almost up to the rising ground immediately east of Esmery Hallon and on the flank of the guns. With the enemy established on this vantage point, the guns would be cut off. Fortunately Lieut. Patten, M.C., who had been sent to warn the batteries of the situation, fell in with the limbers already on their way up, and pushing on at the gallop succeeded in withdrawing the guns under the nose of the enemy.

The guns then crossed the canal and took up their former positions. By this time Esmery Hallon was

partially enveloped by the enemy, whose infantry, just
north of the village, was engaged by C/92. The French,
who had come up during the night, were making a
gallant stand opposite the western exits of the village.
In order to help them the 92nd Field Artillery Brigade
maintained constant fire throughout the day, inflicting
heavy casualties on the enemy. Further south the
situation was somewhat quieter ; Libermont had been
occupied by the French and liaison had been established
betweeen them and B/92 and D/92 Batteries. At the
request of the battalion commander in Libermont
these two batteries searched and swept the Bois de
l'Hôpital. This wood, lying east and south of Libermont and extending right up to the canal, hid all the
movements of the enemy at this point. By dawn on
the 25th the enemy had drawn up to the bridge-heads,
but all attacks that morning were beaten off with
heavy loss. The French had no guns east of Ognolles
(one mile south-west of Ercheu), so the 92nd Brigade
found itself responsible for the immediate support of
the French infantry. B/92 and D/92 were in and near
Ercheu, covering Libermont and the crossings in its
neighbourhood ; A/92 and C/92 were further north,
covering the bridge at Ramecourt and the roads from
Esmery Hallon. These two latter batteries accounted
for a large number of the enemy, who in this area was
forced to attack down an exposed slope. Opposite
Libermont the problem was very different. It had
become increasingly evident that there was no defensive
line on the right, where officers' patrols had failed to
gain touch with anybody except scattered parties of
French infantry. It was also reported that the enemy
was working his way through the Bois de l'Hôpital.
At 12.30 P.M. the enemy was known to be across the
canal south-west of Libermont.

At 1 P.M. French infantry began to take up an outpost line south-west of Ercheu, and to dig in along the railway further to the rear, in front of Ognolles.

The position of B/92 and D/92 was becoming critical, as the ground on their right flank not only commanded their positions, but with its scattered copses, orchards and straggling hedgerows gave excellent cover to small parties of the enemy and machine guns which might now be momentarily expected. Libermont, too, had been turned, and French infantry, after putting up a most gallant defence, began to retire.

Both batteries were then ordered to withdraw to Ognolles, leaving one gun of B/92 and three howitzers of D/92 in close support to oppose any machine guns which might try to establish themselves on the slight ridge which commanded Ercheu from the south.

These guns dispersed the first machine-gun detachment which appeared and, firing at close range, most successfully held the enemy at bay until the remainder of the brigade had withdrawn and the enemy, working through the enclosed country further south, had completely turned the position. They then rejoined the rest of the brigade, which at dusk moved to Roiglise.

We must now go back to the 61st Brigade and the 91st Field Artillery Brigade, which we left on the 21st of March near St Simon and Tugny under the 36th Division, and follow the actions of these troops until on the 25th the 61st Brigade returned to the Division and the 91st Field Artillery Brigade came under the French. By dark on the 21st of March the 61st Brigade was east of the St Quentin Canal, covering the perimeter of the St Simon and Tugny bridge-heads, the 7th D.C.L.I. (Lieut.-Colonel Burges-Short) on the right, east of Avesne (one mile east of St Simon), the 12th King's (Lieut.-Colonel Vince) on the left as far as

Pont de Tugny. The 7th Somerset L.I. (Lieut.-Colonel Troyte-Bullock) were in reserve on a line north-east of St Simon. The German advance on this day forced the 36th Division to retire during the night to the line Tugny—Happencourt—Fontaine. The 61st Brigade covered this retirement, and at 11.30 P.M. received orders from the 36th Division to withdraw to the west bank of the canal. By the morning of the 22nd the Somersets had taken up a position on the south-west bank of the St Quentin Canal from a point about one and a half miles north-west of Jussy to the canal junction west of St Simon. On their right the only troops of the 14th Division whom they met were odd patrols. The 12th King's continued the line northwards to a point half a mile north-east of Tugny, where they joined the right of the 36th Division and gained touch also with the 60th Brigade. These two battalions thus held a front of 6000 yards.

From mid-day on the 22nd the 7th D.C.L.I. (less one company) held the south bank of the Somme Canal from the left of the Somersets at the canal junction to half a mile west of the Dury–Ollezy road. They were in touch on their left with a brigade of the 36th Division. By 11 P.M. this division had another brigade at Cugny and another at Brouchy. One company of the D.C.L.I. had been sent shortly before mid-day to fill the gap between the right of the 7th Somerset L.I. and the 14th Division. This company got into touch with the 6th Somerset L.I. (14th Division) and helped to stem the heavy attacks on Jussy before rejoining the battalion on the morning of the 23rd.

" C " Company, 20th Machine Gun Battalion, was distributed so as to cover the front of the 7th Somerset L.I. and the 7th D.C.L.I., and " D " Company 11th

D.L.I., under the 12th King's, dug trenches near Dury and Tugny. The 61st T.M.B. and Brigade Headquarters were at Ollezy.

The retirement on the 21st necessitated a reorganisation of the artillery covering the 36th Division. Three groups were formed. The Right Group under Lieut.-Colonel Erskine, consisting of A/91 and C/91 Batteries and the 232nd Heavy Battery, was detailed to cover the 61st Brigade. B/91 was attached to the Centre Group, under Lieut.-Colonel Potter, and D/91 to the Left Group, under Lieut.-Colonel Eley, both covering the 36th Division. On the night 21st/22nd Lieut.-Colonel Erskine established his headquarters at Ollezy, and placed his batteries west and north-west of the village to cover the crossings near St Simon.

During the 22nd the 61st Brigade maintained its position along the canal. Enemy patrols crossed near Artemps in the morning and entered St Simon at 1.40 P.M., when the Somersets came under gun and trench mortar fire. During the evening the 91st Field Artillery Brigade, now reinforced by D/173 (Howitzer) Battery, was withdrawn to positions near Eaucourt, where the crossings of the canal could be as easily covered while the guns were less exposed.

That night a company of the 12th King's was driven out of Tugny, and soon afterwards, owing to the retirement of the 36th Division, the battalion, with " D " Company 11th D.L.I., fell back through the 7th D.C.L.I. to the railway, leaving one company to reinforce the D.C.L.I. at the Ollezy—Dury crossing.

At 7.45 A.M. on the 23rd the 12th King's were sent back to positions guarding Cugny. At 11.30 A.M. came the serious news that the Germans were advancing on both flanks. On the right they were reported to be approaching Cugny from the east, on

the left they had broken through at Ham and were
advancing south on Brouchy. Here they were held
up by the 36th Division, which formed a defensive
flank on the line Brouchy—Golancourt, and also sent
up troops to fill the gap between that line and the
left of the 61st Brigade on the Somme Canal. Near
Cugny a company of the 12th King's, supported by
three platoons of the 11th D.L.I., beat off an attack
and drove the enemy back into the woods east of
the village. The remaining platoon of the 11th
D.L.I. was last seen advancing to support another
company of the 12th King's. During this fighting,
Lieut.-Colonel Vince, commanding the 12th King's,
was killed.

During the morning the enemy forced the passage
of the canal at Jussy, on the front of the 14th Division.
This completely turned the flank of the three companies of the 7th Somerset L.I. on the canal bank.
" A " Company was in reserve and was then the only
company in touch with battalion headquarters, which
had moved back, by order of the Brigade Commander,
to the railway west of Annois, so as to be in more
direct communication with Brigade Headquarters at
Eaucourt. " A " Company endeavoured to form a
defensive flank between battalion headquarters and
the companies on the canal, but owing to the fog and
marshy ground this was found to be impossible.

The three companies on the canal were eventually
surrounded, but they fought on until all ammunition
and bombs were spent before the survivors fell into
the hands of the enemy. Battalion headquarters
and " A " Company fell back fighting, with both
flanks turned, and joined the headquarters and
one company of the 7th D.C.L.I., who by this time
were on the railway embankment south of Ollezy.

During this fighting, Lieut.-Colonel Troyte-Bullock, their commanding officer, had been badly wounded.

At the time when the enemy broke through at Jussy the 7th D.C.L.I. were disposed as follows : one company, with the attached company of the 12th King's, was holding the Somme Canal north of Ollezy; one company was east of Ollezy, supporting the left company of the Somersets ; one company and battalion headquarters were on the railway embankment south of Ollezy; the company which had returned from fighting with the 14th Division was posted south-east of Ollezy, south of the railway.

Shortly after mid-day Lieut.-Colonel Troyte-Bullock arrived at the headquarters of the 7th D.C.L.I. Although he was very exhausted as the result of his severe wound, he managed to give Lieut.-Colonel Burges-Short most valuable information. The attack on the 7th D.C.L.I. developed in great strength against the company east of Ollezy, but was repulsed about 6 P.M., largely by enfilade fire from the company south of the railway. On the evening of the 23rd, owing to the enemy's advance at Annois and to the retirement of the 36th Division from the canal to a position north of Eaucourt, Lieut.-Colonel Burges-Short withdrew the forward companies of the 7th D.C.L.I. and the attached company of the 12th King's to the railway embankment.

The front then held extended from the stream running north from Cugny to the Eaucourt—Ollezy road. The remnants of the 7th Somerset L.I., about 120 men, were disposed between Eaucourt and the railway facing north-west.

All batteries of the 91st Brigade barraged the canal bank during the morning, and later, when the attack on Brouchy developed, were ordered back, A/91 to a

Q

position one mile south-east of Brouchy, C/91 to north of Beaumont, and D/173 to Villeselve, where the headquarters of the 61st Brigade and of the 91st Field Artillery Brigade were then established. The 232nd (Heavy) Battery was transferred at this period to another command.

Soon after 6 P.M. the enemy took Brouchy, forcing back the troops of the 36th Division on to the gun position of A/91 Battery south-east of the village, where the gunners helped the worn-out infantry to dig trenches alongside the guns.

At the same time the position about Eaucourt was obscure. It was decided that Brouchy should be retaken by the 36th Division, and that the 61st Brigade should clear up the situation at Eaucourt. The attack on Brouchy did not take place, but about 11 P.M. 100 men of the 284th A.T. Company R.E., under Lieut. Jones (7th Somerset L.I.), the intelligence officer of the 61st Brigade, and 2nd Lieut. Arnold (12th King's), the brigade gas officer, advanced to Eaucourt. The party consolidated a position on the north side of the village, joining up with the D.C.L.I. on the railway.

The 62nd Field Ambulance had been established at Dury on the 21st. On the morning of the 22nd, leaving squads of bearers in Dury and Ollezy, and sending a party to Eaucourt to form an A.D.S., the unit moved back to Brouchy. From the A.D.S. at Eaucourt the only way to get the wounded to Brouchy was by horse ambulance over high ground and across open country. Time after time this journey was made under shell-fire in full view of the enemy.

The bearers who had been left at Dury were cut off on the morning of the 23rd on the far side of the canal. By that time the bridges had been blown up and all crossing points were being shelled by our guns, so that with no way of escape left open the party fell into the enemy's hands. The field ambulance moved back from Brouchy to Guiscard and in the evening opened an A.D.S. at Villeselve.

In the early hours of the 24th the 7th D.C.L.I. on the railway became almost isolated; they nevertheless held on until they were ordered to withdraw at 11 P.M. to Villeselve. By that time the enemy was in Golancourt and Brouchy on the left, and on the right was advancing on Cugny, out of which he drove our troops at 1.30 P.M. No attack on the D.C.L.I. developed from Ollezy, but the company on the right had to fight a hard rearguard action to gain time for the remainder to withdraw. This was successfully accomplished, and the battalion reached Villeselve at about 12.30 P.M.

The 91st Field Artillery Brigade, to which B/91 Battery had returned, took up positions of readiness in the morning in a thick fog south-west of Villeselve. At 1.10 P.M. 61st Brigade Headquarters left Villeselve for Beines.

When the troops at Cugny were driven back at 1.30 P.M. they also retired on Villeselve. By the time the remnants of the 7th D.C.L.I. and 12th King's reached that place a number of French troops with various details of other divisions were occupying a line east and north-east of the village. To cover the right flank of these troops three companies of the D.C.L.I. took up a position on a ridge about 500 yards south-west of Beaumont; the remaining company of this battalion was in Villeselve, and a company of the 12th King's supported the French.

The 91st Field Artillery Brigade had meanwhile been ordered to take up a position at Beines to cover

the approaches to Villeselve. The troops of the 14th
Division were falling back through Beines at 2.30 P.M.
French troops also were coming back, and there was
considerable confusion. What was left of the 61st
Brigade was almost isolated, and the enemy was
threatening Beaumont and was advancing from
Brouchy and Golancourt.

Realising that immediate action was necessary to
save the brigade from being surrounded, and being
unable to communicate with the headquarters of
the 36th Division, Brig.-General Cochrane explained
the situation to Brig.-General Harman, 3rd Cavalry
Division, who also was most anxious to do anything
he could to check the retreat. Under the orders of
Brig.-General Harman a composite squadron of cavalry,
commanded by Major E. H. Watkins Williams, 10th
Hussars, made a most gallant charge on the Germans
north-west of Villeselve, killing a great many and
taking 107 prisoners. This action of the cavalry
considerably eased the situation on that flank.

From their position south-west of Beaumont the
three companies of the D.C.L.I were able to prevent
the Germans from entering Beaumont until 4.30 P.M.
when, under cover of an intense trench mortar barrage,
parties of the enemy began to filter through the
village. At the same time the enemy was seen
moving south-westwards across the Brouchy—Villeselve
road. At 5 P.M. Lieut-Colonel Burges-Short was
severely wounded, and shortly afterwards was taken
prisoner as the enemy advanced.

" D " Company of the 11th D.L.I. had become
separated from the 12th King's in the fighting north
of Cugny on the 23rd and retired on the village, carrying
back two wounded officers of the King's with them.
No troops could be found except a company belonging

to the 36th Division, whose line the D.L.I. prolonged
until at 6.45 P.M. the enemy was reported to be working round their right. It was then decided to withdraw. Second-Lieut. Banks went to the assistance
of the company of the 36th Division. Touch with
this company was lost in the darkness, and 2nd
Lieut. Banks was not seen again. " D " Company
of the D.L.I. retired to Villeselve, meeting no organised
body of troops before coming within three-quarters
of a mile of the villge. Having reported to Brigade
Headquarters and procured three boxes of ammunition
and a few badly-needed rations, the company commander led his company forward at 6 A.M. on the 24th,
to try and get into touch with the rest of the brigade.
In the thick mist he was unable to do so and dug in
about a mile north-east of Villeselve, facing north,
with a section of the machine gun company and a
company of the 36th Division on his left, and some
troops of the 14th Division facing east on his right.
At noon the mist cleared, and the company, coming
under heavy shell-fire from the east and south, had
to swing round to the east. Although about this
time the remnants of the 61st Brigade fell back, covering
Villeselve further to the right, " D " Company was
not in touch with them.

The troops on the left retired at 3 P.M., and after
holding on for another half hour " D " Company fell
back to a sunken road on the eastern outskirts of
Villeselve. There a little later it gained touch with
the reserve company of the 7th D.C.L.I. The Germans
gradually worked their machine guns forward and
swept the bank of the sunken road with fire ; their
field guns came into action about 6 P.M. at a
range of 1500 yards, firing shrapnel which burst most
effectively right on to the line. Half an hour later

the troops were shelled out of the position, and retired along the road to Villeselve, which for the first 200 yards was swept by the enemy's machine guns.

The batteries of the 91st Field Artillery Brigade held on in their position near Beines until 5.30 P.M., when orders were received to retire the brigade to Guiscard with a view to joining the 9th French Division. All batteries were accordingly withdrawn to Guiscard except C/91, which remained in position until dark, and was able to give most valuable support to the French on the right and to the cavalry on the north of the Villeselve—Guiscard road. C/91 managed to get back by the last available road after the enemy had captured Berlancourt and was close to Buchoire, about a mile south-east of Guiscard.

By 7 P.M. the remnants of the 61st Brigade, now very much mixed and scattered, had retired to a line covering Guiscard and Buchoire ; Brigade Headquarters was 2000 yards south-west of Guiscard on the main road to Noyon. Large numbers of troops and stragglers retiring from Guiscard were stopped by a party of 100 men of various units of the brigade, who were formed up at 9 P.M. on a defensive line across the main road 400 yards in front of Brigade Headquarters. At 10 P.M. the right of the 61st Brigade line was found to be in the hands of the enemy.

The A.D.S. at Villeselve was abandoned shortly before the enemy entered the village. In consequence of the rapid advance of the Germans, all transport and surplus personnel of the 62nd Field Ambulance in Guiscard were sent back. A small party under Lieut.-Colonel Stack, the commanding officer, remained in the village collecting, dressing and evacuating crowds of wounded, British and French. Shells fell into the garden of the house which served as a dressing station.

but Lieut.-Colonel Stack refused to go until all cases had been cleared.

The 91st Field Artillery Brigade came in the evening under the G.O.C. 9th French Division, from whom orders were received at 10 P.M. to move to Crisolles. Guiscard was being heavily shelled at this time, and soon afterwards was captured by the enemy. Having lost a certain number of men during the shelling of the town the brigade successfully withdrew at 11 P.M., although the enemy had advanced by then to within a few hundred yards of the guns.

What remained of the 61st Brigade was withdrawn to Neuvilly, where it was reorganised on the morning of the 25th into a composite battalion of four companies, one from each battalion in the brigade, with a head-quarters company in addition. The total strength was then nine junior officers and 440 other ranks. At 1.45 P.M. the brigade marched to Avricourt and then moved by 'bus to Gruny to rejoin the 20th Division, under which in the course of two days' intense fighting the three battalions together were destined to be reduced to under 100 men.

CHAPTER XII

THE GERMAN OFFENSIVE ON THE SOMME
(Continued)

26th March to 28th April 1918

The March to Le Quesnel—Defence of Le Quesnoy—Actions at
Arvillers and Mézières—Retirement to the line of the
Luce—Relief of the Division—Actions of the 91st Field
Artillery Brigade under the French—Divisional Artillery
at the Battle of Villers-Bretonneux.

WE left the 20th Division on the evening of
the 25th of March holding the line Cressy—
Billancourt—Réthonvillers, with the 60th
Brigade on the right, the 59th on the left, and
Divisional Headquarters at Roye.

By that time all local reserves on this part of the
battle-front had been thrown into the fighting, but
French forces were coming up in increasing numbers
to reinforce the British line. On the 25th the French
took over the whole of the front south of the Somme,[1]
the 20th Division coming under the orders of the G.O.C.
133rd French Division. '' The situation still remained
critical, however, as every mile of the German advance
added to the length of the front to be held, and while
the exhaustion '' of the British divisions '' was hourly
growing more acute, some days had yet to pass before
the French could bring up troops in sufficient strength
to arrest the enemy's progress.'' [1]

The Division was under orders from XVIIIth Corps

[1] Sir Douglas Haig's Despatches. p. 204.

to conform with the retirement of the French towards Roye, should such retirement become necessary. On arrival at Roye the Division was to move north-west to Le Quesnel, covered by the 61st Brigade as a left flank guard. The 133rd French Division, which was to have relieved the 20th, had orders to retire during the night, and French and British troops were so mixed that a relief in the ordinary sense of the word would have been impossible. At an interview between Lieut.-Colonel Haskard, G.S.O.I. of the 20th Division, and the G.O.C. 133rd French Division, it was decided that the 20th should withdraw at midnight, at the same time as the French. The French Divisional Commander, however, said that he could give no orders as to the withdrawal of the 20th Division, as his line of retreat was towards the south. He had no objection to the 20th moving on Le Quesnel, although as the enemy was already in Liancourt he doubted if this could be done.

It was obviously a difficult task, for it meant a flank march in the face of an advancing enemy who at the beginning was not more than four miles away, and who before the march was completed penetrated to within half a mile of the road on which the troops were moving. It is due to the exceptionally gallant action of the 61st Brigade that this operation was brought to a successful close.

On arrival at Gruny late in the evening of the 25th, the 61st Brigade moved into its allotted position. The battalion headquarters company was on the eastern outskirts of Gruny, the Somerset L.I. company on the eastern outskirts of Cremery, and the D.C.L.I. and King's companies at Liancourt. The headquarters and Somerset L.I. companies took up their positions without incident. The D.C.L.I. and King's, on the other hand, had some difficulty at Liancourt, as although a line was established in touch with the French on the east side of the village, German machine guns and patrols were in occupation of the south-west outskirts. No touch was obtained with the 24th Division on the left. and during the night the position in the village it-elf was not quite clear, as British, French and German patrols were continually challenging each other in different languages.

The 60th and 59th Brigades withdrew to Roye at midnight, and before dawn this difficult manœuvre was successfully accomplished and outposts were thrown out east, north and west of the town.

The march from Roye to Le Quesnel was timed to begin at 7 A.M. on the 26th. By that time the 61st Brigade had slowly fallen back to the line Fresnoy— La Chavette. During the day, in order to cover the flank of the Division, detachments of the 61st Brigade occupied in turn the villages of Parvillers, Damery and Le Quesnoy, establishing posts on all roads leading to the enemy and pushing out patrols to the north with the object of keeping touch, which had then been gained with the 24th Division.

The chief action of the day was fought in defence of Le Quesnoy, where the garrison, one officer and 100 men of the 7th D.C.L.I., with two Lewis guns, was commanded by Captain E. C. Combe, M.C., the brigade major of the 61st Brigade. During the morning Capt. Combe was ordered to hold the village until relieved by troops of the 30th Division, some of whom had already taken over the defence of Bouchoir. At noon the enemy moved out from Parvillers towards Le Quesnoy. The Lewis gunners seized their chance and fired four drums into the advancing lines at 500 yards range with great effect. Both guns were put out of

action, however, at 1.30 P.M., when the enemy opened
heavy machine-gun and trench mortar fire. By two
o'clock, after hand-to-hand fighting, the Germans
gained the east edge of the village and had machine
guns trained on the exits. At this point Capt. Combe
was ordered to withdraw to Beaufort, but considering
it impossible to do this in daylight and in close contact
with the enemy, he decided to hold on till it was
sufficiently dark to give his troops a chance of getting
back in safety. At 3 P.M. the enemy again attacked
and reached the centre of the village, but the few men
of the garrison who remained held on to the west edge
until 6.40 P.M., when the enemy closed in on both flanks.
Then the only survivors—two officers and nine men—
withdrew, still firing with good effect on the Germans
as they over-ran the position. Sir Douglas Haig refers
in his despatch [1] to this " very gallant feat of arms."

The Division only just completed the march in time,
for the troops did not reach Le Quesnel till noon, and at
11.15 A.M. patrols of the enemy had crossed the road
south-west of Damery, thus severing all communication with the French in the neighbourhood of Roye.

The fact that the French troops were being forced
south-west, while the British retired west, left a gap
between the two armies of which the enemy took full
advantage. To fill this gap the 36th and 30th Divisions,
which had been withdrawn to rest the previous day,
were put back into the line, and offering a gallant
resistance, played no small part in preventing the
enemy from breaking through.[2]

On arrival at Le Quesnel the Division came again
under the command of the XVIIIth Corps and was
ordered to consolidate a line just east of the village
with the 59th and 60th Brigades, while the 61st con-

---

[1] Sir Douglas Haig's Despatches, p. 206.   [2] Ibid., p. 206.

centrated at Beaufort. This placed the 20th Division
in support of the 30th, which at this time held the line
Bouchoir—Rouvroy-En-Santerre. Touch was gained
with the 24th Division at Warvillers. The enemy
was reported soon after mid-day to be advancing in
large numbers along the Roye—Amiens road. Four
motor machine-guns, in action near the cross-roads
north-west of Rouvroy, did most useful work, delaying
the enemy's advance and causing great loss to his
troops.

At 6.30 P.M. XVIIIth Corps ordered the 61st
Division to take over the defence of Le Quesnel
and the 20th to hold a line in immediate support of
the 30th. The 60th Brigade accordingly moved to
Arvillers and the 59th to Folies ; the 61st was at
Beaufort, and the Divisional Reinforcement Battalion
in reserve at Le Quesnel. To assist in carrying out
reconnaissance duties twelve Corps cyclists, under
Lieut. Quartermain, were attached to the Division :
they were most ably handled, and proved of the greatest
value in the operations of the following day.

Most of the fighting on this line fell to the lot of the
60th Brigade on the south-eastern and eastern outskirts
of Arvillers. The front was held from right to left by
the 11th D.L.I., the 12th K.R.R.C., and the 6th K.S.L.I.
The 12th R.B., to whom the 60th T.M.B. had been
permanently attached as riflemen, were in support
in the village.

On the morning of the 27th Arvillers was heavily
shelled, and the German attack developed towards
Erches and Rouvroy about 10 o'clock. Major-General
Douglas Smith then ordered the 25th Entrenching
Battalion to be transferred from the 59th Brigade to
the 61st—a valuable addition to the strength of the
left flank, as this battalion numbered 38 officers and

640 men. The 59th Brigade being then very weak, asked urgently for reinforcements in the afternoon, and was given two companies of the Divisional Reinforcement Battalion.

At 10.40 A.M. Erches was captured and at 12.30 troops of the 30th Division were driven out of Bouchoir. Brig.-General Duncan therefore ordered the 12th R.B. to send one company to prolong the line of the 11th D.L.I. to the right. Before mid-day large numbers of troops were streaming back from the direction of Erches towards Le Quesnel. Lieut.-Colonel Welch, commanding the 6th K.S.L.I., rallied many of these men and placed them on his left flank, and other troops retiring along the Erches—Arvillers road were stopped by the 12th K.R.R.C. Beyond elements of other divisions on the right of the D.L.I. there were no troops on the right of the 60th Brigade for 1200 yards. Some of the 30th Division were in Hangest. During the day four German cyclists dressed in British uniform, evidently having lost their way, rode into the lines of the 60th Brigade; three of these were shot by the 12th K.R.R.C. before they could get through, and the fourth was made a prisoner.

On the front of the 59th Brigade the 11th R.B. repulsed by a counter attack a German advance from the direction of Bouchoir.

The following was the situation at 6.30 P.M. The 60th Brigade held a line round the south and east of Arvillers. North-east of the village, on the main Roye-Amiens road, were elements of the 30th Division which had been driven out of Bouchoir. From this road to the left the 24th Division held a line which ran north-west and north of Bouchoir and then followed the road to Warvillers. The 59th Brigade was at Folies and the 61st at Beaufort. Hangest was held by the 61st

254 HISTORY OF THE 20TH DIVISION [CH. XII.

Division and elements of the 30th, Le Quesnel by the
61st Division and the French.

At midnight the enemy made a local attack on
Folies, but this was very effectively repulsed by the
11th K.R.R.C., who inflicted a number of casualties
and captured a machine gun.

Before dawn on the 28th the 59th and 61st Brigades
had been relieved by the 401st Regiment of the 133rd
French Division. They marched along the main Roye-
Amiens road to a wood south-east of Demuin, which
they reached by mid-day. The relief of the 60th
Brigade presented a good deal of difficulty, chiefly
because the relieving troops belonged to two separate
French formations. Before it could be completed,
about 8.30 A.M. the enemy put down a heavy barrage,
which he followed by an attack on the whole brigade
front. After severe fighting, in which the enemy lost
heavily, an advanced platoon of the 11th D.L.I. was
driven in and the right flank of the battalion became
exposed. A counter attack failed to restore the situation. The enemy then advanced on the front of the
6th K.S.L.I., and also worked round to the right of
Arvillers. As it was evident that a serious attack
was developing, Brig.-General Duncan ordered the
brigade to withdraw. At this time the mixed troops
on the right, who had occupied a ridge of great importance, and whose task was to hold on until the
60th Brigade began to leave the village, were seen
to have fallen back. The position was then precarious. The enemy was only a few hundred yards
away from the ridge, from which he could cut off the
retreat of all troops from Arvillers. The situation
was saved by the soldierly instincts and most gallant
leading of Capt. Tait, the adjutant of the 12th
R.B., who seeing what had happened, swung round

a company of his battalion to the right, opened fire
on the Germans at short range, and drove them off.
At 11 A.M., under unusually heavy shell and machine-
gun fire, the brigade withdrew in very good order,
and at 3 P.M. rejoined the rest of the Division.

An A.D.S. of the 60th Field Ambulance under the
commanding officer, Major R. V. C. Ash, had remained
near Réthonvillers on the 25th until the enemy came
within 500 yards. Having withdrawn from this
position, Major Ash moved the whole field ambulance
south to a village about a mile north-east of Roiglise.
As the enemy was reported that evening to be advancing on both flanks, it was decided, after consultation
with Divisional Headquarters, to retire through Roye
to a point about two miles south-west of it on the
Montdidier road. By the time this position was
reached, about 3.20 A.M. on the 26th, information
was received from the French that the enemy was
on the point of entering Roye and that French troops
were about to form a defensive line through the village
in which the 60th Field Ambulance was established.
No further information could be obtained. Major
Ash continued to withdraw along the road towards
Montdidier, stopping on the way to help the 53rd
C.C.S. to evacuate its wounded, and collecting a large
number of cases along the road. At Faverolles communication with the Division was obtained and the
field ambulance marched north to rejoin, eventually
arriving at Domart on the 28th.

It was then decided that the Divisional transport
and two out of the three field ambulances should
be sent back out of the way to Abbeville. The 60th
and 62nd Field Ambulances accordingly moved back
that day.

From this time until the 1st of April the only remaining

field ambulance—the 61st—did great work. Except
for a small detachment from the cavalry field
ambulances there seemed to be no other medical
units near. Wounded and sick from the whole Corps,
from Army troops and cavalry, and from the French
had to be dealt with. Every man was fed and dressed,
had his case diagnosed, and was properly ticketed before
being sent back.

The 92nd Field Artillery Brigade was last mentioned
moving back to Roiglise on the 25th, under the orders
of the 30th Division. A further retirement to Beau-
vraignes became necessary on the morning of the 26th;
and that afternoon, covered by a section of D/148
Battery and one of C/92 firing on the enemy in
the open south-west of Roiglise, the rest of the
brigade withdrew to positions between Laboissière and
Guerbigny and opened fire on Andechy.

At 10 A.M. on the morning of the 27th the brigade
came under heavy shell-fire from the direction of
Erches. Shortly afterwards the French were forced
out of Laboissière and the brigade was compelled
to fall back to positions south-west of Favorelles,
covered by the fire of B/92. At this time orders were
received for the brigade to rejoin the 20th Divisional
Artillery, but as the French were being hard pressed
it was decided to stop and fight with the French
until all ammunition was expended.

The whole afternoon the enemy pressed his attack
between Piennes and Favorelles, keeping up a barrage
on the main road through Montdidier, which increased
in intensity as more guns came up. One enemy motor
machine gun which tried to get into Favorelles was
knocked out at close range by C/92. A good many
casualties were caused by enemy machine-gun fire.

At 5 P.M. nearly all ammunition had been expended,

MAJOR-GENERAL G. G. S. CAREY, C.B., C.M.G.

[*To face p* 256.

and the batteries retired under mutual covering fire to the bridge at Le Monchel, about a mile and a half south of Montdidier. The last battery crossed at 6.30 P.M., when all ammunition had been fired. The brigade marched back to Serevillers, and on the 28th moved north to join the 20th Division, arriving at Rouvrel on the 29th.

On arrival in the Dormat area on the 28th the 20th Division came under the XIXth Corps (Lieut.-General Sir H. E. Watts). This Corps had been very heavily pressed all day, and its right was reported to be in a critical position. Accordingly, the Division was ordered to occupy a defensive line between Mézières and Demuin, exclusive of both villages. The 59th Brigade, with a strength of 770, held the right as far as the Roye—Amiens road, the 61st held the left, and the 60th was in reserve west of the road from Demuin to Moreuil.

The orders stated that the Corps line would be held on the 29th by the 20th Division between Mézières and Demuin, and by Carey's Force from Demuin to the Somme. The 24th Division was to concentrate just west of Mézières and the 8th Division in Cavalry Wood to protect the right flank. The 50th Division was to assemble south of Demuin as reserve to the 20th.

At 8.35 A.M. on the 29th the 59th Brigade gained touch with the French, who held Mézières and a line from there back towards Moreuil, but no trace of the 8th and 24th Divisions could be found.

About mid-day, as the French were reported to be heavily engaged, the 50th Division was asked to send a battalion forward to the north of Villers, and the 60th Brigade was ordered to form a defensive flank on the right of the 59th.

R

The French withdrew from Mézières about 1 P.M. The 59th Brigade held out with its flank turned until 1.30; then, having exhausted all available reserves, the brigade was forced to fall back on Villers. At this point the 60th Brigade came up and formed a defensive flank with the 12th K.R.R.C. and the 12th R.B., keeping the 6th K.S.L.I. and the 11th D.L.I. just north of Villers in reserve. Here there was a good deal of shelling, and Lieut.-Colonel Welch, commanding the 6th K.S.L.I, was killed.

Just before 3 P.M. Brig.-General Duncan received orders from the Division to recapture Mézières in conjunction with the 59th Brigade. The 12th K.R.R.C. on the right and the 12th R.B. were ordered to attack the village from the south-west, while on the left the 11th D.L.I., with the 11th R.B. of the 59th Brigade on their right, worked through a wood on the northwest. About a company of the 2nd Scottish Rifles operated on the right of the 11th R.B. The artillery covering the Division was on the move, so that there were no guns to support this attack. Brig.-General Duncan and Brig.-General Hyslop asked such batteries as could be found in the neighbourhood to give their help, but very little artillery support was possible.

Zero was fixed at 4 P.M. As the 12th R.B. received the orders at 3.45 P.M. and the 12th K.R.R.C. only at 3.55, these two battalions did fine work in carrying out their instructions and taking their place in the attack. They got right through the village, where they killed a large number of the enemy and took fifty prisoners. The 11th D.L.I., 10 officers and 130 men strong, came under a trench mortar barrage and enfilade machine-gun fire about 300 yards west of Mézières and lost heavily. Nevertheless the survivors worked their way forward. Lieut. King on the left got into the village and retired only when all his men had been hit. Capt. Pemberton with a small party succeeded in pushing right through, but as he had then only two men left, he also had to fall back. Another party entered the square and destroyed three German trench mortars which were found in position there.

The 12th K.R.R.C. and the 12th R.B., however, were unable to hold the village, as they were caught in the rear by concealed parties of the enemy, who was also massing on their right front, and all battalions were forced to retire again. It appears that the Germans were attacking Villers at the same time as we attacked Mézières. Some of the prisoners captured stated that in their attack they had lost very heavily, and that three of their companies had been completely wiped out.

The line was then established along the Demuin-Moreuil road. The 60th Brigade on the right had its right flank about the north-east corner of Cavalry Wood, where it was in touch with the French; the remnants of the 50th Division were placed under the 59th Brigade, which held the centre, with its left on the main road from Roye to Amiens; the 61st Brigade gradually fell back from positions south of Demuin during the night, and by the morning of the 30th continued the line from the left of the 59th Brigade along the road to the river Luce at Demuin. The 92nd Field Artillery Brigade came into action south of Hailles.

About 11 A.M., as the troops north of the Luce retired towards Hangard, the 61st Brigade had to draw back its left flank to the west of Demuin.

The Germans repeatedly attacked the position of the 20th Division in the early morning without success, but at 4 P.M. they penetrated the line of the 60th Brigade.

In order to clear up the situation on this flank the 12th K.R.R.C. and the 12th R.B., now very much depleted and exhausted, were ordered to counter attack in conjunction with the 59th Brigade and some French troops and elements of the 50th Division. At this time the 2nd Cavalry Division was in action in Cavalry Wood, with the 8th Division coming up in support.

For the first time since the retirement began, the infantry was given really good artillery support. After a very effective bombardment for twenty minutes the attack was launched with complete success. Fifty-three prisoners and nine machine guns were captured and the original line was restored. In appreciation of this very fine action by troops tired out by incessant fighting, the G.O.C. XIXth Corps wired to the Division : " Well done the 20th. Such a counter attack after all your hard work is splendid. Please congratulate your troops."

The situation on the left was relieved in the evening by an attack of the 9th Australian Brigade north of the Luce ; the 61st Brigade was then able to gain touch with the 18th Division across the river.

The line held on the morning of the 31st was substantially the same as that taken up during the night of the 29/30th. Demuin, however, was in the hands of the enemy, and the 61st Brigade was just west of the town, with a bridge-head established between Demuin and Hangard. On the right the 60th Brigade was in touch with the 8th Division. French troops were in Moreuil.

All was quiet until mid-day, when the enemy advanced against the French at Moreuil and the 8th

Division in Cavalry Wood. A heavy barrage fell on the line of the 20th Division, and the attack gradually spread northwards along the whole Divisional front. The 8th Division was driven back, leaving the right flank of the 60th Brigade in the air. The 12th K.R.R.C. and the 12th R.B. were then attacked from the right and rear, " D " Company of the 12th K.R.R.C. being almost annihilated. The 6th K.S.L.I. were ordered up from a position south-east of Domart to protect the right flank, and succeeded in stopping the enemy's advance for a time and in causing him severe loss.

The flank was again turned, however, and the 59th and 60th Brigades were forced to swing round to a line south of the Roye-Amiens road, facing south. Here they held on until 4 P.M., when the enemy had again worked round to their right. The Division then fell back—for the last time—to a line just south of the river Luce.

Brig.-General Duncan then asked the cavalry for assistance. Realising that the real danger lay on his right flank, as soon as he saw the cavalry advancing from the direction of Domart, he ordered what was left of the 6th K.S.L.I. (about 120 men) and the remnants of the D.L.I. to support the attack. Details of various units were collected and placed south-east of Domart. The action of the cavalry succeeded in securing the right flank, and at 8 P.M. Brig.-General Duncan offered the 6th K.S.L.I. and the 11th D.L.I. to the cavalry commander, Brig.-General Bell-Smythe, under whose orders these two battalions served until the Division was relieved. These operations were seen from Divisional Headquarters, established on the high ground just north-west of Domart, and the artillery support was forthcoming before infantry brigades had time to ask for it. The 92nd Field Artillery Brigade inflicted great loss on the Germans as they advanced in the open just north of Cavalry Wood.

" By the supreme efforts of all concerned, and as the result of counter attacks by elements of the 20th, 8th, and Cavalry Divisions," [1] the following line was gained and held by 7.30 P.M. The cavalry occupied a position running from the north-west corner of Cavalry Wood north for about half a mile. From this point the 60th Brigade held a line facing south and south-east about half-way between Cavalry Wood and the Luce. The 61st Brigade, covering the Luce almost as far as Demuin, occupied a pronounced salient, as the troops on the north of the river were some way further back. The 59th Brigade withdrew to the bridge-head at Domart. That evening the following wire was received from the G.O.C. XIXth Corps : " Please accept and convey to all ranks my thanks for the splendid work which you have done since joining the XIXth Corps. The fighting spirit and power of endurance displayed by all ranks under very trying conditions have been wonderful."

On the morning of the 1st of April the 2nd Cavalry Division delivered a successful counter attack, supported by 100 men of the 59th Brigade, and occupied positions south-west of Demuin. The 92nd Field Artillery Brigade did valuable work in covering this attack. No further action developed on this front, and at night the 20th Division, less the artillery, was at last withdrawn to rest.

The headquarters of the Divisional Artillery and the 92nd Field Artillery Brigade remained in the line and were attached to the French 2nd Dismounted Cavalry Division, which held the front from Moreuil to the north-east corner of Cavalry Wood. The 92nd Brigade

[1] Official Report.

covered the northern half of the east edge of the wood.

On the 3rd the enemy took Moreuil and pushed forward some distance to the west. In a further attack delivered on the following morning after a heavy bombardment he reached a line just east of Rouvrel, and by the evening was only a mile south of Hailles. This forced the 92nd Brigade to withdraw about mid-day to the neighbourhood of Fouencamps, 12 miles north-west of Hailles. The French counter attacked on the evening of the 4th, and again on the 5th, and drove back the enemy from part of the ground he had gained. Then, on the 6th, the 20th Divisional Artillery Headquarters and the 92nd Field Artillery Brigade withdrew to Poix, 15 miles south-west of Amiens, to rest and refit.

The 91st Field Artillery Brigade, when last mentioned, had successfully withdrawn from Guiscard on the night of the 24th/25th of March. Under the orders of the 9th French Division the brigade moved that night to Crisolles, and from there to Lagny, where positions were taken up south of the village in the early morning of the 25th, to cover the crossings over the canal near Bussy. At 4 P.M. the French retired across the canal, and the batteries took up forward positions about a mile and a half south-east of Lagny, to cover the withdrawal of the French artillery, which was still in position on the canal bank. By dusk the French batteries had been successfully withdrawn, and those of the 91st Brigade, after an exciting fight for half an hour with the Germans who were crossing the canal, returned to their former positions. The brigade then marched back through Cuy and Thiescourt, along roads blocked with troops of every kind. The last battery reached Chevincourt, two miles south-south-east of Elincourt, at 8 A.M., on the 26th. No billets were available, and no rations ;

no one had had any sleep for days, and men and horses were dead beat.

On the 27th the batteries took up positions on the Thiescourt Massif, which gave a wonderful view over miles of the country below, in order to cover the line from Thiescourt to the south-east. Although dust columns could be seen at Cuy, no action developed opposite the 9th French Division, although there was considerable activity on the left flank about Lassigny, in which D/91 Battery was taking part. Since the 21st of March D/91 had been attached to the 153rd Field Artillery Brigade under the C.R.A. 36th Division. It had fought its way back in a succession of rearguard actions through Tugny, Ham, Buverchy, Flavy-Le-Meldeux (1½ miles north-west of Berlancourt), Freniches, and Beaulieu (one mile north of Ecuvilly), to Gury (three miles south-west of Lassigny), where it came into action on 26th of March, and covered the 177th French Division. Before the battery rejoined the 91st Field Artillery Brigade, a week later, it had taken part in a heavy attack by the Germans on the 30th of March, when the French were forced back through the guns but retrieved the situation by a brilliant counter attack, taking 700 prisoners.

On the 29th, having received orders to rejoin the British Army, the 91st Field Artillery Brigade started on a five days' march to the neighbourhood of Poix. Here on the 3rd and 4th of April D/91 Battery and No. 1 Section of the Divisional Ammunition Column rejoined the brigade and D/173 Battery returned to its own formation. Large reinforcements of N.C.O.'s and men were available, but no horses.

At a conference held on the 4th, the C.R.A. 14th Division, who commanded all the artillery units concentrated in this area, urged brigade commanders to report at the earliest possible moment when their commands were fit to take the field again. The 91st Brigade, although tired out by continuous fighting, volunteered to carry on at once. The next day accordingly found the brigade once more on the move, and by the 7th the batteries were in position north-west of Villers Bretonneux.

The 91st Field Artillery Brigade was now in the IIIrd Corps (Lieut.-General Sir R. H. K. Butler) and under the 58th Divisional Artillery, and from the 9th covered part of the front of the 58th Division, from the main road east of the village to the south. Lieut.-Colonel Erskine took over the Left Artillery Section of the Right Division, IIIrd Corps, and had at first two and later three artillery brigades under his command.

By the 17th of April the 92nd Field Artillery Brigade was in the line north and north-west of Villers Bretonneux, under the 5th Australian Division, covering the front from the main road east of the village to the north. The 5th Australian Division side-stepped to the left to join its own Corps on the 22nd, when the 8th Division took its place. From that time the Southern Group, under Lieut.-Colonel Erskine (91st, 291st and 179th Brigades), and the Northern Group, under Lieut.-Colonel Balston (92nd Brigade), came under the C.R.A. 20th Division, who had moved up into the line two days earlier to take command of the 8th Divisional Artillery Group, covering the front of the 8th Division.

Between the 5th and the 24th of April the only important action on this part of the front was a German attack on Hangard on the 11th. The enemy succeeded in taking the village and a wood to the north of it, but was driven back to his original position the same day. On the 17th, however, the German guns poured so many gas shells into Villers Bretonneux as to make it uninhabitable. The whole detachment of an 18-pdr. gun, which had been placed in the eastern outskirts of Villers Bretonneux as an anti-tank gun, was gassed. Attempts were made to keep this gun in action, but every man sent up to replace the casualties met the same fate, so the gun had to be withdrawn. Up to this time the artillery had had observation posts in the village —an unpleasant place even then, as it was shelled frequently with gas. After the bombardment on the 17th, it was fairly obvious that the Germans intended to make a supreme effort to capture Villers Bretonneux, from where they would have observation over all the country to the west as far as Amiens. Accordingly intense harassing and counter-preparations were carried out nightly, and all gun teams were moved up close to the battery positions. Batteries which had been discovered by the enemy moved to new positions.

About 6.30 A.M. on the 24th, after a heavy bombardment lasting three hours, the Germans launched an attack on both sides of the village with four divisions. Taking advantage of the undulating ground, German tanks— now used for the first time—broke through south-west of Villers Bretonneux and opened a way for the infantry.

The battery positions of the artillery were north of the Bois l'Abbé. Those of the 91st Brigade were on the Cachy—Fouilloy road and with the exception of D/91 were just north of the railway; D/91 was just south of the railway, which at that point ran on a high embankment. The 92nd Brigade was on the left of the 91st, with the exception of C/92, which was just north of the railway, three-quarters of a mile west of the Cachy—Fouilloy road.

By 9 A.M. the enemy had worked round the south of Villers Bretonneux and was in the village, and began dribbling troops down the railway line towards the Bois l'Abbé. The batteries had suffered very severely from the bombardment ; Major Poer of A/91 had been killed, and D/91 had lost all officers at the battery positions, including the commanding officer, Major E. G. Earle, D.S.O., severely wounded. As the advance of the Germans on the south side of the railway rendered the position of D/91 a very precarious one, Capt. Gwyn, M.C., was sent up from the wagon lines with orders to move the guns at all costs to the north side of the embankment. The teams came up from the wood under a hail of bursting shells and succeeded in getting the guns through a bridge under the embankment to the north side, where the battery came into action again. Shortly after this the German infantry advanced down the main road from Villers Bretonneux and occupied the east edge of the Bois l'Abbé. Gunners from some of the nearest batteries manned the embankment with rifles and prevented the enemy from breaking through to the north. At about the same time Lieut.-Colonel Balston ordered C/92 (Major A. Currie), to move to a position close to his other battery on the left of the 91st Brigade. Before moving, the battery had lost fifty per cent. of its personnel and had two guns put out of action by enemy shell fire.

The position at this time was curious, for the enemy had advanced south of the railway to the Bois l'Abbé, but north of the railway his line was no further forward than Villers Bretonneux, and British troops were still holding out along the road to Fouilloy.

At 11 A.M., when this situation became definitely known, orders were received to withdraw the artillery from the threatened flank. The 91st Brigade and the other brigades of the group moved back into the valleys east of Blangy Tronville. The 92nd Brigade sent

A/92 to a position south-east of Aubigny. B/92 and D/92 remained in their original positions throughout the day, exposed to a galling fire from all natures of artillery, and when the enemy attempted to advance through Villers Bretonneux north of the main road, drove them back by direct fire over open sights.

In the afternoon orders were received that a counter attack would be launched at 10 P.M., by a brigade of the 18th Division and the 13th and 15th Brigades of the 4th and 5th Australian Divisions. The plan was to pinch out Villers Bretonneux by driving the enemy back across the ground he had gained south of the village, and by pressing forward at the same time on the north. To cover the attack those batteries which had been withdrawn were ordered to move forward again after dark.

Although the attack was delivered at such short notice it was brilliantly carried out and met with complete success. At dawn on the 25th, Villers Bretonneux was practically surrounded, and during the morning two brigades of the 8th Division overcame the resistance of such parties of the enemy as still held out in the village. By the night of the 25th, Villers Bretonneux was again completely in our hands. A thousand prisoners were taken, and a German tank was left derelict in our lines.[1]

The salient feature of the battle was the part taken by the artillery on both sides. By 5 P.M. on the 24th, one 18-pdr. battery alone had fired over 4000 rounds. Throughout that day the gunners had to fight in gas masks, and the various changes of position added greatly to the fatigue.

The supply of ammunition threw extremely heavy work upon the battery drivers and the Divisional

---

[1] Sir Douglas Haig's Despatches, p. 232

Ammunition Column. They had to make innumerable and incessant journeys between the dumps and the batteries, whole teams being sometimes completely wiped out.

The many rewards for gallant action given to the 20th Divisional Artillery on this day included the D.S.O. to Major Price-Williams, M.C., commanding C/91 Battery, and the M.M. to Fitter Robson of B/92. The latter, though wounded in the head, refused to go to the dressing station until he had put into action again two guns which had been knocked out by shell-fire. Having had his wounds dressed, he returned to the battery with a splinter still in his head, and rendered invaluable service for four days until the battery came out of action.

On the evening of the 25th, the 91st Field Artillery Brigade was relieved. The 92nd, which remained in action for a few days longer, helped to repulse several attacks, the two most important of which took place on the 27th, when the brigade inflicted extremely heavy losses on the enemy, who dispersed and fled before reaching the front line.

With the relief of the Headquarters 20th Divisional Artillery and the 92nd Field Artillery Brigade on the 28th of April, the last troops of the Division moved out of action, having fought continuously throughout the retreat and having taken their part in the battle that marked the last effort of the Germans to break through on the Somme.

CHAPTER XIII

LENS AND AVION

2nd April to 8th October 1918.

The Division at rest—Move to the Lens and Avion sectors—
Major-General Douglas Smith succeeded by Major-General
Carey—Raids—The last German attacks and opening of
the Allied offensive—Extension of the Divisional line—
Attack of 7th D.C.L.I. south-west of Acheville—Retire-
ment of the enemy south of Lens—Advance on the whole
Divisional front.

(*Vide* Sketch C.)

THE ten days' incessant fighting in March, and
the extremely heavy losses suffered during
that time, left the Division no longer fit to
take the field. For the 20th, and for many other
divisions, a rest was imperative, and large reinforcements were needed before units could be brought up
to their former strength. At the same time it was
unlikely that the Germans would rest long before
renewing their offensive, and although by this time
preparations for an attack north of La Bassée were
known to be nearly complete, the strong forces still
concentrated in the Somme battlefield directly
threatened our positions east of Amiens.

On the 9th of April the Germans attacked between
La Bassée and Armentières, driving back the British
troops from positions that had been held since the
autumn of 1914. On the 10th they advanced as

far north as Wytschaete, and in the following days drove a deep wedge into our position. Merville and Bailleul fell, and it became necessary on the 15th to withdraw from the Ypres salient to a line nearer the town, giving up the ground which had been gained at such heavy cost in the summer and autumn of the year before.

After the 18th there was a lull in the fighting, broken on the 24th by the battle of Villers Bretonneux in the Somme area and on the northern battle front on the 25th by fierce German attacks which ended in the capture of Kemmel Hill. This marked the end of the enemy's successes south of Ypres, and with the failure of all attempts to penetrate further in the following days the second phase of the German offensive came to an end.

The 20th Division, less the artillery, withdrew on the 2nd of April to Quevauvillers, ten miles southwest of Amiens. In the week spent in this area all units were busily employed re-organising and absorbing large drafts.

On the 3rd of April the Division suffered a severe loss when Major-General W. Douglas Smith, who had commanded the Division so ably through all its most serious fighting, departed to take up a command in England. He was succeeded by Major-General G. S. Carey, C.B., who had been on his way from England to take up the command of the Division on March 26th, when he was placed in command of the force of details that became so well known as Carey's Force.

About the same time Brig.-General Hyslop handed over command of the 59th Brigade to Brig.-General R. M. Ovens, C.M.G.

From Quevauvillers the Division went back to the

country south-west of Abbeville and there carried on the work of training and of taking in reinforcements until the 17th, when it moved into the First Army area with Divisional Headquarters at Villers Châtel about ten miles north-west of Arras. The Division then came back again to the XVIIIth Corps. In the last days of April units began to move forward again towards the line, and between the 1st and 3rd of May the 20th took over from the 3rd Canadian Division the Avion and Lens sectors of the front.

The outpost line (shown by the dotted line in Sketch C) extended from 1000 yards south of Avion to the north-west corner of Lens. Behind this ran several other lines, covering altogether a depth of three miles. The Souchez river and the canal which ran by its side formed a natural boundary between the two sectors. Two spurs known as Hirondelle Ridge and Hill 65, standing up on either side of the river, formed bastions to the various defensive lines and gave observation over a large extent of ground.

About two miles west-south-west of Avion rise the slopes of the northern end of Vimy Ridge, giving a magnificent view over many miles of the open country to the east. An O.P. on Vimy Ridge was always occupied, for though it was too far back for observation of artillery fire it was useful for obtaining information of movements behind the enemy's line, and for spotting flashes.

East of Avion the enemy occupied the high railway embankment which ran in the form of an oval to the north of Méricourt and back. This was known as the Bull Ring. For a long time the Canadians had tried to get a prisoner from this place, but had never succeeded. The Division carried out many raids

LENS AND AVION, 1918.

Sketch C.

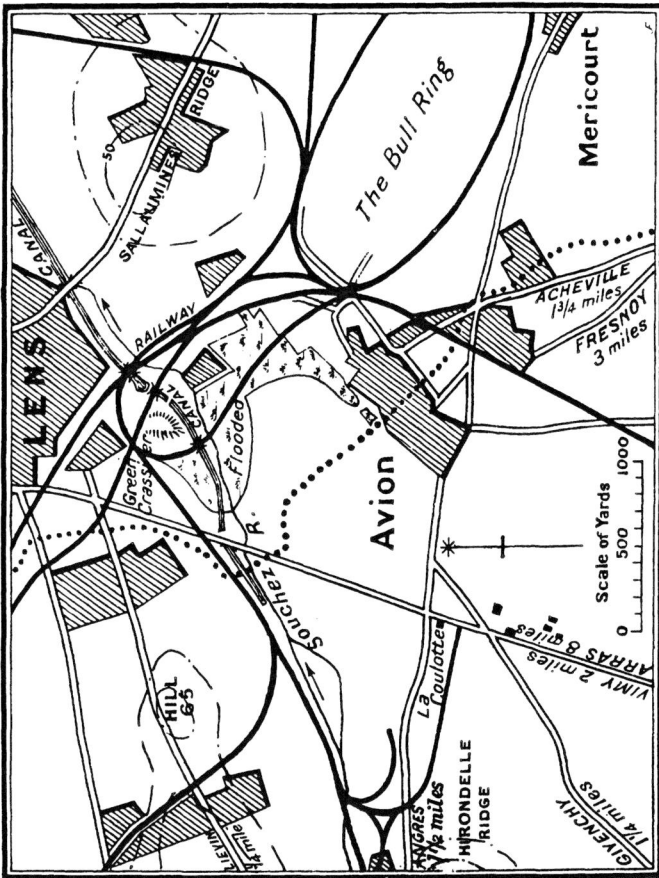

LENS

CANAL

SALLAUMINES RIDGE

50

RAILWAY

CANAL

Green Crassier

Flooded

R. Souchez

HILL 65

Liévin

4 mile

The Bull Ring

Mericourt

ACHEVILLE 1¾ miles

FRESNOY 3 miles

Avion

La Coulotte

ANGRES 1½ miles

HIRONDELLE RIDGE

GIVENCHY 1¼ miles

VIMY 2 miles

ARRAS 8 miles

Scale of Yards

0   500   1000

[*To face p.* 272.

.

here with the same object, but although prisoners
were taken from advanced posts on this front, it was
only rarely that the Bull Ring itself could be entered.
It was indeed a very formidable position especially
at the Avion end, where the south-west face of the
embankment consisted of a high and solid wall of
masonry. Here the only point which gave any hope
of success was a gap near the north-east corner of
Avion, where the railway bridge over the road had
been broken, leaving a gap in the embankment. The
other railway lines converging at this point also ran
on embankments which were held by the enemy as
advanced positions.

Between Avion and Lens a large area of ground
had been flooded sufficiently deeply to prevent any
advance by either side on that front. This flooded
area was completely overlooked by the Green Crassier,
a large slag heap, which formed part of the enemy's
defences.

North of the Souchez river the whole of the ground
in front of the line was a mass of ruins, the remains
of the continuous succession of mining villages which
encircled Lens. Behind our line the mining town
of Lièvin was still standing, but every house had
been damaged by shells. South-east of Lens the
horizon was bounded by the houses which stood on
the crest of the Sallaumines Ridge.

By the 3rd of May the 60th Brigade had taken over
the Avion sector on the right and the 61st the Lens
sector on the left; the 59th Brigade was in reserve
at Souchez, four miles south-west of Lens. Divisional
Headquarters was at Villers au Bois until the 7th of May,
when it was removed a mile further north to Château
de la Haie. Both these places are about three and
a half miles west of Souchez. The 24th Division was

S

on the left of the 20th, and by the 7th of May the
52nd had relieved the 4th Canadian Division on the
right.

The front was covered by the 20th Divisional
Artillery, which rejoined at this time. The 91st Field
Artillery Brigade came into action behind Hirondelle
Ridge, covering the right sector; the 92nd Brigade
moved to Liévin on the 13th to cover the left.
Excellent observation could be obtained from O.P.s
on Hirondelle Ridge and Hill 65.

As soon as the artillery came into the line, battery
commanders came up to the front trenches to see
the country and discuss with infantry commanders
the question of artillery support. All through the
four months spent in this area the co-operation between
the two arms was particularly close.

Among the many railway lines which ran between
Lens, Liévin, and the various mining villages, several
were found which some little distance behind our
front trenches ran towards the enemy. Both artillery
brigades used these lines to run single guns forward
on specially constructed trucks at night to fire on
certain points at close range. After firing a number
of rounds the gun was withdrawn. The Germans
soon got to know pretty well from which bits of line
our guns fired, and then shelled the lines to prevent
the guns from getting back. These expeditions consequently became rather exciting, but as a matter of
fact no guns were lost and very few casualties were
suffered in this way. The 91st Brigade had one gun
two miles away from all the others among the houses
north-west of Lens, where it did most useful work
as it was able to take in reverse the enemy's dug-outs
in the Bull Ring.

The 92nd Brigade had not been long in this sector

before Major F. Butcher, commanding A/92 Battery, was killed by a direct hit on the O.P. on Hirondelle Ridge.

An excellent system of buried cable communications was in process of being laid when the Division took over the sector. This was completed by the 20th Division. Owing to the enormous difficulty of digging among the ruined houses in Liévin full use was made of the gas mains, whereby several miles of practically indestructible cable were laid. By the time the Division left this area, the system of communication was about as perfect as it could be.

From the beginning of May to the first week in October, when the enemy at last retired on this front, the battalions in the line carried out a succession of raids with the principal object of obtaining identifications to show what movements the enemy was carrying out in order to reinforce other parts of his line. For the first month our activity was not so marked, but as the operations in the south developed these raids increased in scope and importance. Gas was successfully discharged on the Divisional front twice during May, and on many other days when all arrangements were complete the orders had to be cancelled at the last moment because the wind was unfavourable. Battle patrols from several of the battalions attempted to raid parts of the enemy's line, but at that time none of them succeeded in taking a prisoner.

When the Division first took over this sector a German attack was expected, so that for the first two or three months all efforts were concentrated on maintaining an adequate defence. With a view to meeting any attempt by the Germans to recapture Vimy Ridge, the troops in reserve were practised in occupying defensive positions and in delivering counter attacks,

sometimes under the personal supervision of the
Corps Commander. Units were chiefly composed of
new drafts, fresh from England. These had to be
trained. Great attention was paid to patrolling, to
the inculcation of the fighting spirit, and to leadership by subordinate commanders, with the result that
the efficiency of the Division rapidly improved. By the
middle of July the conditions had completely changed;
a moral ascendency had been obtained over the Germans
and our patrols were masters of No Man's Land.

On the 4th of June two officers and 84 other ranks
of the 12th R.B. raided a point on the south-west
face of the Bull Ring east of Avion with the co-operation of the 20th and 52nd Divisional Artilleries and
the 20th Machine Gun Battalion. As the raiders
approached the enemy retired hurriedly from his
advanced posts, but on reaching the Bull Ring the
party came under heavy fire from the north-east and
suffered severely, losing both officers and several of
the N.C.O.s. Company Sgt.-Major Whitmore took
command and bombed the dug-outs on the north-east
side of the embankment. A German greatcoat was
found and brought back, but as the enemy had retired
no prisoners were taken.

Early in June the command of two of the infantry
brigades changed hands. On the 5th, Brig.-General
Duncan, who had been appointed to command the 61st
Division, handed over the 60th Brigade to Brig.-General
W. R. H. Dann, D.S.O., and on the 7th, Brig.-General
Ovens commanding the 59th Brigade was succeeded by
Brig.-General A. C. Baylay, D.S.O.

Up to the middle of June each brigade had held
its sector with two battalions in the line, the reserve
battalions each sending one company to hold the
defences on Hill 65 and the Hirondelle Ridge. Be-

tween the 18th and the 22nd the defensive scheme
was modified so that from that time onward each
brigade held its front with three battalions distributed
in depth.

A raid on the Bull Ring just north-west of the outlying houses of Méricourt was very well carried out by
the 2nd Scottish Rifles, commanded by Lieut.-Colonel
Sandilands, in the early morning of the 23rd of June.
At 3.5 A.M. the Divisional Artillery, with the assistance of Stokes, medium, and heavy trench mortars,
barraged the enemy's position. Two minutes later
" A " and " B " Companies of the Scottish Rifles
advanced, and after crossing two belts of wire concealed in long grass reached the embankment. Up
to this time very few of the enemy were seen. Out
of four who tried to run away two were shot and gave
the identification required. Behind the embankment
there were many deep dug-outs, and it is clear that
the Germans had retired into these and were surprised
by the raid. A few of them attempted to come out
and showed some fight, but bombs were thrown into
the dug-outs before they had time to do much. The
raiding party included six men of the 96th Field
Company R.E. who carried mobile charges and blew
up six deep dug-outs. According to statements made
later by prisoners, great damage was done and many
Germans were killed.

When the party had been seven minutes in the lines
the enemy began to barrage the embankment. Both
companies then withdrew, having carried out a very
successful raid, killed many of the enemy, and obtained
an identification with a total loss of ten men. Capt.
D. F. Campbell, who commanded the raiding party,
was awarded the M.C., and Cpl. E. Pow and Lance-
Cpl. W. Henderson the M.M.

On the 13th of July a gas beam attack was carried out on the First Army front at 12.15 A.M. In the Divisional area gas was liberated from four railheads on the light railway, two in each sector, and altogether 4000 cylinders were used. A prisoner captured a few days later stated that in one company forty casualties were caused by our gas.

A new system of allotting the work of the R.E. field companies came into force on the 14th. Instead of being attached to an infantry brigade, and going into and out of the line with it, each field company took over a definite part of the front and became responsible for the work in its own area. The 83rd Field Company took over the right, the 96th the centre, and the 84th the left.

On the night of the 18th/19th, a thousand Stokes gas shells were fired in the Avion sector. Two sections of twelve guns each were employed, each section firing 250 rounds lethal and 250 rounds lachrymatory.

A marked characteristic of the Lens sector was the frequent and heavy shelling with mustard gas which the enemy poured into Liévin. On the night of the 26th/27th of May between four and five thousand shells are estimated to have fallen in the town, followed by some three thousand more the next night. Several times in July Liévin was heavily shelled, chiefly with mustard gas. The men of the 92nd Field Artillery Brigade then began to suffer rather badly from the effects of the gas, although most of them remained at duty. In a heavy bombardment on the 29th of July Major P. Belcher, commanding C/92 Battery, was mortally wounded.

Meanwhile, on other parts of the front, battles of decisive importance had been fought. Except during the first week of October the 20th Division came hardly

LIÈVIN

[To face p. 278.

at all into any large operations after the retreat in
March, but by the end of August the battle area had
spread to within a few miles of the Divisional front,
and even by the last week in July raids were made in
the Lens and Avion sectors with the definite object
of assisting operations in other parts of the line.

The rôle of the Allied armies up to the middle of
July was to preserve the front unbroken until fresh
reinforcements and the increasing strength of the
American army should make it possible once more to
resume the offensive.

During this period the Germans continued to seek
a decision by delivering attacks in great strength on
various parts of the southern battle front. The first
of these attacks was unexpectedly launched on the
27th of May west of Rheims and across the Chemin des
Dames, involving not only the French but also several
British divisions which had been sent to that area to
rest. The German forces penetrated to the Marne,
where after intense fighting they were held on the 6th
of June.

Hardly had the offensive on this front been checked
when on the 7th of June the Germans attacked the
French between Noyon and Montdidier, and forced
them to withdraw. On the 15th of July the Germans
made a final effort to break through, this time east and
south-west of Rheims. After making some progress at
first this attack was soon held at all points, and definitely
failed.

Three days later, on the 18th of July, Marshal Foch
delivered the successful counter-attack between Château
Thierry and Soissons which so dramatically marked
the turn of the tide. Thenceforward the history of
the war is an unbroken record of Allied successes.[1]

[1] Sir Douglas Haig's Despatches, pp. 248 to 256.

To assist the operations in the south by obtaining identifications and killing as many of the enemy as possible, raids were carried out on the night of the 22nd–23rd of July by a company of the 11th K.R.R.C. in the Avion sector, and by all three battalions of the 61st Brigade opposite Lens, one company of the 12th King's on the right, two platoons of the 7th D.C.L.I. in the centre, and one platoon of the 7th Somerset L.I. on the left.

The three raids of the 61st Brigade began at 11.30 p.m. under a creeping barrage ; parties of the 84th and 96th Field Companies R.E., carrying mobile charges, went forward with the infantry to blow up the enemy's dug-outs. The 11th K.R.R.C. with a party of the 83rd Field Company R.E., started at 12.30 a.m., behind a smoke-screen put up to simulate a gas cloud, and a barrage in rear of the objective.

The enemy's trenches opposite the Lens sector were in many places extremely difficult to raid. The ground between the lines was very much cut up by shellholes and was a mass of débris. East of the Lens—Arras road not only did the ruined houses constitute a formidable obstacle in themselves, but the gaps between the ruins and the spaces inside the houses were filled with barbed wire. The enemy had a number of forward machine guns in strong concrete emplacements which were difficult to silence. During the operation a medium trench mortar bomb was seen to drop directly on to one of these emplacements without apparently making any impression on the firing of the gun. The fact that on the whole the enemy's trench mortars and machine guns gave comparatively little trouble says a great deal for the excellent way in which our artillery and trench mortar barrages were carried out.

The chief defensive work on the front to be raided

by the 12th King's was known as the Fosse St Louis, just north-west of the Green Crassier. The company of this battalion moved forward in four parties, without coming under any machine-gun fire until four minutes after zero, when the enemy opened fire from the direction of the Fosse and the Crassier. Two platoons successfully worked through the houses north of the Fosse, thoroughly bombing the cellars on their way. Their return was delayed by a trench mortar barrage, which the enemy put down on the Lens—Arras road, but they reached their own lines again at 12.15 A.M. The other two platoons attacked the northern and southern flanks of the Fosse. On the north the party was bombed from one of the houses and came under heavy machine-gun fire at point-blank range. On the south, 2nd Lieut. Hughes led his platoon most gallantly, and reached the southern face of the Fosse, where he fell riddled with bullets. Throughout the operation all ranks behaved with great courage. The losses in this battalion were ten, including one man who was seen after the party returned but was afterwards reported to be missing. It is probable that he fell during one of the attempts that were made to recover the body of 2nd Lieut. Hughes.

In the centre the 7th D.C.L.I. found great difficulty in advancing through the mass of ruins and wire, especially east of the Lens—Arras road. Only the two officers—2nd Lieut. Howe and 2nd Lieut. Wedge— and six men finally succeeded in forcing a way through the houses. This party pressed forward to an enemy machine-gun post consisting of four men. In the fight that ensued three of the enemy were killed, and the fourth was wounded and taken prisoner. The machine gun also was captured, and bombs were thrown into a dug-out which could not be blown up as the R.E. party had not been able to get through. By this time the half-hour allotted to the raid had expired, so the party turned back, being guided by the German prisoner through a gap in the wire on the Lens—Arras road. A nest of machine guns fired a little during the raid, but for the most part this fire was kept down by our artillery and trench mortars.

The total casualties in the D.C.L.I. were ten men wounded. Four or five of the enemy were actually killed, and judging from the number of ambulances seen from our observation post on the following day our artillery and trench mortars must have inflicted considerable loss.

The report on this raid states : " Too much cannot be said for the splendid co-operation of the artillery, trench mortars, and M.G.C., which meant such a lot towards the success of the venture."

There is no doubt that the raid was a complete surprise. The enemy's first S.O.S. did not go up until seven minutes after zero.

The platoon of the 7th Somerset L.I. on the left advanced in two parties. These succeeded in penetrating the enemy's defences, but they were unable to secure an identification. Eventually the parties returned with only three casualties.

The raid of the 11th K.R.R.C., timed to begin at 12.30 A.M., was carried out by " C " Company with one N.C.O. and six men of the 83rd Field Company R.E. The objective was a trench between the north-east corner of Avion and the Bull Ring.

It was intended that the sappers should advance first under the smoke cloud with torpedoes and blow two gaps in the wire. As soon as the torpedoes went off the infantry parties were to rush the gaps and do what damage they could. Fifteen minutes after zero.

the artillery was to fire on certain selected targets. Unfortunately the wind dropped and the smoke cloud, which was supposed to come over five minutes before zero, never reached the objective. At zero, therefore, the sappers had to crawl forward without it and place the torpedoes. Five minutes later one torpedo was in position. The other could not be placed, as an enemy patrol suddenly appeared on the opposite side of the wire. Accordingly the one torpedo was fired fifteen minutes after zero, whereupon the infantry dashed through the gap and successfully entered the trench. No identification could be secured, as the enemy offered little resistance, and after firing a few shots and throwing some bombs ran back to the main line. The party stayed twenty-five minutes in the German line and brought back a machine gun complete with all its equipment. The casualties were six men wounded.

Further raids took place in both sectors on the night of the 30th/31st, when the 7th Somerset L.I. entered the enemy's posts on the western edge of Lens and brought back a prisoner. Lieut. B. W. Hall, 12th R.B., received the M.C. for his prompt and fearless action on the night of the 1st/2nd of August. He was out with a patrol which was bombed by the enemy. Several unexploded bombs fell close to Lieut. Hall, who immediately picked them up and threw them back at the enemy, so saving many lives.

During this time Lieut.-Colonel Haskard, G.S.O.I., was succeeded by Lieut.-Colonel M. O. Clarke, D.S.O.

The following week was very quiet, but on the night of the 9th/10th of August a very successful little raid was undertaken on the front of the 59th Brigade, which at that time held the Lens sector. The raid was carried out by No. 7 Platoon, " B " Company, of the 11th R.B., under Lieut. Stonham, M.C. It was a difficult place to raid, as a heavily wired railway embankment had to be crossed.

A " box " barrage was put down two hours before the raid took place to simulate a raid, and a bugle was blown from the front trenches a few minutes after the artillery fire had ceased, to make the Germans think that the raiding party was being withdrawn. During the real attack only smoke shells were used. Within half an hour two prisoners, both wearing iron crosses, had been taken, the enemy's dug-outs had been blown up by two sappers, and the whole party had returned without a scratch.

By this time the British offensive had opened with an attack east of Amiens, launched in the early morning of the 8th of August. Success was rapid and complete. In five days the enemy was driven back to his old Somme defences of 1916, with the loss of nearly 22,000 prisoners and over 400 guns.

This was followed by a larger operation on the whole Somme front. The main attack was delivered on the 23rd of August on a front of 33 miles from our junction with the French near Chaulnes to Mercatel, four miles south-east of Arras. Again our troops met with immediate success. By the 1st of September they had driven the Germans with very heavy loss across the old Somme battlefield to the line Peronne—east of Bapaume—Bullecourt.

The battle front extended northwards on the 26th of August, when the right of the First Army attacked the German positions astride the Scarpe, east of Arras. By the 27th these troops had approached to within assaulting distance of the strong trench system which ran from the Hindenburg Line at Quéant to Drocourt, five miles south-east of Lens. Once this line was broken the whole of the enemy's organised positions on a wide front southwards would be turned.

On the northern front the enemy began to withdraw from the Lys salient on the 18th of August, closely pressed by our troops. By the 6th of September he had fallen back to a line just west of Armentières.[1]

The 20th Divisional front meanwhile had been considerably extended. On the 14th of August the 60th Brigade, which had then just moved into reserve, came up into the line again, taking over the Méricourt sectoi on the right from the 8th Division. This front was covered by the 242nd (Army) Field Artillery Brigade. The 59th Brigade was then in the centre holding the Avion sector, with the 61st in the Lens sector on the left. Five days later the 24th Division on the left took over one battalion front from the 61st Brigade, and the brigade boundaries were readjusted.

Owing to the operations east and south of Arras the Division side-slipped to the right on the 27th, taking over from the 8th Division the Acheville sector. The Lens sector on the left then passed to the 24th Division.

The result of these changes was to bring the Divisional left flank down to the Souchez river, thus giving up about 2000 yards of the old line, and to extend the right to a point over 4000 yards south of the original boundary. By the evening of the 28th, when the necessary re-distribution of troops had been made, the 61st Brigade held the Acheville sector, the 60th the Méricourt sector, and the 59th the Avion sector on the left.

The 59th Brigade was then under the command of Brig.-General H. D. O. Ward, C.B., C.M.G., during the temporary absence of Brig.-General Baylay. At the

---

[1] Sir Douglas Haig's Despatches, pp. 258–274.

same time the 92nd Field Artillery Brigade moved from the Lens to the Acheville sector to cover the 61st Infantry Brigade. The 242nd (Army) Field Artillery Brigade and the 91st Field Artillery Brigade remained, covering the 60th and 59th Infantry Brigades respectively.

Early in September the enemy began to show greater activity. Our patrols were constantly out, and frequently came into contact with those of the enemy, but for nearly a month longer the Germans held on to most of their positions opposite the Division, although they withdrew in the Lens sector on the 1st, when the 24th Division occupied the Green Crassier.

As patrols had reported that the enemy was evacuating his forward positions, the 2nd Scottish Rifles sent out a daylight patrol of two men, under Lieut. A. S. Martin, on the 1st of September. Having reached the railway embankment, Lieut. Martin crept round by a ruined bridge and found a German N.C.O. sitting in a dug-out. He brought up his two men, and as the German tried to fight, he shot him. Identification was obtained, and the patrol returned without drawing fire, Lieut. Martin was awarded the M.C.

On the 2nd of September the Drocourt—Quéant line south-east of Arras was broken, and the enemy was thrown into precipitate retreat on the whole front south of it. By the 8th he had fallen back to the defences of the Hindenburg Line.

Battalions of the 20th Division attempted to establish posts on the railway embankment on the 1st and 2nd of September, but on the 1st the enemy was too alert, and on the 2nd, although the posts were temporarily established, hostile shelling and a trench mortar bombardment made their positions untenable.

During the first week of September the enemy

shelled the Divisional area very heavily with gas. On the night of the 4th/5th 4000 shells are estimated to have fallen on the front of the 12th K.R.R.C., at that time the right battalion of the 60th Brigade. Our artillery fired in retaliation the following day, but the enemy put down a very heavy gas bombardment in the Avion sector that night, and on the 7th shelled the area around La Coulotte, again with gas.

On our side constant activity was maintained; gas was successfully discharged several times during the month, and fighting patrols continued to raid the German lines.

A very useful raid was carried out near Méricourt on the 20th by two platoons of the 12th K.R.R.C. under 2nd Lieut. C. E. Austin and 2nd Lieut. F. R. Cleeves. One section of the Light Trench Mortar Battery carried Stokes bombs to destroy the dug-outs, and two sappers carried a torpedo to blow a gap in the enemy's wire.

At zero, 2.30 A.M., " F " Special Company R.E. discharged smoke with unqualified success, and the machine-gun barrage opened. The torpedo was fired, and both platoons got through the wire without difficulty. On the right no Germans were met, but on the left they offered a good deal of opposition, and here Cpl. Arscott, Lance.-Cpl. Taylor, and Rfm. Young did very good work. Several Germans are believed to have been killed, one was taken prisoner, and at 4 A.M. the whole party returned to the line without loss. The Divisional Commander sent his congratulations to the battalion for securing an identification which was very badly needed.

On the 19th of September Lieut.-Colonel F. W. Gosset, C.M.G., D.S.O., arrived to take over temporarily the duties of G.S.O.I. from Lieut.-Colonel Clarke.

Later in the month he was succeeded by Lieut.-Colonel A. W. Stericker, D.S.O.

By the end of September the development of the general situation began directly to affect the position on the Divisional front. The operations of the British Army formed part of a comprehensive scheme by which four converging offensives were launched by the Allies on the whole front from the Meuse to Flanders. On the 26th of September French and American forces attacked on both sides of the Argonne; on the 27th troops of the First and Third British Armies captured the outlying German defences west of Cambrai, as a prelude to a British attack on the whole Hindenburg Line; on the 28th the Second Army and the Belgians attacked in Flanders, where the success gained forced the enemy to retire on the 2nd of October on the whole front from Armentières south to Lens. The British assault on the Hindenburg Line, begun on the 29th, resulted in the capture of the whole of this formidable position from St Quentin, which was taken by French troops operating on our right, to Cambrai. By the 5th of October the enemy's defence in the last and strongest of his prepared positions had been shattered, and the way was opened to the vital railway centre at Maubeuge.[1]

At the time when those battles opened the enemy still held his line opposite the 20th Division, and during the whole of this period, up to the 6th of October, although pressed by fighting patrols from each brigade, he gave up comparatively little ground except immediately south of Lens.

On the night of the 26th/27th of September the 7th D.C.L.I., the right battalion of the 61st Brigade, attacked the enemy's trenches south-west of Acheville

---

[1] Sir Douglas Haig's Despatches, pp. 277–278.

in conjunction with the 8th Division on the right.
At the same time the 59th and 60th Brigades assisted
with trench mortar and machine-gun fire, and gas was
projected in the Avion sector.

The front attacked by the 7th D.C.L.I. extended
for some 1200 yards and contained seven posts strongly
held by light machine guns and trench mortars, effectively wired in. For over ten days patrols of this
battalion had shown considerable enterprise and
boldness in making constant reconnaissances of the
objective, gaining definite knowledge of the obstacles
to be encountered, and of the enemy's dispositions.
The information obtained was passed on to all ranks,
so that every man knew what to do.

The night was dark and overcast, and for some
time heavy rain fell, making movement more difficult
but helping to conceal the assembly. In order to
prevent enemy patrols from obtaining information of
the preparations, and also to make the night's pro-
ceedings appear normal, a platoon of " D " Company
patrolled the front until shortly before zero.

The assaulting troops, "A" Company, under Captain
Waters, and " B " Company, under 2nd Lieut. Lobb,
assembled along a road known as Winnipeg Road,
which ran parallel to the objective and about 300 yards
west of it. At midnight the Divisional Artillery,
with some other batteries attached for the purpose,
opened a particularly well-timed and effective barrage,
and continued to fire for three-quarters of an hour.
The 61st L.T.M.B. fired about 1500 rounds with good
effect during the operations, and a skilfully arranged
and well-executed programme was carried out by the
20th Battalion M.G.C. The co-operation of the artillery,
trench mortars and machine guns in this operation was
splendid.

T

Close under the barrage—in places within thirty yards of it—the infantry advanced, " A " Company on the right, " B " Company on the left. " A " Company, in close touch with the assaulting troops of the 8th Division, attacked the enemy in front. One platoon of " B " Company advanced on the left of " A."

The enemy was undoubtedly surprised by the rapidity with which these troops reached the line, and left his trench, making a stand on the far side. The fight was brief. Under very effective fire from rifles, Lewis guns and rifle grenades, many of the enemy fell. Posts were quickly established in the captured trench and consolidation was begun at once.

The three remaining platoons of " B " Company turned the trench from the north, and by this manœuvre effectively took the garrison by surprise. After a short fight at close quarters all opposition was overcome, and leaving many dead in the trench and several prisoners and a machine gun in our hands, the rest of the enemy retreated under rifle and Lewis gun fire.

As soon as the objective had been captured, " C " Company sent up trench parties, accompanied by R.E. These parties removed the enemy's blocks in the communication trenches leading into the captured line, and with the material which they carried forward established blocks in the communication trenches leading from the new line towards the enemy.

" D " Company was in support of the attack, but was not needed, and when the protective barrage ended, three platoons of this company moved up to act as battle patrols, carrying with them R.E. material and tools, which they dropped in the new line as they passed through.

In this very successful operation " A " and " B " Companies, with slight loss to themselves, captured a machine gun and 12 prisoners, thereby gaining valuable identifications, and inflicted many casualties on the enemy. The Corps, Divisional and Brigade Commanders sent their congratulations.

The Corps Commander's letter ran as follows :

" MY DEAR CAREY,—Please express to the Brigade and Battalion concerned my appreciation of the excellent work done by your Division during the recent operations, which, in conjunction with the 8th Division, have led to the capture of Arleux and the trenches to the north of it on the important Bois Bernard spur. They were well conceived, carefully prepared, and boldly and gallantly executed.

" I congratulate each one and all. The operation reflects credit not only on the individuals concerned but on the Division as a whole.

" All good luck to you and to your fine Division.—Yours sincerely,

" AYLMER HUNTER-WESTON."

On the following night the enemy attempted to regain his lost line. A strong reconnoitring patrol was driven off at 9.15 P.M. At 1.15 A.M., under cover of a heavy bombardment, the enemy delivered two attacks, one frontal and one on the left flank, each of an estimated strength of two companies. On the front, parties of the enemy worked their way up the communication trenches and tried to force the posts of the D.C.L.I. by rifle fire and bombing, while the main attack came across the open. Owing to the splendid effect of the Lewis gun and rifle fire of this battalion none of the enemy reached the trenches. On the left the attack was directed against the exposed flank of the D.C.L.I., but here also the enemy was driven back by Lewis gun and rifle fire.

The S.O.S. signal was fired by the right company when the attack began, and the effective barrage, which was put down very promptly, especially by the Machine Gun Battalion, must have caused the enemy great loss.

In the first week of October all three brigades were able to advance, at least as far as the enemy's front line, before the Division was relieved between the 5th and 7th of the month. Only on the left, however, could the advance be pushed to any great depth, for south of Avion the enemy defended with determination the only part of his line from which he had not yet withdrawn.

Before these operations were carried out the Divisional line was extended still further to the right, where the Willerval sector was taken over from the 8th Division.

In anticipation of the enemy's withdrawal, fighting patrols went out by day and night to obtain certain information of his dispositions. As a rule the enemy withdrew from his forward positions on the approach of our patrols, relying on machine guns to defend his line.

On the 2nd, several explosions and fires were noticed behind the German lines, and our aeroplanes flew over Sallaumines and Méricourt without drawing any fire. On the morning of the 3rd, the 59th Brigade found the enemy's positions in the Avion sector unoccupied, and immediately advanced. At 3.30 P.M. Divisional Headquarters sent out the order for an advance by battle patrols on the whole front to be begun at 5.30. Schemes had been prepared for some time, so that all units moved on receipt of the code word " Berlin."

At this time the dispositions were as follows. The

AVION SECTOR

The Green Crassier and Flooded Area

[To face p. 292.

61st Brigade on the right held the line opposite the German positions between Fresnoy and Acheville, the 60th Brigade in the centre faced the trenches between Acheville and Méricourt, and the 59th Brigade on the left carried on the line to the Souchez river. The front line was held from right to left by the 7th D.C.L.I., the 12th King's, the 12th K.R.R.C., the 6th K.S.L.I., the 2nd Scottish Rifles, and the 11th K.R.R.C. In reserve were the 7th Somerset L.I., the 12th R.B., and the 11th R.B.

The 8th Division was on the right of the 20th and the 58th on the left.

The operations began on the left, where on the morning of the 3rd the enemy was found to have withdrawn. " A " and " B " Companies of the 11th K.R.R.C. advanced at 9 A.M. An hour later, although fired on by snipers and isolated machine guns, these two companies established an outpost line north of the Bull Ring and a thousand yards in front of their former line. On the following day " D " Company moved forward through " A " and " B," and occupied the Sallaumines Ridge. Patrols penetrated as far as Noyelles, 2500 yards east of Lens, but coming under heavy shell-fire they were forced to withdraw. The line gained on this day was held until the 6th, when the battalion was relieved.

On the right of the 11th K.R.R.C., " C " Company of the 2nd Scottish Rifles occupied the near embankment of the Bull Ring on the morning of the 3rd, while patrols of " D " Company passed through. These patrols came under heavy machine-gun fire from the south, but they rapidly gained the far side of the Bull Ring and the village of Sallaumines. The only point at which they were held up was on the right, where the enemy opened very heavy fire from machine guns in Méricourt and at the south-east end of the Bull Ring.

To support the advance of these two battalions, the batteries of the 91st Field Artillery Brigade moved forward on the 3rd to positions along the Lens—Arras road.

In order to improve the unsatisfactory position on the right flank of " D " Company, 2nd Scottish Rifles, it was decided on the 4th to attack a triangle of railway lines at the south-east end of the Bull Ring and to clear out the machine guns there which had delayed the advance. This operation was most successfully carried out by " B " Company of the 2nd Scottish Rifles, under Capt. D. F. Campbell, with artillery co-operation. " B " Company took the Germans by surprise, gained the objective and a trench on the north side of Méricourt, and captured two prisoners, a machine gun, four carrier pigeons and a considerable quantity of arms and equipment. Touch was gained with " D " Company on the left, and later with the 6th K.S.L.I. west of Méricourt. At this time, although the 2nd Scottish Rifles were on the north of Méricourt, the village was still in the hands of the enemy.

Accordingly, on the 6th an attempt to clear Méricourt was made. The artillery shelled the village at dawn. It was arranged that as soon as the shelling ceased strong patrols of the 2nd Scottish Rifles should be pushed forward. A patrol of " C " Company penetrated the village from the west, but was heavily fired on by machine guns and snipers. A patrol of " B " Company, under 2nd Lieut. W. R. Jack, moved along the northern outskirts to the north-east corner and then suddenly came under fire from three directions. The position of this patrol was very difficult, as the only line of retreat crossed some 200 yards of open ground swept by rifle and machine-gun fire. When the other patrols had been driven back it became essential that 2nd Lieut. Jack should be informed of the situation and that his patrol should be withdrawn.

Five runners attempted to deliver this important message, but they were all killed or wounded.

It was then that Pte. J. Towers, 2nd Scottish Rifles, won the V.C. Well aware of the fate of the previous runners, he at once volunteered to make a sixth attempt. As soon as he showed himself heavy machine-gun fire was opened on him, but running from cover to cover he went straight through and eventually delivered the message. He remained with 2nd Lieut Jack. until dusk, when he guided the patrol back to the line. He showed the greatest courage and determination and an utter disregard for his personal safety, and set a magnificent example to his comrades. Second-Lieut. Jack was awarded the M.C., Private W. McGinty received a bar to his M.M., and Pte. J. Allan and Lance-Cpl. S. Smith the M.M. for their gallant conduct during these operations. That night the battalion was relieved.

Fighting patrols of the 60th Brigade had to overcome determined opposition before they could gain a footing in the enemy's line between Acheville and Méricourt.

Two platoons of " A " Company of the 6th K.S.L.I. moved forward against the German line south of Méricourt on the 3rd of October. They came under heavy fire while crossing " No Man's Land," and were unable to get further than the German front line before dark. There they remained, more or less scattered, in isolated positions during the night.

On the morning of the 4th the company commander

took over his two remaining platoons, accompanied by
a section of the Light Trench Mortar Battery, and
having lost a certain number of men from machine-
gun fire, joined the first two platoons. Posts were
established in the captured front line trench and
repeated efforts were made throughout the day to
gain the support trench some four hundred yards
further on. The enemy, however, showed great activity
with machine guns and bombs, and although parties
of the K.S.L.I. pushed forward along the communication trenches no posts could be established in the
support trench. No. 4 platoon met strong opposition
from an enemy bombing post. In the course of the
fighting one of the enemy was shot, and later Sgt.
Naylor, at great personal risk, went over and secured
the identification. The enemy attempted a counter
attack and was held back only with great difficulty,
as by then the supply of bombs had run out. Efforts
to get forward were made until darkness came on and
all trench mortar ammunition had been spent.

On the morning of the 5th a platoon was sent to
work down the front line, while two platoons of
" C " Company reinforced " A " Company. Both met
considerable opposition. The Light Trench Mortar
Section having received more ammunition, knocked
out an enemy machine gun, and at least two Germans
were shot as they ran away from the position.
Excellent work was done throughout the operations
by this trench mortar section, whose shooting was
very accurate. A platoon of " B " Company was
also sent up to secure the left flank. The enemy then
opened a very heavy bombardment on our position
and resisted strongly everywhere. One platoon of
" C " Company lost nearly every man. The enemy
again attempted a counter attack, but was unsuccessful.

Eventually a patrol of the 6th K.S.L.I. succeeded in entering the support trench and pushing up northwards, gaining touch with the Scottish Rifles near Méricourt.

The positions gained were held until the night of the 5th/6th, when the battalion was relieved.

The 12th K.R.R.C. on the 3rd sent forward a platoon of " A " Company, under 2nd Lieut. J. C. Mackenzie, and a platoon of " B " Company, under 2nd Lieut. J. S. Langworth. In spite of strong resistance the platoon of " A " Company established a post in the enemy's front line. Second-Lieut. Langworth was wounded, and after heavy fighting his platoon was surrounded and only two men got back. Second-Lieut. Mackenzie, although hard pressed, held on to his position throughout the following day, and on the 5th " D " Company established two more posts in the German line south of Acheville. Heavy machine-gun fire prevented any further advance.

On the front of the 61st Brigade, on the 3rd, parties of the 12th King's bombed their way up several communication trenches but met with strong opposition, and the battalion made no progress that day. On the right the 7th D.C.L.I. advanced on a two company front, with " D " Company, under Lieut. Chegwin, on the right, " B " Company, under Capt. Davis, on the left. Both made good progress and occupied the German front line beween Fresnoy and Acheville, where they captured twelve prisoners and a machine gun, and a number of documents, aeroplane photographs and maps, which gave very valuable information. The D.C.L.I. then found themselves in advance of both the units on their flanks, as the troops on their immediate right had also been unable to gain their objective.

On the following day the 12th King's, attacking

behind an artillery barrage, entered the German trenches, thus advancing their line 500 yards. On the front of the D.C.L.I. " D " Company was relieved by " A " Company, under Lieut. Parkes. Well supported by artillery, by machine guns and by the 61st Light Trench Mortar Battery, the leading companies gained Fresnoy Wood ; they pushed from there to the village, but being unsupported on the flanks withdrew to the wood again.

On the 5th the line of both battalions was established in the German trench system between Fresnoy and Acheville. The King's established themselves in the trenches north of Fresnoy, and in the evening pushed two platoons of the right company forward to the west end of Fresnoy Park. Patrols which entered the park met a good deal of opposition, entirely from machine guns. During the day touch was gained with the 11th K.R.R.C. on the left, and the battalion was relieved on the night of the 6/7th.

A patrol of the 7th D.C.L.I., under 2nd Lieut. Spargo, located an enemy trench mortar on the morning of the 5th. A Stokes gun of the 61st L.T.M.B. opened fire on it, scattered the team and knocked out the trench mortar, which was then captured by the patrol. Soon after mid-day the enemy, approaching under cover of Fresnoy Wood, launched a strong counter attack on " B " Company of the D.C.L.I. The company suffered a certain number of casualties, but successfully repulsed the attack. Most useful work was done throughout the operations by the second in command, Capt. J. W. Rawle, who remained with the front companies, helping to organise the defence of the captured trenches, and keeping battalion headquarters informed of the situation.

On the night of the 5/6th the 7th D.C.L.I. were relieved by the 7th Somerset L.I., who on the following day pushed forward battle patrols of " B " and " D " Companies. These patrols were engaged all day with the enemy rearguards, and the line of the battalion had been advanced to 400 yards in front of Fresnoy when the battalion was relieved that night.

By the 8th the relief of the 20th Division by the 12th Division was complete.

CHAPTER XIV

THE FINAL ADVANCE

9th October to 11th November 1918

The Division at rest in the Monchy Breton area —Move to
Cambrai —Advance to the line Mons-Maubeuge.
(*Vide* Sketch D.)

L ITTLE remains to be said. After the fighting
between Fresnoy and Lens the Division moved
to the neighbourhood of Monchy Breton. The
Divisional Artillery was sent on the 9th of October to
the Chérisy—Fontaine area. All units were occupied
in training until the end of the month.

During this period the Allied line was carried forward
on the whole front. While the French and American
armies advanced in the south, the British army
by the end of October reached a line well east of
Le Cateau, and just west of Valenciennes and Tournai.
At this point in the operations the 20th Division was
moved at short notice on the 30th of October to
Cambrai, to join the XVIIth Corps of the Third Army
(General Sir Julian Byng).

The Divisional Artillery came under the 19th
Division of the XVIIth Corps on the 1st of November,
when both brigades moved forward from Cambrai to
the east-north-east. The road was so blocked with
traffic that frequent halts were necessary, sometimes for as long as an hour, while the enemy shelled
the neighbourhood with gas, but the batteries came

into action in the course of the day behind the
villages of the Maresches and Preseau, 16 or 17 miles
from Cambrai. The 91st Field Artillery Brigade,
under Lieut.-Colonel Allcard, lost 2 men killed and
5 wounded, and 28 horses ; most of these casualties
occurred when the teams were withdrawing to the
wagon lines at Vendegies, as the enemy was making
good shooting on the road. During the night Maresches
and the valley behind it were heavily shelled.

The Divisional Artillery was required to support an
attack by the 19th Division on the 4th, and spent the
3rd getting up the necessary ammunition, with the
help of the Divisional Ammunitional Column. The
enemy retired on this front during the 3rd, as a
result of the capture of Valenciennes, and the
infantry reached Jenlain, three miles north-east of
Maresches and two and a half miles east of Preseau,
by 4 P.M. that day. Further progress was made by
the infantry during the night of the 3rd/4th, so that
when the barrage opened at 6 A.M. on the 4th the guns
had to fire at very long range, and B/92 Battery was
unable to fire at all. Half an hour after zero the
batteries began to move forward to positions west of
Jenlain. At this time Major Gwyn, commanding D/91
Battery, and two men were wounded while carrying
out a reconnaissance. The infantry of the 19th Division
had gained the high ground east of Jenlain by 10 A.M.
At 4.30 P.M. both artillery brigades supported another
attack in which the 19th Division surprised and defeated
the enemy, who again retired during the night. The
infantry passed Bry on the 5th and occupied La
Flamengrie, a mile and a half further east, and the
92nd Field Artillery Brigade moved to Wargnies le
Grand. It poured all that day, and the supply of
ammunition became a very difficult matter. These

operations formed part of a decisive attack which was launched by the Fourth, Third, and First Armies on a front of thirty miles from the Sambre to Valenciennes, and which definitely broke the enemy's resistance.

By the morning of the 6th both brigades had gone forward and come into action south-east of Roisin. This advance presented some difficulty, as the ground was too waterlogged to allow guns or wagons to take cross-country cuts. The roads were being heavily shelled, and all bridges and culverts over the numerous streams which crossed the route had been destroyed.

On approaching the allotted position the 92nd Brigade found the eastern exits of Roisin under a heavy barrage. The bridge south-east of the town had been blown up and the Rivière de Roisin, with its marshy banks sodden from the heavy rain, barred the way. A double avenue of trees running parallel with the stream, although it formed no obstacle to the howitzers, masked the fire of the 18-pdrs. and made it essential to get them across. The brigade and battery staffs, under a harassing fire, built a bridge with German ammunition baskets, materials from some gun-pits near by, straw mattresses and earth, completing their work in time to allow the leading battery to cross after only a few minutes' delay.

D/92 Battery, coming into action west of the stream, was unfortunately spotted by a low-flying aeroplane, and soon afterwards came under accurate fire from the German guns. The first shot knocked out a howitzer, and the searching and sweeping of the area caused a good many casualties. In spite of these difficulties all batteries were in action at the time ordered.

From these positions south-east of Roisin both brigades during the 6th engaged enemy machine guns which were holding up the advance.

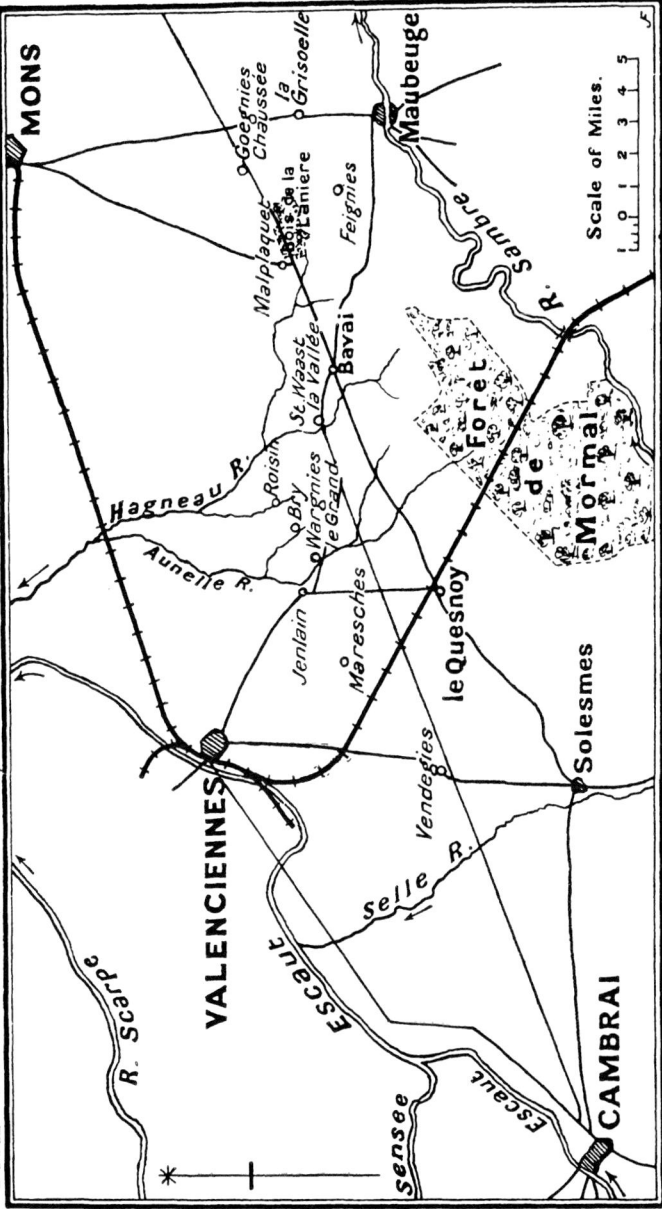

Sketch D.

THE FINAL ADVANCE, Nov.r 1918.

MONS

Goegnies Chaussée

la Grisoelle

Maubeuge

Malplaquet

Bois de la
St. Waast Lanière

Feignies

Bavai

R. Sambre

St. Waast
la Vallée

Foret de Mormal

Hagneau R.

Roisin

Bry

Wargnies
le Grand

Aunelle R.

Jenlain

Maresches

le Quesnoy

VALENCIENNES

Vendegies

Solesmes

Selle R.

R. Scarpe

Escaut

Escaut

sensee

CAMBRAI

Scale of Miles.

0 1 2 3 4 5

[To face p. 302.

This was another day of pouring rain, and the
ammunition supply was critical. The enemy, who was
apparently using up his ammunition, shelled the whole
area. D/91 Battery lost twelve horses during a very
heavy bombardment of the 91st Brigade horse lines
at Bry.

After a further retirement by the enemy during the
night, the infantry advanced at 6 A.M. on the 7th
behind an artillery barrage, drove in the German rearguard, occupied the high ground east of the Hagneau
river, and finally pushed on to the north of Bavai.
Both artillery brigades of the 20th Division moved at
mid-day to the neighbourhood of Breaugies, about a
mile north-east of St Waast. The 91st Brigade had
difficulty at St Waast, as the bridge broke down,
leaving C/91 and D/91 Batteries stranded there for
three hours. Divisional Artillery Headquarters moved
to Bettrechies, but having been shelled out, went a mile
back to La Flamengrie. During the night the enemy
shelling was again heavy ; Lieut. Vincent, C/91 Battery,
and a driver were killed, and several dumps of ammunition were blown up.

As the 19th Division had advanced more rapidly than
the 11th Division on its left, the left flank of the 19th
had become uncovered. Owing, however, to the situation on other parts of the front, the 19th Division
was ordered to push on at all costs regardless of the
exposed left flank.

On the 8th the 91st Field Artillery Brigade moved
to positions of readiness north-east of Bavai, an advance
of about twenty-eight miles from Cambrai ; the 92nd
went to Houdain, north of Bavai, to guard the left
flank. Divisional Artillery Headquarters moved up
to Breaugies, and later to a point about a mile
east of Bavai. On the 9th both brigades advanced

a further five miles to the north and north-east of Feignies.

The 20th Division meanwhile had been moving up behind the leading troops. Starting from Cambrai on the 3rd of November, the Division spent three days in the Avesnes area and two days round Vendegies. On the 8th, Divisional Headquarters was at Wargnies le Grand, with the brigades at Jenlain, Bry and Wargnies le Petit ; on the 9th, Divisional Headquarters moved to Bavai.

Owing to the amount of traffic on the road, battalions frequently advanced across country. Heavy rain fell during the week, making the march a very trying one. The billets occupied by the troops, having been lately in the possession of the Germans, were filthy, and a great deal of time had to be spent in cleaning them up.

Those civilians who had been left in the villages welcomed the troops with enthusiasm. Much destruction had been done by the Germans in some of these places. The 11th K.R.R.C. found Vendegies unoccupied on the 7th, and badly damaged. When the 7th D.C.L.I. arrived at Wargnies on the 8th there were many obvious cases of wanton destruction, particularly in the church. The inhabitants here complained of harsh treatment, and in some cases of cruelty, at the hands of the Germans. From the 7th the Division became responsible for rationing the civilians in the reoccupied villages in its area. The rationing of each village was to have been taken over by the French Government after four days, but as the French were unable to do this, the Division, with the help of supplies left by a Neutral Relief Committee, carried on until other arrangements could be made. A difficulty arose owing to large numbers of civilian refugees from the area further east continually passing through the Divisional area. It was found possible, however, to maintain a soup kitchen and provide a meal for these people before sending them by lorries to concentration camps in rear.

By the 10th of November the enemy was in full retreat. That day at 11 A.M., VIth Corps took over the Third Army front, and formed an advanced guard to keep touch with the enemy. The 60th Brigade passed to the command of the 24th Division at 3 P.M., relieving the 72nd and 73rd Brigades, which were then holding the front line. The main line of resistance was the high ground immediately east of the Mons—Maubeuge road.

The 12th K.R.R.C. and the 12th R.B. took over the front line; the 6th K.S.L.I. and the 60th L.T.M.B. were in reserve. Brigade Headquarters was at La Grisoelle. The 20th Battalion M.G.C. covered the line with " C " and " D " Companies, disposed by sections along the front so that they might co-operate effectively with the infantry and cover important points. As the 12th K.R.R.C. were moving up, hostile guns heavily shelled the Mons—Maubeuge road. Regimental Sergeant-Major Rawson, who had come out with the battalion and had served with it the whole time it had been in France, was mortally wounded. He died that evening.

The command of the 20th Divisional Artillery had passed to the C.R.A. 24th Division on the 9th; on the 10th Brig.-General Christie, the C.R.A. 20th Division, took over command of the 61st, 19th and 24th Divisional Artilleries and two brigades R.G.A.

There was little activity on this front on the 11th, and the situation remained substantially the same. The 91st Field Artillery Brigade remained north-east

U

of Feignies ; the 92nd advanced to Goegnies-Chaussée, north-east of the Bois de Lanière. When hostilities ceased at 11 A.M. the most forward troops of the Division were holding a line about thirty-five miles east of Cambrai.

The Division took no part in the advance to the Rhine. Major-General Carey took over command of the XVIIth Corps sector during the 11th. The 61st Brigade moved to Feignies that day and the 59th Brigade to the Malplaquet area on the 12th. Three days later the 60th Brigade moved back to La Flamengrie, south-east of Roisin.

On the 23rd of November the Division began to withdraw through Cambrai to the district round Marieux, where all units had arrived by the 2nd of December.

With the beginning of demobilisation in January 1919 the 20th Division ceased to exist as a fighting force. It had fulfilled its rôle ; its record is one of which it may well be proud.

INDEX

ABBEVILLE, 255, 272.
Acheville, 288, 293, 297, 298.
— Sector, 285, 286.
Adam, Captain G., 164.
Aeroplanes—
    activities of German, 117, 150, 163, 167, 194, 198, 228.
    artillery assisted by, 146.
    troops assisted by, 229.
Aisne River, 144.
Aldershot, 4.
Allan, 2nd Lieut., 171.
— Private J., 295.
Allcard, Lieut.-Col., 301.
American Forces, 279, 288, 300.
Amesbury, 7.
Amiens, 110, 111, 252, 254, 257, 259, 261, 263, 266, 270, 271, 284.
Ammunition—
    dump exploded, 117, 303.
    exhaustion of, 257.
    restriction in use of, 23.
    transport of, 99, 147, 150, 175, 269, 301, 302, 303.
Ancre River, 61, 62, 118, 119.
— Valley, 119.
Andechy, 256.
Anderson, Lieut.-Col. A. T., 13.
Anneux, 189.
Annois, 240, 241.
Ardagh, Lieut., 206.
Argonne, 288.
Armentières, 7, 8, 270, 285, 288.
Army—
    First, 7, 15, 35, 272, 284, 288, 302.
    Second, 8, 288.
    Third, 8, 178, 219, 220, 288, 300, 302, 305.
    Fourth, 63, 67, 86, 90, 102, 133, 138, 139, 210, 211, 302.
    Fifth, 120, 122, 139, 217, 218, 219, 220.
— Corps—
    I., 10.
    III., 7, 8, 10, 15, 25, 90, 178, 190, 205, 219, 265.
    IV., 139.
    V., 15, 60, 139.
    VI., 36, 305.
    VII., 219.
    VIII., 62, 63, 88, 125.

Army Corps—*continued.*
    IX., 141, 210, 211, 215.
    XI., 29.
    XIV., 35, 37, 53, 56, 62, 67, 78, 86, 88, 89, 90, 94, 101, 110, 111, 113, 114, 116, 120, 122, 125, 126, 128, 143, 145, 147, 151, 157, 174, 176.
    XV., 90, 91, 94, 98, 101, 110, 111, 125, 138.
    XVII., 300, 306.
    XVIII., 168, 218, 219, 220, 251, 252, 272.
    XIX., 219, 220, 257.
    XXII., 215, 216, 217.
Arnold, 2nd Lieut., 242.
Arras, 8, 118, 119, 122, 143, 144, 272, 280, 282, 284, 285, 286, 294.
Arrow Head Copse, 71, 75, 77, 80, 114.
Arscott, Corporal, 287.
Artemps, 239.
Artillery—
    bombardments by, 43, 57, 58, 63, 67, 76, 88, 109, 136, 146, 168, 171, 260.
    camouflage screens for, 145, 180.
    co-operation between infantry and, 33, 163, 260, 261, 274, 290, 294.
    divisional, *see* Divisional.
    French, withdrawal of, 263.
    German, 27, 51, 102.
    horses of, 46.
    reorganisation of, 47, 89.
Arvillers, 252, 253, 254.
Ash, Major R. V. C., 204, 255.
Ashwell, Captain T. G. L., 171, 189.
Attacks—
    bombing, 38, 39, 40, 48, 97, 114, 127, 162, 171, 208.
    feint, 17, 25, 26, 27.
    gas, 29, 33, 48, 49, 54, 89, 193, 220, 266, 275, 278, 289.
    night, 55, 56, 57, 58, 115, 127, 141, 155, 190, 214, 280, 283, 284, 289, 291, 295.
    surprise, 133, 134, 179, 180, 181, 281, 282.
Aubers, 12.
Aubers-Radinghem Ridge, 16.
Aubigny, 268.
Au Bon Gite, 151, 153, 154, 155, 157, 158, 159, 168.

INDEX 311

Fire, liquid, 75.
Fish, 2nd Lieut., 40.
Flammenwerfer, 118.
Flavy-Le-Meldeux, 264.
Flesquières, 189, 191, 209.
Fletcher, Corporal, 111.
Fleurbaix, 14, 24, 59.
Fluquières, 221, 222.
Foch, Marshal, 279.
Folies, 252, 253, 254.
Folkestone, 7.
Fontaine, 238, 300.
Forked Tree Camp, 84, 90.
Forestier, Captain W. W., 45.
Foster, Lieut.-Col. J. R. 4, 47.
Fosse St Louis, 281.
Fouencamps, 263.
Fouilloy, 266, 267.
France, journey of Division to, 7.
Fraser, Captain, 185.
French Army, co-operation with, 8, 37, 45, 65, 66, 67, 98, 108, 110, 119, 144, 234, 236, 243, 246, 247, 248, 249, 250, 251, 254, 256, 260, 262, 264, 284, 288, 300.
Freniches, 218, 264.
Fresnoy, 250, 293, 297, 299, 300.
— Wood, 298.
Fricourt, 65, 110, 143.
Fromelles, 12.
Frost, Lance-Corporal J., 56.

Gallwitz Farm, 164, 172.
Gardiner, Captain D., 50.
Gas attacks, 29, 33, 48, 49, 54, 58, 89, 146, 147, 193, 220, 266, 275, 278, 289.
— helmets, 148.
— invisible, 148.
— masks, 9, 94.
Germaine-Forestre area, 221.
Germans—
  bombardments by, 44, 51, 58, 88, 102, 117, 140, 146, 166, 170, 193, 220, 261, 266, 287, 291.
  exhaustion of, 209.
  intelligence system of, 13.
  losses sustained by, 38, 39, 259, 277, 284.
  mines exploded by, 52.
  new system of defence by, 166, 167.
  reinforcement of, 66.
  retreat of, 122 et seq. ; 284 et seq.
  traps left by, 124.
Geognies-Chaussée, 306.
Gharwal Brigade, 16, 18.
Gheluvelt, 156, 210, 211.
Gibbs, Private A. J., 141.
Gilbey, Captain G. H., 24, 25, 111.
Gill, Lieut.-Col. J. G., 15.

Ginchy, 65, 70, 71, 72, 78, 79, 80, 81, 83, 84, 89, 91.
— Wood, 81.
Givenchy, 15.
Glossop, 2nd Lieut. G. C., 149.
Godalming, 5.
Godley, Lieut.-Gen. Sir A., 215.
Golancourt, 221, 240, 243, 244.
Gonnelieu, 178, 180, 200, 201, 206, 207, 208.
Goodman, Sergeant S., 161.
Gordon, Lieut.-Gen. Sir A. Hamilton, 210.
Gosset, Lieut.-Col. F. W., 287.
Gough, Lieut.-Gen. Sir Hubert, 139, 172, 173, 219.
Gouzeaucourt, 178, 180, 183, 186, 191, 200, 201, 202, 203, 204, 205, 206, 219.
— Wood, 129, 131, 206.
Grand Seraucourt, 220.
Grant, General, 36.
— Lieut., 25.
— 2nd Lieut. H., 233.
Grattan, Colonel O'D. C., D.S.O., 4.
Green Crassier, 273, 281, 286.
" Greenjacket Ridge," 132.
Green, Lieut., 164.
— Sergeant O., 32.
Grenadier Guards, 62, 176.
Grenay, 8, 15.
Grévillers, 119.
Gribble, Lieut., 38.
Gricourt, 219.
Gruny, 247, 249.
Guards Division, 37, 48, 62, 63, 64, 88, 90, 91, 93, 94, 98, 108, 109, 110, 113, 119, 122, 145, 148, 168, 175, 176, 177, 178, 201, 206, 207.
Guerbigny, 256.
Gueudecourt, 90, 91, 98, 119, 139.
Guildford, 5.
Guillemont, 64, 65, 66, 67, 70, 71, 72, 74, 78, 79, 80, 81, 83, 86, 87, 89, 91, 97, 124, 126, 129, 139.
Guillemont-Montauban road, 64, 68.
Guiscard, 243, 246, 247, 263.
Gully Farm, 52.
Gury, 264.
Gwyn, Major, 267, 301.

Hagneau River, 303.
Haig, Sir Douglas, 8, 65, 87, 119, 144, 174, 175, 209, 231, 248, 251, 268, 279, 285, 288.
Hailles, 263.
Hall, Lieut. B. W., 283.
Ham, 123, 218, 221, 223, 224, 226, 227, 229, 231, 232, 240, 264.
Hamilton, Corporal J., 134.

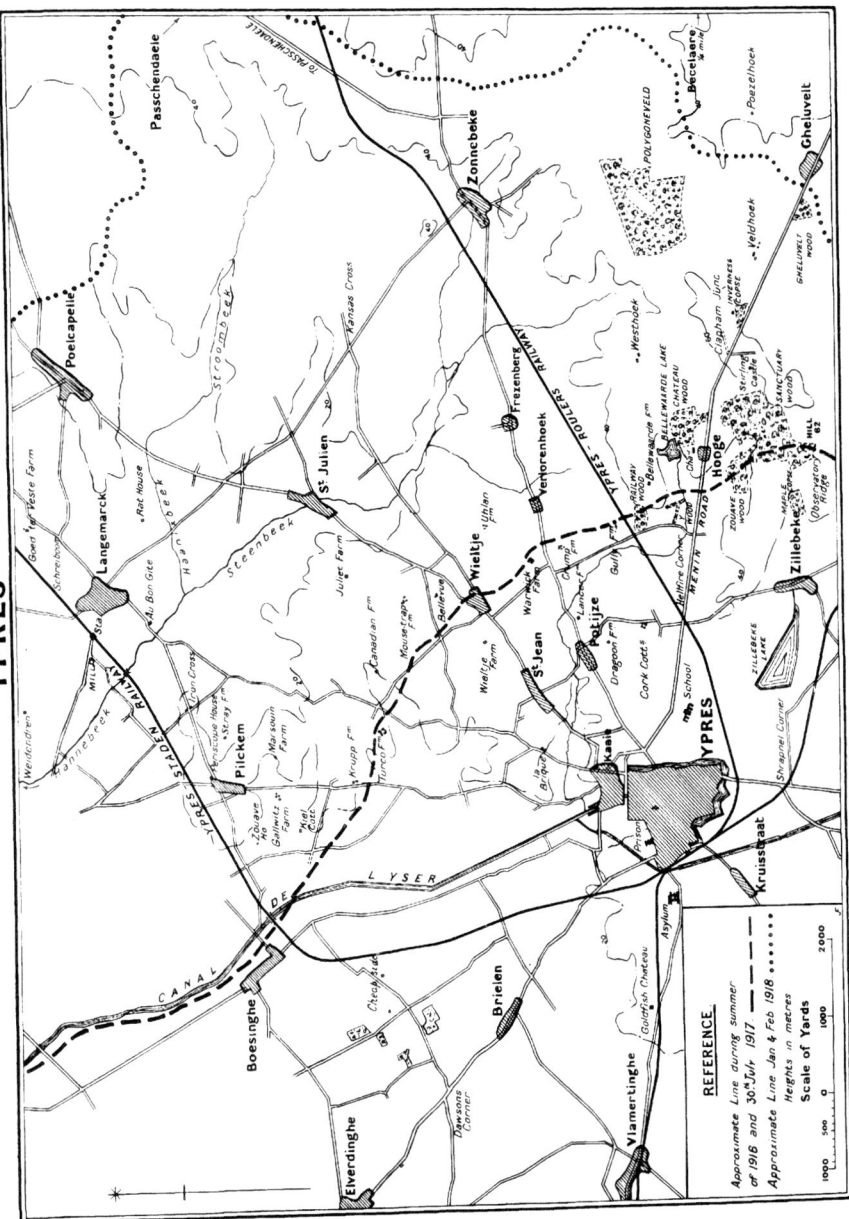

YPRES

Passchendaele
Becelaere
Zonnebeke
Gheluvelt
Poelcapelle
POLYGONEVELD
Poezelhoek
Veldhoek
GHELUVELT WOOD
Westhoek
RAILWAY WOOD
Frezenberg
Verlorenhoek
Hooge
INVERNESS COPSE
Kansas Cross
St Julien
CLAPHAM JUNC
BELLEWAARDE LAKE
HILL 60
SANCTUARY WOOD
Observatory Ridge
Rat House
Au Bon Gite
Langemarck
MENIN ROAD
ZOUAVE WOOD
Zillebeke
ZILLEBEKE LAKE
Wieltje
St Jean
Potijze
Pilckem
Plickem
Shrapnel Corner
Kruisstraat
L Y S E R
DE
CANAL
Boesinghe
Brielen
Vlamertinghe
Elverdinghe
Goldfish Chateau
Dawsons Corner
Asylum
Prison

REFERENCE
Approximate Line during summer
of 1916 and 30 July 1917 -----
Approximate Line Jan & Feb 1918 ••••••
Heights in metres
Scale of Yards
1000 500 0 1000 2000